M & E HANDBOOKS

M & E Handbooks are recommended reading for examination syllabuses all over the world. Because each Handbook covers its subject clearly and concisely books in the series form a vital part of many college, university, school and home study courses.

Handbooks contain detailed information stripped of unnecessary padding, making each title a comprehensive self-tuition course. They are amplified with numerous self-testing questions in the form of Progress Tests at the end of each chapter, each text-referenced for easy checking. Every Handbook closes with an appendix which advises on examination technique. For all these reasons, Handbooks are ideal for pre-examination revision.

The handy pocket-book size and competitive price make Handbooks the perfect choice for anyone who wants to grasp the essentials of a subject quickly and easily.

THE M & E HANDBOOK SERIES

Basic Computer Science

J. K. Atkin
B.Sc (Hons), M.Sc, M.Inst.P

Lecturer in Physics and Computer Science,
Richmond College of Further Education,
Sheffield

MACDONALD AND EVANS

Macdonald and Evans Ltd.
Estover, Plymouth PL6 7PZ

First published 1978

0 7121 0265 5

Printed in Great Britain by
Richard Clay (The Chaucer Press) Ltd,
Bungay, Suffolk

Preface

The aim of this HANDBOOK is to provide a sound introduction to computer science. Emphasis has been placed on the fundamental principles of the subject with the purpose of educating the reader rather than training him in the specific details of a particular machine or programming language.

The book should serve the needs of students taking a variety of courses connected with computing. For example, those embarking on A-level Computer Science in schools and Colleges of Further Education will find here more than adequate coverage of the syllabus. The text is also suitable for first-year polytechnic introduction to hardware design and programming. Certain universities (such as Strathclyde) will also find the book of considerable relevance to their courses.

A brief history of calculating machines leads the reader on to general system concepts, information and its representation, combinational logic circuits, sequential circuits, arithmetic methods, memories, how instructions are executed, peripheral devices, programming and computer applications.

The importance of low-level programming concepts has been underlined in Chapter VIII by means of the author's hypothetical LOCO language, which illustrates in one simple form vital ideas such as the use of literals, relative addressing, indirect addressing and indexing.

It is envisaged that most users of this book will be using BASIC as part of their studies in computer science. Consequently, the high-level program examples in the book are written exclusively in this widely used language. BASIC is now available on most commercial and educational time-sharing systems and has the combined advantage of simplicity and great power, permitting early investigation of fundamental programming concepts such as looping, use of subroutines and intrinsic functions.

Although interdomain conversions are dealt with in Chapter IX, operational details of analog computers have not been included in the text as it is felt that these machines represent a specialist area deserving a separate description (*see* Appendix II, Further Reading, for a recommended book).

Progress Tests appear throughout the book and answers to numerical questions are provided in Appendix I. Answers to non-numerical questions are not given as many of these are of the open-ended variety, calling for explanations and discussion which should provide a basis for stimulating tutorial sessions.

Reactions, comments, corrections and suggestions for improvement will be gratefully received.

December 1977 J. K. A.

Contents

CHAPTER I

History of Calculating Machines

The last thirty years have produced unprecedented interest in computers, and digital machines in particular have attracted considerable publicity. This has given many people the idea that computers are a recent invention, whereas recent developments are a continuation of ideas applied hundreds of years ago. In order to give the reader some idea of the historical background of this subject, the high-points in the evolution of aids to calculation are set out below. The calculating machines range in time from the most primitive counting frames to the microcomputer of today.

EARLY DEVELOPMENTS

1. The Abacus. The first civilisations in Egypt and in the river valleys of Asia represented numbers by pebbles arranged in heaps of ten. This system was the forerunner of the ABACUS (Greek: abax), a manually operated storage device which aids the human calculator. It consists of a row of any number of parallel wires, rods, or grooves on or in which slide small beads or blocks. The groups of beads are divided into two sections by means of a bar perpendicular to the rods. One section has one or two beads, representing 0 and 5 depending on their position along the rod. The second section has four or five beads, representing units. Each bar represents a significant digit, with the least significant digit on the right.

2. Napier's bones. In 1617 John Napier, the inventor of logarithms, published a work describing methods for performing multiplication and division by means of "rods" or "bones". His technique, combined with the use of original data tables marks one of the historical contributions to computation by mechanical means.

3. Pascal's arithmetic machine. In 1642, the Frenchman Blaise Pascal built a digital calculating machine to assist with his father's business accounts. The machine consisted of a train of number wheels whose positions could be seen through windows in the cover of an enclosing box. Numbers were entered by means of dial wheels. The machine was able to perform addition during which "carrying" occurred by means of a gear chain, arranged so that the next left wheel turned one unit when the dial exceeded the digit 9.

4. Leibniz's Stepped Reckoner. In 1694, the German mathematician G. W. Leibniz completed a machine called the "stepped reckoner". This was more advanced than Pascal's machine as it could not only count, but could also multiply, divide and extract square roots. This was achieved by a series of repeated additions similar to that used today in modern digital computers. The major contribution of Leibniz was his demonstration of the advantages of the binary over the decimal system for mechanical computers.

5. Babbage's Analytical Engine. In 1835, in England, Charles Babbage formulated an entirely new device called the "analytical engine" which was able to combine arithmetic processes with decisions based on its own computation. The machine had two basic components:

(*a*) a storage unit containing fifty counter wheels that could store 1000 numbers of fifty digits each, and

(*b*) *an arithmetic unit* or "mill".

Input to the machine was by means of three types of punched cards:

(*a*) *Number cards*, with the constants of a problem.

(*b*) *Directive cards*, for controlling the movement of numbers in the machine.

(*c*) *Operation cards*, for selecting the operation of addition, subtraction, multiplication or division, as required.

Babbage's machine is best known for two important innovations. The first was the concept of *conditional transfer*, which enabled the machine to compare quantities and branch to another instruction as a result of the comparison. The second feature permitted the results of a calculation to change other numbers and instructions, making it possible for the machine to *modify* its own program. The plans for the machine were complete in every detail but were forgotten until Babbage's writings were rediscovered in 1937.

6. Boole's logic. George Boole was an English logician to whom all computer scientists are indebted for his development of symbolic logic, especially of the binary logic operators such as AND, OR and NOT. He pointed out an analogy between the symbols of punched cards : cartes perforées

algebra and those of logic as used to represent logical forms. Boole's formalism, showing the way to mechanise logic and using only the truth values 0 and 1, is the basis of what is now called Boolean algebra and binary switching, upon which modern computing is based.

7. Jacquard and Hollerith. A loom invented by Joseph-Marie Jacquard in the early 1800s was the first use of a punched card to control the loom. In 1886, the American statistician, Herman Hollerith, working on the 1880 census, developed the idea of using holes in punched cards to represent arithmetic sums. These could be sensed by a machine which could perform the arithmetic. Thus, Hollerith, inspired by Jacquard, invented the punched card, which is still one of the basic input media to modern computers. In 1911, Hollerith joined with two companies to form the Computing Tabulating Recording Company, which later became International Business Machines Corporation (IBM).

THE TWENTIETH CENTURY

8. Aiken and the Harvard Mark 1. From 1939 to 1944 Howard Aiken of Harvard University worked with IBM engineers to construct a fully automatic calculator. This was known as *The Automatic Sequence Controlled Calculator* (otherwise known as Harvard Mark 1), an electromechanical machine, 15 metres long and 2.4 metres high. The machine was sequenced by punched paper tape and could perform five basic operations: addition, subtraction, multiplication, division and table reference. Numbers were held to twenty-three decimal digits. Input was via punched cards and output was either on cards or by an electric typewriter.

9. ENIAC. In 1946 J. P. Eckert and J. W. Mauchly of the University of Pennsylvania completed ENIAC (Electronic Numerical Integrator and Calculator), the first all-purpose, all-electronic digital computer. ENIAC was more than a 1000 times faster than the Harvard Mark 1, contained around 10 000 vacuum tubes, and had a power consumption of 150 kW. Problems for the machine had to be set up by hand using a cumbersome plug-and-lead system, but, despite this, it was estimated that the early nuclear physics calculations carried out on the machine in two hours would have taken 100 physicists one year to perform by hand.

10. Von Neumann. In 1947, the mathematician John von Neumann devised a means for superseding the concept of the externally programmed machine (like ENIAC). The new concept was that of the *stored-program computer*. Von Neumann suggested that such a machine should contain a selection of permanently wired units which could be placed under central control. He also suggested that instruction codes be treated as numbers which could be stored electronically just as numeric data were stored. This would eliminate special instruction wiring.

This stored-program concept led to the construction of the EDVAC (Electronic Discrete Variable Automatic Computer) with its electronically alterable memory which could store both the instructions and the numbers to be used in a calculation.

11. EDSAC. In 1949 a stored-program computer called EDSAC (Electronic Delay Storage Automatic Computer) was constructed at the University of Cambridge. EDSAC contained 3800 vacuum tubes and used a mercury delay line store of sixteen 35-bit words.

12. BINAC and Univac 1. In 1950, while running their own company, Eckert and Mauchly conceived the BINAC (Binary Automatic Computer), the first machine to use self-checking devices. In 1951 the company was sold to Remington Rand but the two men were instrumental in completing Univac 1 for the U.S. Bureau of the Census. Univac 1 was the first machine to process both numeric and alphabetic information with equal ease.

13. LEO 1. In 1951 the LEO 1 (Lyons Electronic Office) computer went into service. The machine contained 7000 vacuum tubes and used magnetic tape as a storage medium.

14. Magnetic-core storage. In 1955 the magnetic core store was invented. This development revolutionised the concept of high-speed computer memories.

15. Second-generation computers. Between 1957 and 1958 the first transistorised computers came into service; such machines are called *second-generation* machines. The use of transistors, rather than vacuum tubes, brought about increased reliability and a very significant reduction in the physical size of the computer.

16. Third-generation computers. In the late 1960s discrete electronic components were replaced by *integrated circuits*. Computers based on this kind of construction are called *third-generation* machines.

17. Microprocessors. In 1971 the first *microprocessor* was introduced by Intel. A microprocessor is a complete central processor etched on a single chip of silicon. The addition of peripheral devices with which to communicate with the microprocessor resulted in the creation of the first *microcomputer*. The trend today is towards increasingly small computer circuitry. These dramatic reductions in size (*microminiaturisation*) bring enormous advantages both in speed, reliability and cost.

PROGRESS TEST 1

1. Describe briefly the contribution of Charles Babbage to the development of the computer. In what ways did Babbage's machine differ from a modern electronic computer system? **(5)**
2. What do you understand by the term "conditional transfer"? **(5)**
3. Why is the name of George Boole famous in the history of computer development? **(6)**
4. In what fundamental way did the EDVAC computer differ from the ENIAC machine? **(9, 10)**
5. What is meant by the expression "computer generations"? **(15, 16)**

CHAPTER II

The Computer as an Information System

FUNDAMENTAL IDEAS

1. Definition of a computer. A computer is an electronic device which can accept data, apply a series of logical operations and supply the results of these operations as information. Computers are used to perform complex series of mathematical calculations at very great speed; this makes them of great use for diverse purposes, such as routine business calculations, the control of industrial processes or the guidance of vehicles in space. Their ability to perform these operations depends not only on their mathematical capabilities, but also on their ability to store and retrieve specified pieces of information in the appropriate circumstances.

2. The types of computer. There are three principal categories:

(*a*) *Analog computers*, which represent the values of variables or numbers by physical quantities (usually potential differences), the magnitudes of which are made directly proportional to the variables or to suitable functions of the variables. Such machines operate on *continuous* rather than discrete units.

(*b*) *Digital computers*, which count specifically or discretely, never varying or responding in degrees but only to exact signals that exist or do not exist. Data are represented by means of characters, numbers and symbols.

(*c*) *Hybrid computers*, which combine the advantages of the above two categories. There are different definitions as to what constitutes a hybrid machine, but the simplest is probably the combination of a general-purpose analog computer with a digital computer. Signals are sent between the two subsystems via a set of analog-digital and digital-analog converters, examples of which are described later in this book (*see* IX). At the present time there are relatively few hybrid machines in existence and, as the digital machine is generally more versatile than the analog machine, prime consideration to the digital computer is given in this book.

3. The essential structure of the digital computer. In broad outline a typical digital computer can be regarded as two basic electronic systems, the *central processor* (or CPU) and the *peripheral subsystem*, linked by a switching unit termed the *peripheral interface.* These systems are schematically depicted in Fig. 1, where each system is seen to consist of smaller units or subsystems.

4. The central processor. This system contains [CPU]

(*a*) *internal memory* which is a high-speed storage device used to hold the immediately needed instructions (program) and data;

(*b*) *The arithmetic unit* which can both temporarily hold and arithmetically process numbers fed into it, as well as carry out certain elementary but very useful logic operations;

(*c*) *a control unit* which must interpret the information and instructions held in memory and which transmits the results of its interpreting to other subsystems for carrying out computations. This unit also contains the *clock*—an electronic pulse generator which sends precisely synchronised streams of pulses to many different parts of the computer.

5. The peripheral subsystem. This system contains

(*a*) *input devices* by means of which numerical data, alphabetic data, and instructions can be supplied to the machine;

(*b*) *output devices* for converting the results of calculations into forms which are suitable for human appreciation;

(*c*) *storage devices* which supplement the internal memory by providing areas into which vast amounts of data can be fed and subsequently retained prior to some further processing or outputting in permanent form.

6. The peripheral interface. This unit provides input/output channels between the various peripheral devices and the CPU. Each peripheral device is coupled into the interface using standard multiway connector plugs which carry all the wiring for control signals and data flowing between the CPU and a particular peripheral device.

7. Information. The computer must be capable of storing and processing information. But what *is* information? How do we measure it?

In English we could communicate quite well using a limited character set as follows:

A, B, C, ..., X, Y, Z, space, full-stop.

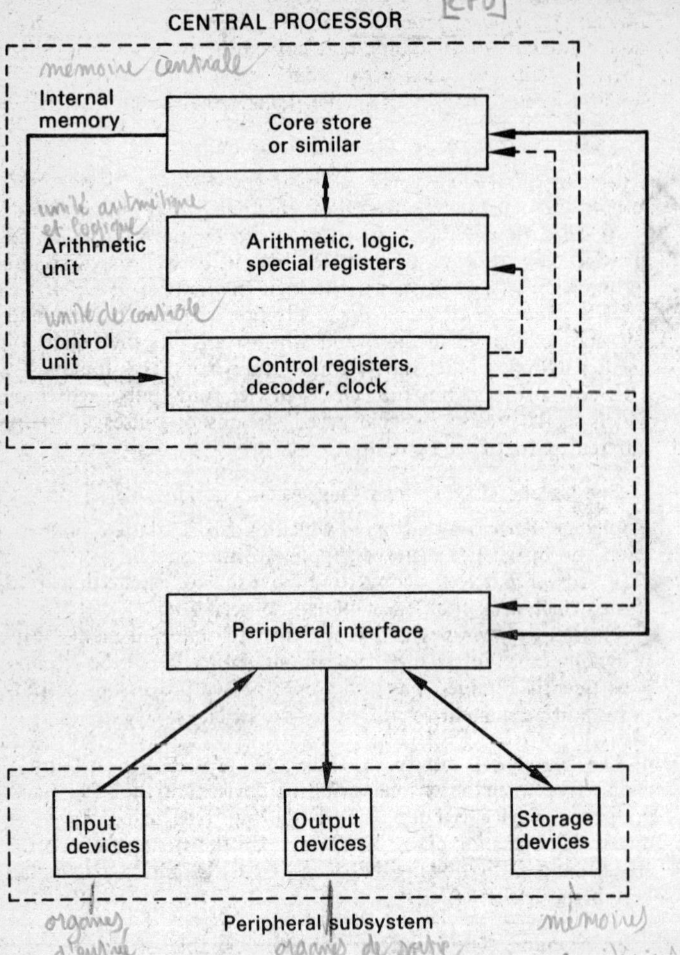

FIG. 1 *Essential digital computer structure.*

Consider a group of ten of these characters written down at random:

e.g. D space X U P J . W H L
or K Y I G Q B T . R S

There are 28^{10} ways in which this can be done. However, not all of these are permitted combinations; the combinations we call *words*.

If a code is used it is possible to arrange that *all* combinations of characters are meaningful. To generalise, consider such a code in which p represents the number of characters in the character set. Let x be the number of characters used to form a message, then the number of possible (and permitted) combinations, N, is given by:

$$N = p^x \qquad (1)$$

We now need to define a *quantity of information*, I. We are led to a useful definition by the reasonable suggestion that quantity of information should be proportional to length of message. From equation (1) we have:

$$\log N = x \log p$$

in which we find the desired proportionality.

Hence, we define quantity of information by:

$$I = x \log p \qquad (2)$$

The simplest imaginable code is one which uses only *two* characters. These characters could be A, B or &, * or H, L or any distinguishable pair of symbols. The symbols conventionally chosen are 1 and 0. So,

$$\text{character set} = (1, 0) \qquad \text{i.e. } p = 2.$$

The simplest message one could send would consist of *one* character. So,

$$x = 1$$

Hence, the information conveyed by this simplest message in the simplest code is

$$I = \log 2$$

The choice of logarithm base is arbitrary, and so base 2 yields

$$I = 1$$

So our message carries unit information, called a bit (for *b*inary dig*it*) and can take the value 1 or 0.

We see that, using this code, the quantity of information is equal to the number of bits, as

$$I = x \log_2 2$$

or

$$I = x \tag{3}$$

Also, the number of possible messages, N, is given by

$$\log_2 N = x \log_2 2$$

or

$$N = 2^x \tag{4}$$

For example, the number of possible messages carrying 3 bits of information each is 2^3 or 8. These messages are 000, 001, 010, 011, 100, 101, 110 and 111.

8. Distinction between computer and calculator. The above messages are recognisable as the first few binary numerals and thus we have a simple and elegant code for the representation of numeric information within a machine. Electronic switches are used to represent the characters 1 and 0, while it is possible to construct electronic circuits to manipulate information in this form, thus rendering calculation by machine a possibility. All this goes on in the arithmetic unit of the computer. However, the ordinary pocket calculator is also capable of addition, subtraction, multiplication, division and often quite sophisticated operations such as the evaluation of square roots or trigonometrical functions. So, what is the difference between a calculator and a computer?

The answer to this question is best arrived at by asking how we use a simple pocket calculator. We may be interested in our personal financial status at the end of the month, in which case we should go through a whole series of steps—adding net pay to any balance from the previous month—deducting amounts corresponding to various bills—adding in any other income—perhaps assessing average weekly expenditure on food—and so on. At each step we should have to *decide* what to do with the data available and, unless our calculator was a very good one, we should have to write down certain intermediate results as well as the final summary of pecuniary ill-health.

The real point to be derived from all this is that we cannot leave the calculator to get on with the job; it requires a constant stream of instructions on the basis of decisions made by the human operator. The computer, however, requires no such human intervention. Its central processor contains not only an arithmetic unit (the calculator) but also an internal memory unit in which are placed the *instructions* required to carry out a specific task. This set of instructions is called a computer *program* and is expressed in a binary-coded form so that it can be retained in the memory.

Once the computer has been provided with a program and a set of data on which to work, it *can* be left to carry out a complex task entirely automatically.

So, the computer has properties similar to those of a calculator in that it can perform arithmetic, but in addition it can make decisions, i.e. select on the basis of stored instructions. This stored-program concept and large memory capability are the two primary characteristics differentiating the computer from a high-speed calculator.

9. Hardware and Software. As we have seen above, the computer is a machine which is capable of automatically executing a large number of instructions at very high speed. The physical units or subsystems are collectively referred to as the *hardware*—the palpable devices and circuits which primarily constitute the province of the physicist and computer engineer. By formal analogy the term *software* is used to describe all programs which can be used on a particular computer system.

HARDWARE

10. Development of hardware. Computer hardware consists basically of elementary switches and amplifiers. Such devices comprise a myriad of types and combinations and are usually referred to as *gates*. In the original electronic computers, gates were constructed from vacuum tubes, but these quickly gave way to gates built using the transistor (developed by W. Shockley in 1948). The transistor amplifies, generates and switches electrical signals in electronic circuits that also contain such other elements as resistors, capacitors and diodes. Resistors impede the flow of signal energy, while capacitors store it. Diodes provide a path for electric current in one direction only, thus facilitating conversion of alternating current to direct current and certain logic operations.

Computers based on the vacuum tube are sometimes referred to as *first-generation machines*, while those built around the transistor are termed *second-generation*. The latter type consisted of millions of transistors and other electronic components. These massive, complex systems were made possible by the low cost, low operating temperature, small size and long life of the transistor.

The millions of discrete components of the second-generation machines had to be handled individually and connected by an enormous number of soldered joints. Such construction methods are necessarily very costly and result in reduced reliability because of the almost astronomical number of connections which have to be made. Also, computer speed is limited by the time taken for a signal to travel from one part of the machine to another. Every 30 cm of circuit separation requires a travel time of about one nanosecond. This travel time can be reduced only by making the circuits and their separations microscopically small.

11. Integrated circuits. Present-day technology almost invariably realises transistors using *integrated circuit* techniques. These techniques give rise to the innovations of *microelectronics* which make it possible to mass-produce on single chips of silicon the very complex circuits that formerly required hundreds of thousands of discrete components. Elements which can store one bit—flip-flops (*see* V)—can, with this technology, occupy an area about 0.1 mm square. Integrated circuit (IC) flip-flops are packaged in three basic styles:

(*a*) the DILIC (dual-in-line integrated circuit) which contains one or two flip-flops with dimensions typically 7 mm × 10 mm;

(*b*) the MSI package (medium-scale integration) containing typically 16 flip-flops (Fig. 2);

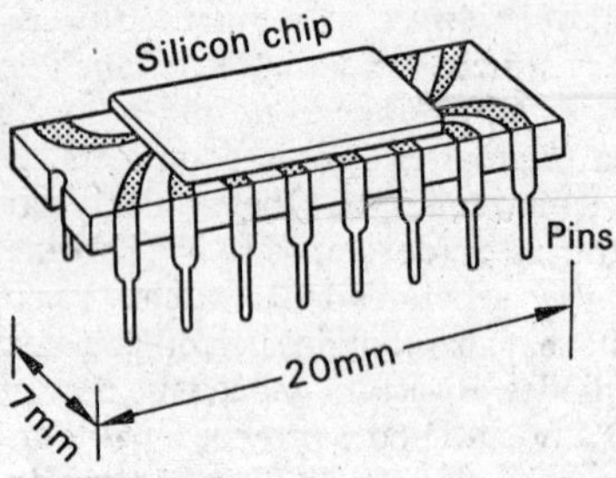

FIG. 2 *MSI package.*

(*c*) the LSI package (large-scale integration) which can contain a very large number of flip-flops in a package only 12 mm × 40 mm. It is now possible to construct LSI elements with enough capacity to be used as main storage devices containing over 8000 flip-flops on a single chip.

The speed of the computer has steadily increased since 1948, when it took around 1 millisecond to add two numbers. Today, the same operation takes less than 1 microsecond with speeds increasing all the time. Some idea of these high-speed operations can be obtained by considering a modern IC flip-flop. These elements can change their state from "1" to "0" in about one nanosecond. It is sobering indeed to think that there are as many nanoseconds in one second as there are seconds in thirty-two years!

12. The microprocessor. The most recent development of LSI technology is the *microprocessor*—a device which performs arithmetic and logic like a computer, but does so all on a single circuit chip of silicon measuring only 6 mm square and containing the equivalent of 14 000 transistors. When combined with memory chips for storing operating instructions and for controlling input/output functions, the device becomes a full *microcomputer*. Microprocessor chips which contain all the associated memory for carrying out complete tasks on their own are already available. The microprocessor has many applications in the day-to-day world, such as controlling petrol consumption in the motor car, or functioning as the "brain" of a fully automatic electric cooker. In the computer field itself the microprocessor offers some truly exciting possibilities for the construction of super-fast computer systems. The idea here is to construct a device consisting of many thousands of microprocessors operating in parallel. The resulting machine is called a distributed array processor (DAP), pilot versions of which have already been successfully tested by ICL's Research And Development Organisation. On this machine a matrix inversion has been run in 35 milliseconds which is equivalent to a speed of about 20 MIPS (million instructions per second), or more than twice the speed of the same problem solved on an IBM 360 computer.

SOFTWARE

13. Need for software. The power of the digital computer rests not only in its high speed and capacity for manipulating large masses of data but also on the fact that it can perform complex sequences of such actions under control of a stored program. This permits the *same* computer to work at a variety of tasks in sequence or even intermittently.

The early computers had to be programmed directly in *machine code*—a coding system to which the hardware is immediately responsive but which bears no resemblance to human languages. Programming in machine code was a very difficult and highly specialised task which meant that programs took a considerable time to prepare and often contained many errors. One way in which the work was eased was in the establishment of thoroughly tested *subroutines*—program segments which were in regular demand and which could be used over and over again.

14. FORTRAN. The world of science and engineering has a great need for expressing problems in algebraic form and it was in response to this need that IBM developed the first *high-level language* called *FORTRAN*, in 1954. FORTRAN stands for FORmula TRANslation. The language permits the engineer or scientist to write programs in a form which bears quite a close resemblance to the equations he uses in his own discipline. Here is a sample instruction:

```
D=I-A+ASIN(N*SIN(A-ASIN(SIN(I)/N)))
```

15. ALGOL. A high-level language with a more logical structure than FORTRAN is *ALGOL* (ALGOrithmic Language) which is also an international language for the communication of algorithms (*see* XI). Here is a sample:

```
            A:=0;
        FOR I:=1 STEP 2 UNTIL 99 DO
            A:=IF X(I) 0 THEN A+2*X(I) ELSE A+X(I);
    DIVIDE: A:=A/50
```

16. COBOL. COmmon Business-Oriented Language is an international computer language developed for commercial use. It was designed to express problems related to business data processing, such as processing a weekly payroll or maintaining inventories. An attempt to give the language the appearance of English makes it very clumsy to write simple instructions, e.g.

```
WRITE LINE-3 AFTER ADVANCING 2 LINES
IF STOCK LESS THAN MINIMUM GO TO REORDER
MOVE SPACES TO LINE-4
```

The language does have special features for handling entire files of information as a single unit, such as all information contained in an employee's personnel record.

17. Batch and time-sharing modes. The mode in which a computer system is operated varies according to purpose. Early attempts to optimise the efficiency of the system resulted in the concept of *batch mode*—each *job* is submitted in its entirety (e.g. in the form of a program and data on punch cards) and results are returned to the submitter at a later time (e.g. in the form of printed tables). The system itself may be internally organised to work on several jobs intermittently, thus improving the total "through-put rate". This has led to the concept of the *time-sharing mode* in which not only are many programs being executed at once, on an intermittent basis, but the user is permitted direct *interaction* with the program during execution through a remotely located *terminal.* Such an *interactive* mode makes possible a fundamentally different style of use, with consequent implications for programming languages. Time-sharing systems and the language *BASIC* (Beginners' All-purpose Symbolic Instruction Code) were pioneered at Dartmouth College, New Hampshire, under the direction of J. G. Kemeny and T. E. Kurtz.

18. BASIC. This has achieved wide recognition as a language of great simplicity. It is very easy to learn but possesses a number of powerful features, such as a useful set of matrix operations. BASIC is commonly used for both scientific and commercial problem solving; it will be encountered again in X and XI.

PROGRESS TEST 2

1. Distinguish briefly between (*a*) digital, (*b*) analog and (*c*) hybrid computers. You should list the relative merits of each type of machine. **(2)**
2. Draw a schematic diagram showing the essential structure of a digital computer as a set of interconnected subsystems. **(3)**
3. What do you understand by the word "information"? **(7)**
4. Describe in your own words, the main difference between a calculator and a computer. **(8)**
5. Explain the terms (*a*) peripheral, (*b*) bit, (*c*) program, (*d*) hardware, (*e*) software, (*f*) microelectronics, (*g*) MIPS. **(4–13)**
6. Name three high-level languages. **(14–18)**
7. Distinguish between batch mode and time-sharing mode as methods of computer operation. **(17)**

CHAPTER III

Representation of Information

The digital computer is an information machine. Information from the environment (data) is combined with information stored within the machine to produce information which is sent back to the environment.

NUMERIC INFORMATION

1. Basic information. The way in which information is represented in a machine depends largely on the available technological devices. At present the simplest and most reliable devices are the two-state devices known as *flip-flops* or *bistables*. Such devices are essentially electronic switches possessing two stable states, an *ON*-state (*YES*) represented by 1, and an *OFF*-state (*NO*) represented by 0. By assembling groups of bistables we can represent information by combinations of 0s and 1s. The symbols 0 and 1 are the only ones necessary in the binary representation of numbers, and so they are called *binary digits* or more often simply *bits*. Two bistables provide us with four combinations of two bits each: 00, 01, 10 and 11. In general, n bistables (providing n bits) will give 2^n combinations, and so with a large set of bits it is possible to represent all the letters, symbols and digits required in computing.

2. Numeric information. A number is, of course, an abstraction and requires a symbol for its representation. Such a symbol is called a *numeral*. In most civilisations numerals consist of an ordered set of *digits*, the numerical weight of each digit increasing by a constant multiplying factor as we move from right to left. The constant multipling factor is called the base or *radix*, and such a system of numeration is termed *positional notation*.

Any number can be represented by the generalised numeral:

$$d_n d_{n-1} \ldots\ldots d_2 d_1 d_0 \cdot d_{-1} d_{-2} \ldots\ldots d_{-(m-1)} d_{-m}$$

which denotes the polynomial

$$d_n r^n + d_{n-1} r^{n-1} + \ldots\ldots + d_2 r^2 + d_1 r^1 + d_0 r^0 + d_{-1} r^{-1} + d_{-2} r^{-2} + \ldots\ldots d_{-(m-1)} r^{-(m-1)} + d_{-m} r^{-m}$$

where d_n to d_0 represent the digits in the *integral part* of the numeral and d_{-1} to d_m represent the digits in the *fractional part* of the numeral. r is the radix and n and m are positive integers. The separator between the integral and fractional parts is termed the *radix point.*

As an example consider the *decimal* system. Here the radix = ten, and the necessary digits, are 0,1,2,3,4,5,6,7,8 and 9. So the numeral 45.2 in fact represents

$$(4\times10^1)+(5\times10^0)+(2\times10^{-1})$$

In this case it is the *decimal point* which separates the integral and fractional parts. Although many different radixes have been used, only a few are of any real importance in computing. These include binary, octal and hexadecimal, all of which we shall examine below.

THE BINARY SYSTEM

3. Binary numeration. In the binary system the radix = two, and the necessary digits are 0 and 1 only.

For example, in this system the numeral 1011.11 means:

$$\begin{array}{ccccccccccc}(1\times2^3)&+&(0\times2^2)&+&(1\times2^1)&+&(1\times2^0)&+&(1\times2^{-1})&+&(1\times2^{-2})\\ 8&+&0&+&2&+&1&+&\frac{1}{2}&+&\frac{1}{4}\end{array}$$

or decimal 11.75.

Using three bits only, the numbers zero through seven would be written:

000
001
010
011
100
101
110
111

It can readily be seen how this system lends itself to machine representation as the number five would, for example, be stored as switch states ON–OFF–ON. The price paid for this simple representation is that a good many more binary digits are required than decimal digits to represent a given number. Consider, for example the quite modest decimal numer 1 073 741 824. This happens to be 2^{30}, or in binary numeration:

1 000 000 000 000 000 000 000 000 000 000

Thus it can be seen that three decimal digits are roughly equivalent to ten bits.

4. Bit groupings. A computer which performs arithmetic in pure binary operates on numbers represented by a standard number of bits. A standard bit-grouping of this kind is referred to as a *word*. Different machines use different word-lengths, but a common length is 32 bits. This length is conveniently broken into 4 *bytes*, a byte being defined as a group of 8 bits. This number of bits to the byte is found useful as 8 bits are more than enough for alphabetic and numeric character representation in input and output devices. The term *field* is used for any sequence of bits which together form a single entity or item of information.

5. Negative number representation. It is obvious that some means of sign representation must be provided if useful arithmetic is to be performed. The commonest methods used for representing both positive and negative numbers are based on the idea of *complementation*. Two methods are in use.

(*a*) *The twos complement method.* We define the twos complement, $T(N)$, of the binary number N by:

$$T(N) = 2^n - N$$

where n is the word-length or number of bits available to represent the number. For example, using a hypothetical 3-bit word, the twos complement of one is

$$\begin{aligned} T(1) &= 2^3 - 1 \\ &= 7 \end{aligned}$$

In other words, $+1$ is represented by 001, and -1 is represented by 111. This will become clear if we list all the possible representations available with our hypothetical 3-bit word.

$$\left.\begin{array}{l} 111-1 \\ 110-2 \\ 101-3 \\ 100-4 \end{array}\right\} \text{negative}$$

$$\left.\begin{array}{l} 011+3 \\ 010+2 \\ 001+1 \\ 000+0 \end{array}\right\} \text{positive}$$

The left-most bit of each of the above numerals is designated the *sign bit*. A positive number has a sign bit equal to 0, while a negative number has a sign bit equal to 1. Thus the computer has a simple means of distinguishing positive from negative numbers. Notice that on this system zero is regarded as a positive number.

Although a defining equation for the twos complement has been given, it is important to be aware of an equivalent *rule of formation* more easily adapted to machine implementation. In order to appreciate this rule we must first define some terms. When we say that a binary numeral is *inverted* we mean that all its 0s are changed to 1s and all its 1s are changed to 0s. For example, if we invert 1101 we obtain 0010. Further, the left-most and right-most bits of a word are frequently called the *most significant bit* (*MSB*) and the *least significant bit* (*LSB*) respectively. Now for our rule of formation.

> *To form the twos complement of a binary numeral, invert and add* 1 *to the* LSB.

For example,

	$011 = +3$
invert:	100
add 1	$101 = -3$

In VI we shall see that this method of using complements to represent negative numbers lends itself to the mechanisation of arithmetic. As a more realistic example of number representation, this is how the numbers +89 and −89 would appear using twos complements in a 32-bit word computer.

$$0\ 0000000000000000000000001011001 = +89$$
$$1\ 1111111111111111111111110100111 = -89$$

By examining the possible representations of the hypothetical 3-bit word, the reader should verify for himself that the RANGE of an n-bit word is given in general by

$$-2^{n-1} \leqslant N \leqslant 2^{n-1} - 1\text{: twos complement method.}$$

(*b*) *The ones complement method.* We define the ones complement, $0(N)$, of the binary number N by:

$$0(N) = 2^n - 1 - N$$

For example, again using our hypothetical 3-bit word, the ones complement of two is $0(2) = 2^3 - 1 - 2 = 8 - 1 - 2 = 5$, i.e. 010 becomes 101.

The possible representations in the 3-bit word are shown below.

111	−0	negative
110	−1	
101	−2	
100	−3	
011	+3	positive
010	+2	
001	+1	
000	+0	

Notice that on this system there are two different numerals for zero. However, this ambiguity is offset by the simpler rule of formation.

To form the ones complement of a binary numeral, simply invert.

The numbers +89 and −89 can again be compared in their 32-bit word forms (the IBM 360 system uses this word length). So, in ones complement mode:

0 0000000000000000000000001011001 = +89
1 1111111111111111111111110100110 = −89

Using this system, the range of an n-bit word is given by

$$-2^{n-1}+1 \leqslant N \leqslant 2^{n-1}-1\text{: ones complement method.}$$

6. Conversion between binary and decimal numerals

(*a*) *Decimal to binary*. The idea behind this conversion is that of finding the powers of two contained in the decimal number. This is achieved by successive division by two, the remainders at each stage becoming the bits of the binary numeral.

For example, to convert 121_{10} to binary:

2)121		
2)60	r 1	LS
2)30	r 0	
2)15	r 0	
2)7	r 1	
2)3	r 1	
2)1	r 1	
0	r 1	MS

i.e. decimal 121 = binary 1111001
Check: 64+32+16+8+0+0+1 = 121

(*b*) *Binary to decimal.* This is the reverse of the above process. We begin with 1 as the most significant bit and multiply by two for each term, adding 1 when the corresponding bit is 1.

For example, convert 11010_2 to decimal

MS	1	1
	1	3
	0	6
	1	13
	0	26

i.e. binary 11010 = decimal 26
Check: 16+8+0+2+0=26

OTHER SYSTEMS

7. Octal and hexadecimal numerals. Binary numerals, despite their obvious advantage in machine representation of numbers, suffer from the fact that large strings of bits are needed to represent quite small numbers. For this reason, it is common practice in computer circles to write numbers down in forms which are more compact and less prone to error than pure binary. The two most frequently used systems are the *octal* and *hexadecimal* scales. Not only do these scales of numeration provide a more compact notation, they have the advantage that both can be very readily converted to pure binary. This is because both scales have radixes which are powers of two.

(*a*) *Octal* (radix $= 8 = 2^3$). In this system, eight digits are used:

0, 1, 2, 3, 4, 5, 6, 7

Instead of hundreds, tens and units, we now count in sixty-fours (8^2), eights (8^1) and units (8^0). Let us compare the decimal, octal and pure binary scales.

Decimal	*Octal*	*Binary*
0	0	000
1	1	001
2	2	010
3	3	011
4	4	100
5	5	101
6	6	110
7	7	111
8	10	1 000

Decimal	*Octal*	*Binary*
9	11	1 001
10	12	1 010
11	13	1 011
12	14	1 100
13	15	1 101
14	16	1 110
15	17	1 111
16	20	10 000

Examination of the above scales shows just how easy it is to convert octal and binary. To convert a binary string to the equivalent octal we simply form groups of 3 bits and write down the corresponding octal digit for each group. For example, the binary numeral 1110110 is converted to octal as follows:

$$1110110 = 001 \quad 110 \quad 110 \text{ (forming groups of 3 bits)}$$
$$= 1 \quad 6 \quad 6$$

i.e. binary $1110110 = \text{octal}\,166$

Check: $(1\times 64)+(6\times 8)+(6\times 1) \quad = 118$ (decimal)

$64+32+16+0+4+2+0 = 118$ (decimal)

Conversion in the other direction is just the reverse of the above procedure. An octal numeral such as 776767 is the compact equivalent of the binary string:

111 111 011 111 110 111

(*b*) *Hexadecimal* (radix $= 16 = 2^4$). An even more compact notation is obtained by extending the familiar range of basic digits to sixteen by the addition of letters A, B, C, D, E and F to represent the numbers ten through fifteen. Again, compare decimal, hexadecimal and pure binary:

Decimal	*Hexadecimal*	*Binary*
0	0	0000
1	1	0001
2	2	0010
3	3	0011
4	4	0100
5	5	0101
6	6	0110
7	7	0111
8	8	1000
9	9	1001
10	A	1010

Decimal	*Hexadecimal*	*Binary*
11	B	1011
12	C	1100
13	D	1101
14	E	1110
15	F	1111
16	10	1 0000

Once again conversion to and from binary is very simple, the difference here being that groups of *four* bits correspond to a single hexadecimal digit. For example, the binary numeral 1110110 is converted to hexadecimal as follows:

$$1110110 = 0111 \quad 0110 \text{ (forming groups of 4 bits)}$$
$$= 7 \quad 6$$

i.e. binary 1110110 = hexadecimal 76

Check: $(7 \times 16) + (6 \times 1) = 118$ (as before)

Again, conversion in the other direction is the reverse of the above. The hexadecimal numeral FO2C is the compact equivalent of the binary string 1111 0000 0010 1100.

8. Binary-coded decimal codes. Human beings are used to the decimal system and so it is often desirable to build systems which can be operated in decimal. A system working in this fashion has to be able to represent each decimal digit (0 through 9) by means of a code consisting of some pattern of bits. It should be obvious that *four* is the minimum number of bits required for such a representation and that six of the 16 possible permutations of four bits are redundant. It follows that the number of possible codes of this type—called *four-bit binary-coded decimal codes*—is given by:

$$\frac{16!}{6!} = 3 \times 10^{10} \text{ (approx.)}$$

Needless to say, we shall consider only a rather small sample of this enormous range.

The actual choice of code used in practice will depend on such considerations as ease of performing arithmetic, gating operations, storage space and error detection and correction. Let us now examine the more important of these codes.

(*a*) *8421–BCD.* This code is so well known that it is often referred to as simple BCD (binary-coded decimal) on account of the fact that the bit positions within each group of four bits (a group being called a *decade*) have the same weightings as pure binary.

decimal	8421–*BCD*
0	0000
1	0001
2	0010
3	0011
4	0100
5	0101
6	0110
7	0111
8	1000
9	1001
10	0001 0000
11	0001 0001
12	0001 0010
13	0001 0011
	and so on.

The decimal numeral 428 would require three decades for its representation and becomes:

0100 0010 1000

8421–BCD is generally used in smaller computers where the amount of actual arithmetic to be carried out is relatively slight, and in circumstances where the effort of conversion from decimal to binary is not justifiable. Pure binary is still the natural form of representation and it should be remembered that it provides more economical storage than either BCD or raw bytes. As an example of this, consider the decimal numeral 321. We have here three decimal digits which yield the equivalent pure binary numeral

101 000 001 (9 bits)

and the 8421–BCD form

0011 0010 0001 (12 bits)

and in the widely used ASCII (American Standard Code for Information Interchange) system each decimal digit requires one byte (8 bits), yielding

00110011 10110010 10110001 (24 bits)

The BCD form of our number is said to be *packed*, while the ASCII byte form is described as *unpacked*.

(*b*) *Excess 3 Code*. This is an example of a non-weighted code. A decimal digit D is represented by the binary equivalent of $(D+3)$.

Decimal	*Excess* 3
0	0011
1	0100
2	0101
3	0110
4	0111
5	1000
6	1001
7	1010
8	1011
9	1100

As an example, the decimal numeral 321 would appear in Excess 3 as

0110 0101 0100

Although the detail cannot be presented here, the apparent strangeness of Excess 3 is justified in terms of the advantages it offers as a BCD code. One of these is that it greatly facilitates subtraction in that it is a self-complementing code. This means that the *nines complement* of any number can be easily obtained by changing all zeros to ones and all ones to zeros.

FLOATING POINT

9. Floating-point numerals. In scientific work it is quite common practice to work with very large or very small quantities; for example, the charge on the electron has the value

0.000 000 000 000 000 000 160 219 2 coulomb

which is not only small but expressed in a clumsy manner. The physicist would express this quantity in the form

$$1.602\ 192 \times 10^{-19}\ \text{C}$$

which is known as scientific notation. In the computer field a slightly different form is adopted:

$$0.160\ 219\ 2 \times 10^{-18}\ \text{C}$$

Here we have a *fraction* and a power of ten but the form is just as compact.

Numbers written in the latter form are called *floating-point numerals* and are defined in general according to the expression

$$N = f \times r^{\varepsilon}$$

where f is a signed fraction called the *mantissa* (or argument)
ε is a signed integer called the *exponent* (or characteristic)
and r is the radix.

10. Decimal floating-point numerals. In the decimal system $r =$ ten.

e.g. decimal 357 000 would be written $0{\cdot}357 \times 10^6$
i.e. $f = +0.357$
and $\varepsilon = +6$

Similarly decimal $-0.000\,012\,3$ becomes -0.123×10^{-4}
i.e. $f = -0.123$
and $\varepsilon = -4$

Notice that if the radix is known, we only need write (or store) the values of f and ε.

11. Binary floating-point numerals. In the binary system $r =$ two (or binary 10).

e.g. binary 10 000.1 would be written $0.100\ 001 \times 10^{101}$
i.e. $f = 0.100\,001$
and $\varepsilon = 101$

Again, if the radix is assumed, it is only necessary to record the values of f and ε. This could be achieved by storing the mantissa and exponent in a single computer word. For example a 16-bit word could be used as follows:

12 bits	4 bits
f-field	ε-field

With this arrangement the number last considered could be stored in the form:

SB	SB
0 100 001 000 00	0 101

In this particular case both mantissa and exponent are positive, as can be seen from the sign-bits of each (both 0).

How could we represent numbers which are less than one, and which also may be negative? Let us answer this with an example.

Suppose we wished to represent decimal −0.171 875 which is binary −0.001 011. Converting to floating-point form we obtain

$$-0.101\ 1 \times 10^{-10}$$

Here both f and ε are negative which means that we shall have to use a complementary representation. If we form the twos complement of f and ε we obtain the contents of our 16-bit floating-point word as below:

1 010 100 000 00	1 110

This is our representation of decimal −0.171 875 in the computer.

12. Normalisation. In order to obtain maximum precision in the storage of floating-point numerals, it is common practice to shift the fraction part as far to the left as possible without losing any significant bits or causing the register storing the numeral to overflow.

For example, the form

0 010 000 100 00	0 110	=decimal +16.5

is *not* normalised. Shifting f one place to the left and reducing the exponent by 1 gives the *normalised* form:

0 100 001 000 00	0 101	normalised

Similarly, the form

1 110 000 000 00	1 101	=decimal −0.031 25
$-\frac{1}{4}$	2^{-3}	

is *not* normalised. Shifting f and adjusting the exponent gives the normalised representation:

1 000 000 000 00	1 011
−1	2^{-5}

This normalisation process is of great importance in floating-point arithmetic operations. If it is not carried out very grave errors would result in the simplest of calculations.

13. Range of mantissa and exponent. The permitted range of the MANTISSA in the normalised form is defined as follows:

$$+\tfrac{1}{2} \leqslant f < +1$$
$$-1 \leqslant f < -\tfrac{1}{2}$$

This range may be better visualised and remembered by referring to Fig. 3 in which a *full* vertical line denotes an included end-of-

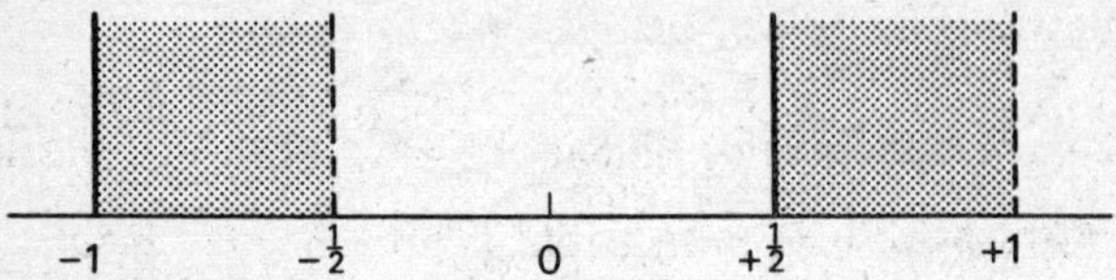

FIG. 3 *Mantissa range.*

range value and a dotted vertical line denotes that the end-of-range value is not included. Again with reference to the 16-bit word, let us summarise the permitted and the forbidden mantissa values.

```
  1.111 111 111 11 = full f-field ┐
  1.111 111 111 10                │
  .                               │
  .                               ├ forbidden values
  .                               │
  1.100 000 000 01                │
  1.100 000 000 00 = −½           ┘
 │1.011 111 111 11│= smallest magnitude in negative range
 │1.011 111 111 10│
 │.               │
−│.               │
 │.               │
 │1.000 000 000 01│
 │1.000 000 000 00│= greatest magnitude in negative range (−1)
 │────────────────│
 │0.111 111 111 11│= greatest magnitude in positive range
 │0.111 111 111 10│
 │.               │
+│.               │
 │.               │
 │0.100 000 000 01│
 │0.100 000 000 00│= smallest magnitude in positive range (+½)
```

$$\left.\begin{array}{l} 0.011\ 111\ 111\ 11 \\ 0.011\ 111\ 111\ 10 \\ \cdot \\ \cdot \\ \cdot \\ 0.000\ 000\ 000\ 01 \\ 0.000\ 000\ 000\ 00 = \text{empty } f\text{-field} \end{array}\right\} \text{forbidden values}$$

Examination of the above summary shows that we can precisely define the permitted mantissa range as follows:

$$+\tfrac{1}{2} \leqslant f \leqslant 1 - 2^{-(m-1)}$$
$$-1 \leqslant f \leqslant -\tfrac{1}{2} - 2^{-(m-1)}$$

where m is the number of bits allocated to the f-field.

Another important observation is that, provided the mantissa is in the permitted range, the two left-most bits of the f-field will be *different*. This provides a simple means of checking to see if a floating-point numeral has been normalised. A floating-point arithmetic unit contains hardware which reduces all numerals to the normalised form before or after operations.

Summarising the exponent values of our 16-bit word, we have:

$$\begin{array}{l} 1111 = -1 \\ 1110 \\ \cdot \\ \cdot \\ \cdot \\ 1000 = -8 \\ 0111 = +7 \\ \cdot \\ \cdot \\ \cdot \\ 0001 = +1 \\ 0000 = 0 \end{array}$$

Here,

$$-8 \leqslant \varepsilon \leqslant +7$$

from which we can write the range of the exponent in general:

$$-2^{p-1} \leqslant \varepsilon \leqslant 2^{p-1} - 1$$

where p is the number of bits allocated to the exponent field.

In practice it is common to encounter quite large values of m and p. For example a 32-bit word could be divided into a 24-bit mantissa and an 8-bit exponent, in which case the largest number

@	100 0000	0	011 0000
A	100 0001	1	011 0001
B	100 0010	2	011 0010
C	100 0011	3	011 0011
D	100 0100	4	011 0100
E	100 0101	5	011 0101
F	100 0110	6	011 0110
G	100 0111	7	011 0111
H	100 1000	8	011 1000
I	100 1001	9	011 1001
J	100 1010	:	011 1010
K	100 1011	;	011 1011
L	100 1100	<	011 1100
M	100 1101	=	011 1101
N	100 1110	>	011 1110
O	100 1111	?	011 1111
P	101 0000	Space	010 0000
Q	101 0001	!	010 0001
R	101 0010	"	010 0010
S	101 0011	#	010 0011
T	101 0100	$	010 0100
U	101 0101	%	010 0101
V	101 0110	&	010 0110
W	101 0111	'	010 0111
X	101 1000	(	010 1000
Y	101 1001	)	010 1001
Z	101 1010	*	010 1010
[	101 1011	+	010 1011
\	101 1100	,	010 1100
]	101 1101	–	010 1101
↑	101 1110	.	010 1110
←	101 1111	/	010 1111

Line feed	000 1010
Carriage return	000 1101
Bell	000 0111
Delete	111 1111

FIG. 4 *American Standard Code for Information Interchange (ASCII). Parity bit omitted.*

able to be represented would correspond to $\varepsilon = 2^{8-1} - 1 = 127$, and $f = 1 - 2^{-(24-1)}$.

i.e. largest positive number $= (1 - 2^{-23}) \times 2^{127}$
$= \text{decimal } 1.7 \times 10^{38}$ approximately.

NON-NUMERIC INFORMATION

14. Non-numeric information. As well as representing numbers, the computer must also have some means of representing letters of the alphabet and other commonly occurring symbols such as &, @, *, ; etc. All methods of representation use a distinctive pattern of bits for each character to be encoded, and from the discussion in II, it is clear that the number of bits in each character is determined by the total number of characters required.

A complete character set would have to contain numerics as well as alphabetics, and so a *minimum* set of *alphanumerics* might be broken down as follows:

10 numerics (0 through 9)
26 alphabetics (A through Z)
16 special characters (£, &, +, ..., =, ?)

This comprises a total of 52 alphanumerics.

Now a 5-bit set would permit the representation of $2^5 = 32$ alphanumerics, which is not enough. A 6-bit set would allow the representation of $2^6 = 64$ alphanumerics, which would be more than enough for our minimum set.

In practice it is found that more than this minimum character set is required. The ASCII (American Standard Code for Information Interchange) system is now widely used; it consists of an 8-bit set, one bit of which (the parity bit) is used for checking purposes and the remaining 7 bits being used to represent a comprehensive set of alphanumerics as shown in Fig. 4. Notice the very important *carriage return* and *line feed* characters, which do not cause printing but signal the carriage of a computer-linked teletypewriter to return to the beginning of the print line and cause vertical paper movement to the next line respectively. The *delete* character has no significance of its own, and being completely ignored by the computer, is useful in the deletion of wrong characters on paper tape.

PROGRESS TEST

1. Find the twos complement of the following: 11 011, 1, 1001, 1011. (**5**)

2. What is the decimal capacity of a 16-bit binary register in (*a*) positive integer form; (*b*) twos complement form? (**5**)

3. Convert the following binary integers to decimal: 101, 1011, 111 101. (**6**)

4. Convert the following decimal integers to binary, octal, and hexadecimal: 396, 16, 100, 64, 32, 768, 0. (**6, 7**)

5. Convert the following octal integers to decimal: 10, 64, 777. (**7**)

6. Convert the following hexadecimal integers to decimal: E3, 3FF, ABC, 9D31. (**7**)

7. Explain the term BCD. How is BCD used in the representation of information? (**8**)

8. A 12-bit register is used to hold numbers in binary floating-point form. The first 8 bits hold the mantissa and the last 4 bits hold the exponent. The assumed point lies between the two left-most bits and twos complements form is used to represent negative numbers. The mantissa ranges are:

$$-1 \leqslant \text{negative mantissa} < -\tfrac{1}{2}$$
$$+\tfrac{1}{2} \leqslant \text{positive mantissa} < +1$$

and the exponent range is -8 through $+7$. Explain how the mantissa limits facilitate a simple overflow check. Display the maximum and minimum of the positive and negative numbers which can be held in floating-point form in the register. (**13**)

CHAPTER IV

The Basic Building-blocks: Logic Gates; Combinational Circuits

LOGIC GATES

1. The need for logic gates. A digital computer may be thought of as a set of interconnected electronic sub-systems, as was described in II. These sub-systems are themselves constructed of simpler elements which are linked in special ways so that the separate functions of the sub-systems can be effectively carried out.

Although the number of elements in a particular sub-system may be very large and the manner in which connections made apparently of overwhelming complexity, a fact of immense use is that the number of *types* of element needed can be reduced to a mere handful. These basic elements, or fundamental building-blocks, are called *logic gates*, electronic circuits which can provide control of information flow, numerous logical and arithmetic functions, memory facility and even the timing circuitry which synchronises the whole machine.

2. Electronic representation of information. As we saw in III, information can be represented by means of patterns of bits, a bit being either a 1 or a 0. Electronic computers invariably use two different fixed voltages to represent information in bit form. A simple system might be to use −6 volts (say) to stand for 1 and zero voltage to stand for 0. With this sort of convention the fundamental logic operations can be carried out with relatively simple electronics.

Gating logic may be implemented through the use of a variety of devices such as transistors and diodes. At the time of writing the available technology enables these semiconductor devices to be formed into complete *integrated circuits* of very small dimensions. In this chapter we shall stress the *principles* of logic rather than the development of hardware, but it will be shown how a single circuit can be used as a basis for all the other possible gates. The approach chosen is based on *resistor–transistor logic* (RTL). The basic circuit is the NOR-gate.

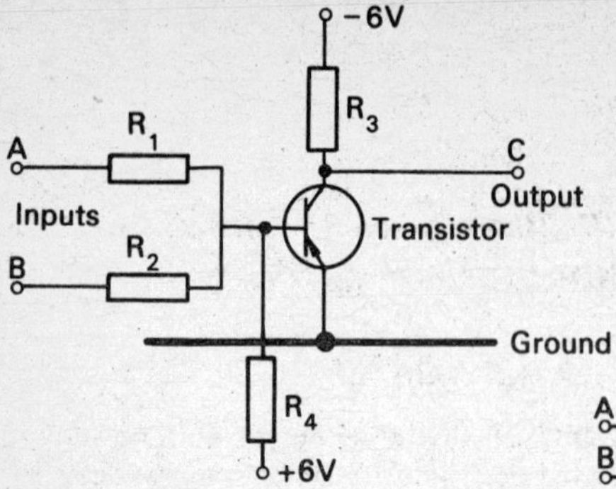

Truth table

A	B	C
1	1	0
1	0	0
0	1	0
0	0	1

FIG. 5 *The NOR-gate.*

3. The NOR-gate. Readers with a little knowledge of electronics will have no difficulty in understanding the operation of this gate which is illustrated in Fig. 5, the operation being briefly as follows.

Normally the transistor is biassed *off* (i.e. non-conducting) by means of the resistor R_4. This means that there will be no current in the resistor R_3 and it follows that the output point, *C*, will be at −6 V, or logic 1. If one of the inputs A or B (or both) is presented with −6 V, this has the effect of turning the transistor *on* (i.e. conducting), the effect of which is to bring the output, C, very close to zero voltage or logic 0. All the possible states of the gate are summarised in a *truth table* which also appears in Fig. 5 along with a *logic gate symbol* which facilitates the drawing of computer logic circuits.

4. The INVERTER. This is an important special case of the NOR-gate, being just a NOR-gate with a *fan-in* (the number of inputs) of *one*. The effect of this gate is to convert a 1 into a 0 and vice versa. One immediately obvious application of this device is the formation of complements as discussed in III. The logic symbol of the inverter and its truth are shown in Fig. 6. Notice that a bar ($\bar{}$) placed over a symbol is used to denote the *inverse* of a logic variable. For example if A = 1 then A (called NOT A) = 0.

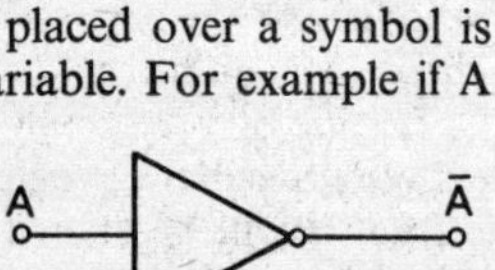

A	Ā
1	0
0	1

FIG. 6 *The INVERTER.*

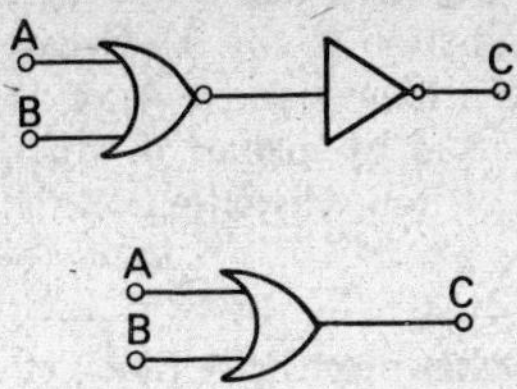

A	B	C
1	1	1
0	1	1
1	0	1
0	0	0

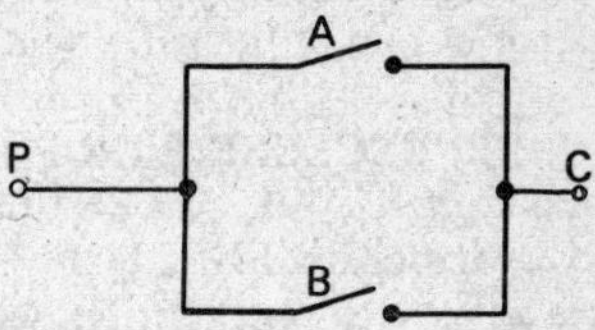

FIG. 7 *The INCLUSIVE OR-gate.*

5. The INCLUSIVE OR-gate. A NOR-gate followed by an inverter creates the device known as an INCLUSIVE OR-gate. Examination of Fig. 7 shows that the output of this gate is just the inverse of the NOR-gate. A 1 appears at the output whenever a 1 appears at either A *or* B and *includes* the case of a 1 appearing at *both* A and B (hence the term INCLUSIVE). This gate provides a *mixing* function in the computer. A single logic symbol for this gate is shown in Fig. 7 together with a simple electric switch analogy. A signal in the form of an electric current can make its way to C if switch A is closed *or* if switch B is closed *or* if both A and B are closed. Thus, the truth table for INCLUSIVE OR applies also to this simple circuit if we use 1 to represent switch closed and 0 to represent switch open.

6. The AND-gate. Inversion of the inputs to a NOR-gate gives us the very important AND-function. By examination of all the possible states of A and B in Fig. 8 the reader will easily verify that the output, C, can only be a 1 when both A *and* B are 1s. This is exactly the function obtained by having two switches A

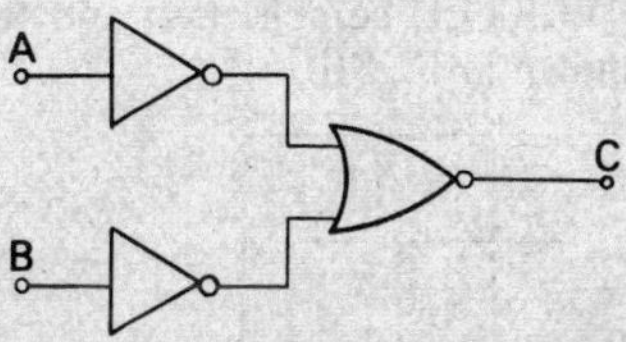

A	B	C
1	1	1
1	0	0
0	1	0
0	0	0

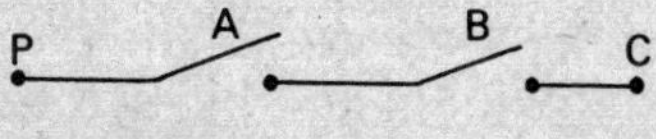

FIG. 8 *The AND-gate.*

and B in series (*see* Fig. 8). A signal from P can only reach C if both A *and* B are closed. The AND-truth table and single logic symbol also appear in the figure. One function of the AND-gate in the computer is in the detection of coincident signals. Another is its application as a sort of electronic tap by means of which a string of bits may be allowed to pass or not, depending on the state of one of the gate inputs.

7. The EXCLUSIVE OR-gate. A somewhat more elaborate combination of ANDs, INVERTERS and or OR-gate gives rise to the very important EXCLUSIVE OR-gate shown in Fig. 9. The reader is advised to verify for himself the associated truth table using his knowledge of the functions of the constituent gates. It will be seen that a 1 appears at the output when A *or* B are 1 but not when both are 1 (i.e. this case is *excluded*, hence the name). Another important name for this function is the *non-equivalence operation*, as a 1 output is only obtained when the input bits are different (i.e. non-equivalent). A single logic symbol for this gate also appears in Fig. 9.

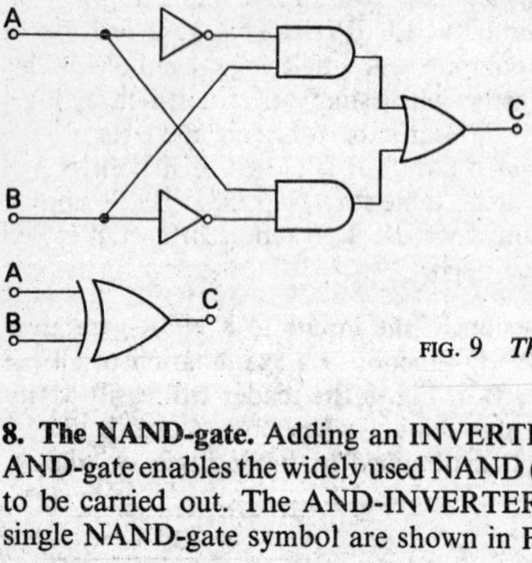

A	B	C
1	1	0
1	0	1
0	1	1
0	0	0

FIG. 9 *The EXCLUSIVE OR-gate.*

8. The NAND-gate. Adding an INVERTER to the output of an AND-gate enables the widely used NAND (NOT-AND) operation to be carried out. The AND-INVERTER combination and the single NAND-gate symbol are shown in Fig. 10.

A	B	$\overline{A.B}$
1	1	0
1	0	1
0	1	1
0	0	1

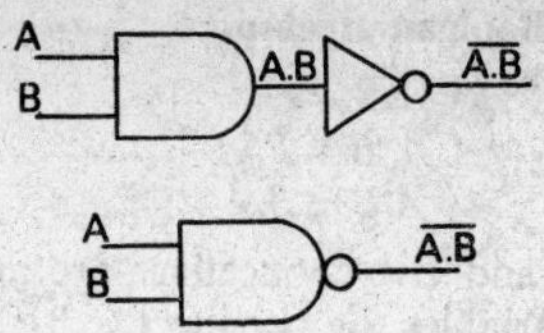

FIG. 10 *The NAND-gate.*

The truth table shows that the output of a NAND-gate is always a 1 unless both (or all, in the case of a multi-input gate) of its inputs are at the 1 level. Some applications of this gate will be described in V.

BOOLEAN ALGEBRA AND LOGIC CIRCUITS

9. Boolean algebra. In 1848 the mathematician George Boole showed that any instruction for dealing with information in binary form can be expressed with the aid of the three logical operations: AND, OR and NOT (i.e. inversion). In 1938 C. E. Shannon pointed out that the operations in Boole's special algebra can be performed by means of a suitable arrangement of electrical switches. Thus we have in our possession a neat and powerful means of describing the behaviour of complex switching networks such as those found in the modern computer.

The variables in Boolean algebra, *A*, *B*, *C*, ... etc., can only take on the values 1 and 0. This is quite unlike ordinary algebra, where a variable can have any value at all. The symbols for the Boolean operators used in this book are presented below:

AND .
OR v
NOT- $\bar{\text{v}}$

For example, the result of combining the variables *A* and *B* under the AND operation would be written

$$A.B$$

and under the OR operation,

$$A_{\text{v}}B$$

while NOT B would appear as

$$\bar{B}$$

10. The postulates of Boolean algebra.

(*a*) *The Commutative laws.*

$$A_{v}B = B_{v}A$$
$$A.B = B.A$$

The results of AND and OR connectives are unaffected by the sequence of logical variables they connect.

(*b*) *The Associative laws.*

$$A_{v}(B_{v}C) = (A_{v}B)_{v}C$$
$$A.(B.C) = (A.B).C$$

The variables may be grouped in any quantity as long as they are connected by the same connective.

(*c*) *The Distributive law.*

$$A.(B_{v}C) = A.B_{v}A.C$$

This should be compared to factoring in ordinary algebra.

(*d*) *The Unit laws.*

$$1.A = A$$
$$1_{v}A = 1$$

(*e*) *The Zero laws.*

$$0.A = 0$$
$$0_{v}A = A$$

(*f*) *The Complement laws.*

$$A.\bar{A} = 0$$
$$A_{v}\bar{A} = 1$$

(*g*) *De Morgan's theorems.*

$$\bar{A}.\bar{B} = \overline{A_{v}B}$$
$$\overline{A.B} = \bar{A}_{v}\bar{B}$$

The laws summarised above are all of great use in the design of logic circuits, in that their careful application can often lead to considerable simplification of the original problem solution. Simplification naturally means a cheaper and less bulky piece of hardware.

11. Perfect induction. The simplest way to show the truth of the above laws is to use the method known as *perfect induction*. Using this approach, all the possible permutations of the relevant variables are listed in a tabular form and the expressions corresponding to each side of the postulated equality are evaluated by means of the basic operators AND, OR and NOT. (Incidentally, the AND and OR operators are called *dyadic*, as they are used to combine two vari-

A	B	C	$A.B$	$B.C$	$A.(B.C)$	$(A.B).C$
1	1	1	1	1	1	1
1	1	0	1	0	0	0
1	0	1	0	0	0	0
1	0	0	0	0	0	0
0	1	1	0	1	0	0
0	1	0	0	0	0	0
0	0	1	0	0	0	0
0	0	0	0	0	0	0

FIG. 11 *Proof of Associative Law.*

ables, while NOT is called a *unary* operator as it is applied to one variable or one group of variables.) The method of perfect induction is illustrated in Fig. 11 where the Associative Law for AND is proved. Fig. 12 shows a proof of the very important De Morgan theorem, a relationship which finds much application in logic circuit design.

Same

A	B	$A_v B$	$\overline{A_v B}$	$\bar{A}$	$\bar{B}$	$\bar{A}.\bar{B}$
1	1	1	0	0	0	0
1	0	1	0	0	1	0
0	1	1	0	1	0	0
0	0	0	1	1	1	1

FIG. 12 *Proof of first De Morgan theorem.*

Manipulation of Boolean algebra bears a striking resemblance to ordinary algebra. The distributive law:

$$A.(B_v C) = A.B_v A.C$$

should be compared to the familiar multiplying out which is commonly used in ordinary algebra, viz.

$$a(b+c) = ab+ac$$

The laws of zero

$$0.A=0;\ 0_{\text{v}}A=A$$

are also reminiscent of the more familiar forms

$$0\times a=0;\ 0+A=A$$

12. Principles of circuit simplification. There are two kinds of approach to the simplification of logic circuits which are in common use:

(*a*) One in which the basic aim is to reduce the number of logic functions in the corresponding Boolean expression. This leads to a smaller number of logic gates and interconnections with a reduction in the overall cost of the system.

(*b*) One in which the aim is to reduce the original circuit to one consisting of various combinations of a limited number of available gate types. There are two basic systems in use—the NOR-system and the NAND-system. This approach can lead to reduced costs and ease of maintenance.

13. Reduction in the number of logic functions. Fig. 13 shows three logic gates connected so as to produce an output given by:

$$D=(A_{\text{v}}B).(B_{\text{v}}C)$$

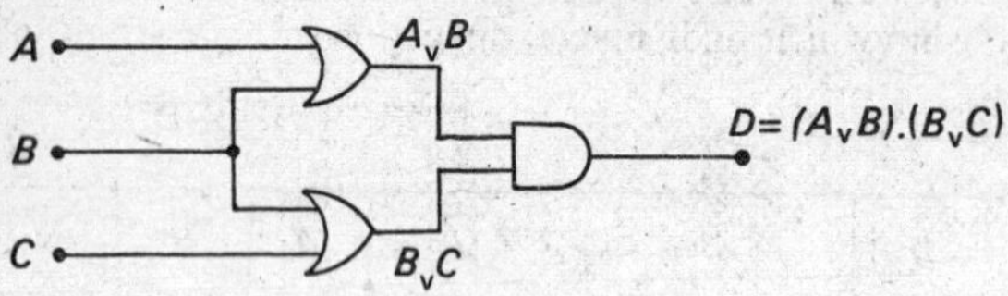

FIG. 13

Using the distributive law, this can be written in the form

$D=A.B_{\text{v}}B.C_{\text{v}}B.B_{\text{v}}B.C$	
$=A.B_{\text{v}}B.C_{\text{v}}B_{\text{v}}B.C$	(as $B.B=B$)
$=A.B_{\text{v}}B.C_{\text{v}}B$	(as $B.C_{\text{v}}B.C.=B.C$)
$=(A_{\text{v}}C_{\text{v}}1).B$	(distributive law)
i.e. $D=(A_{\text{v}}C).B$	(as $C_{\text{v}}1=C$)

Thus we have reduced the original circuit to that in Fig. 14.

In the above example we have eliminated only one gate, so in order to illustrate the considerable gains which can be made we will next take a circuit consisting of *nine* gates and reduce it to only *two*.

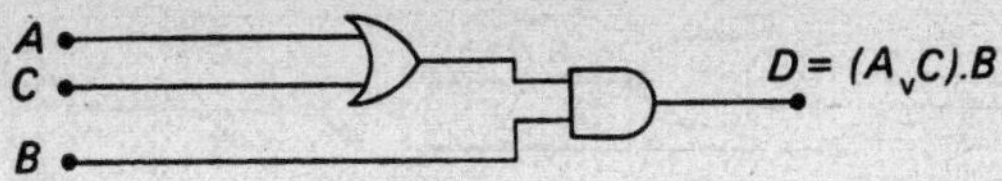

FIG. 14

Referring to Fig. 15 we have a circuit with an output F given by

$$
\begin{aligned}
F &= A.\bar{B}.C.D_{\mathrm{v}}A.(\bar{B}.E_{\mathrm{v}}\bar{B}.\bar{E}) & & \\
&= A.\bar{B}.C.D_{\mathrm{v}}A.\bar{B}.(E_{\mathrm{v}}\bar{E}) & & \text{(distributive law)} \\
&= A.\bar{B}.C.D_{\mathrm{v}}A.\bar{B} & & \text{(as } E_{\mathrm{v}}\bar{E} = 1\text{)} \\
&= A.\bar{B}(C.D_{\mathrm{v}}1) & & \text{(distributive law)} \\
\text{i.e. } F &= A.\bar{B} & & \text{(unit law: } X_{\mathrm{v}}1 = 1\text{)}
\end{aligned}
$$

The above manipulation should convince the reader of the great importance of Boolean algebra for the logic designer. We have completely eliminated *seven* gates and shown that the logic levels on the lines C, D and E are utterly irrelevant to the generation of the function F. The equivalent circuit is shown in Fig. 16.

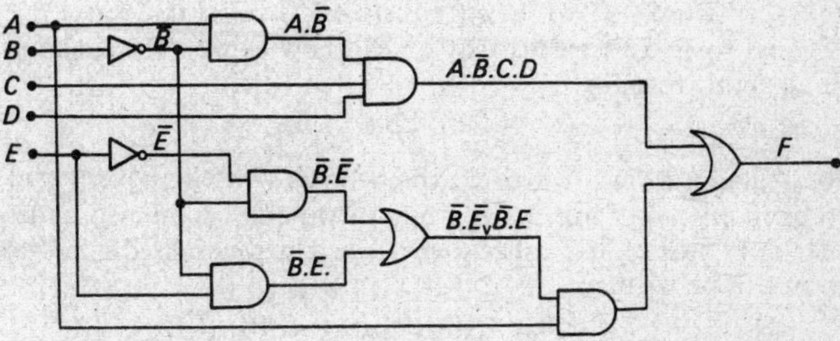

FIG. 15

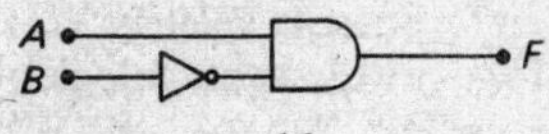

FIG. 16

14. Redundant circuits. It sometimes happens that a logic circuit turns out to be completely redundant; such is the case with the circuit of Fig. 17. Its output is given by

$$
\begin{aligned}
C &= \overline{A.B_{\mathrm{v}}B} & & \\
&= \overline{\overline{A.B}}.\bar{B} & & \text{(De Morgan theorem)} \\
&= A.B.\bar{B} & & \\
\text{i.e. } C &= 0 & & \text{(as } B.\bar{B} = 0\text{)}
\end{aligned}
$$

In other words the output of this circuit is always zero.

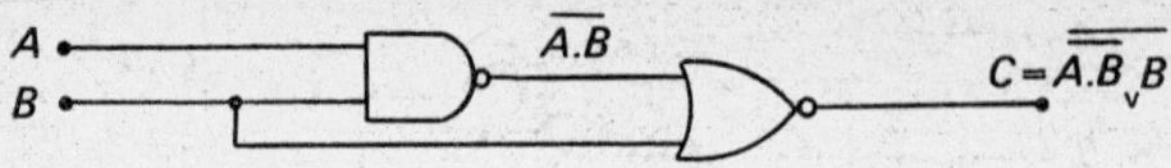

FIG. 17 *A redundant logic circuit.*

15. Functions from truth tables. Chapter VI will show how arithmetic functions can be carried out by suitable combinations of logic gates. We shall there find the need to translate a given truth table into a corresponding Boolean function and so the method of accomplishing this will now be described.

Consider the truth table in Fig. 18. Here the logical variable, D, is a function of the variables A, B and C; in fact, the truth table effectively defines the function. Notice that the function is *true* (i.e. $D=1$) for only three combinations of the variables A, B and C:

100
010
and 001

In other words, $D=1$ when either $A.\bar{B}.\bar{C}$ or $\bar{A}.B.\bar{C}$ or $\bar{A}.\bar{B}.C$ is equal to 1. This means that we can now express the function in algebraic form as

$$D = A.\bar{B}.\bar{C}_{\text{v}}\bar{A}.B.\bar{C}_{\text{v}}\bar{A}.\bar{B}.C$$

16. Minterm forms. A logical expression as written above is said to be in *minterm* form. Each group of variables combined under the AND operation is called a *minterm*. The generalised minterm form can be written:

$$F = m_{0\text{v}}m_{1\text{v}}m_{2\text{v}}m_{3\text{v}} \ldots\ldots \text{etc.}$$

where m_0, m_1, m_2, ... are the minterms making up the function F. Once such a form has been obtained from a truth table it is usually possible to simplify it by Boolean algebra. We shall give an example of this process in VI where we look at the logic of computer addition.

17. Code converters. Although computers operate with various forms of binary code, man prefers to work in the decimal code. It is therefore necessary to be able to construct devices which can convert between binary codes and decimal. Such devices are called *code converters* and are usually classified as either *encoders* or *decoders*. It is probably best to reserve the term *encoder* for conversion into some binary code and use *decoder* to describe a device which converts a given binary code into decimal.

Many methods of code conversion are used in practice but the basic principles of such techniques can be understood by examining two commonly needed converters. The first of these is a *decimal-*

A	*B*	*C*	*D*
1	1	1	0
1	1	0	0
1	0	1	0
1	0	0	1
0	1	1	0
0	1	0	1
0	0	1	1
0	0	0	0

FIG. 18 *Truth table for the function:* $D = A.\bar{B}.\bar{C} \vee \bar{A}.B.\bar{C} \vee \bar{A}.\bar{B}.C$.

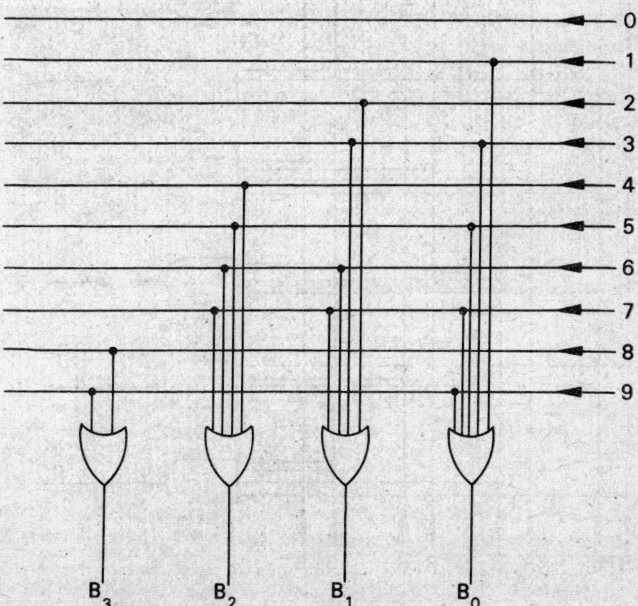

FIG. 19 *DECIMAL-TO- 8421 BCD ENCODER*

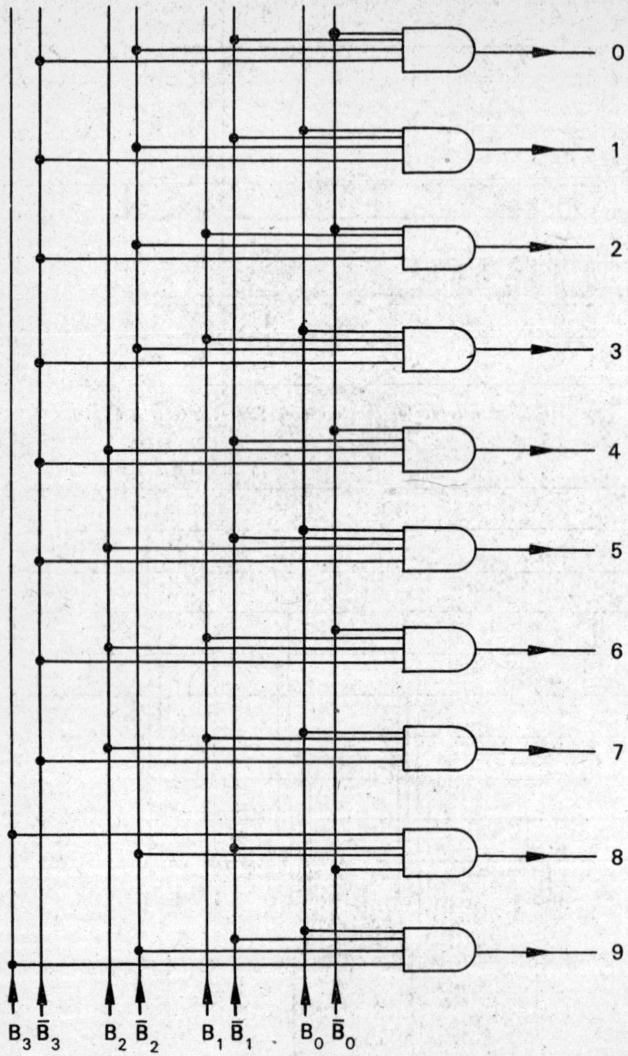

FIG. 20 *8421 BCD-TO-DECIMAL DECODER.*

to-8421 BCD encoder, illustrated in Fig. 19. Decimal inputs to the device are on the right and the output bits appear as B_0, B_1, B_2 and B_3. The reader will be able to verify that, when *one* of the ten input lines is energised, the correct corresponding bit-pattern will appear at the outputs. For example, with line 5 energised, the OR-gate outputs from left to right will be 0, 1, 0, and 1 respectively; i.e. 0101 will be the output.

In Fig. 20 the reverse process is carried out, the input bit-pattern being fed in from the bottom and the decimal output appearing on the right. This circuit uses AND-gates and also requires that the inverse of each input bit is available. This is easily provided by inverters (not shown in the diagram). Again the reader will be able to verify that input of a group of bits such as 0101 (together with the inverse pattern 1010) will cause correct decoding to decimal 5. The output signals may be used to drive display lamps or they may be used to energise printers or other devices.

PROGRESS TEST 4

1.

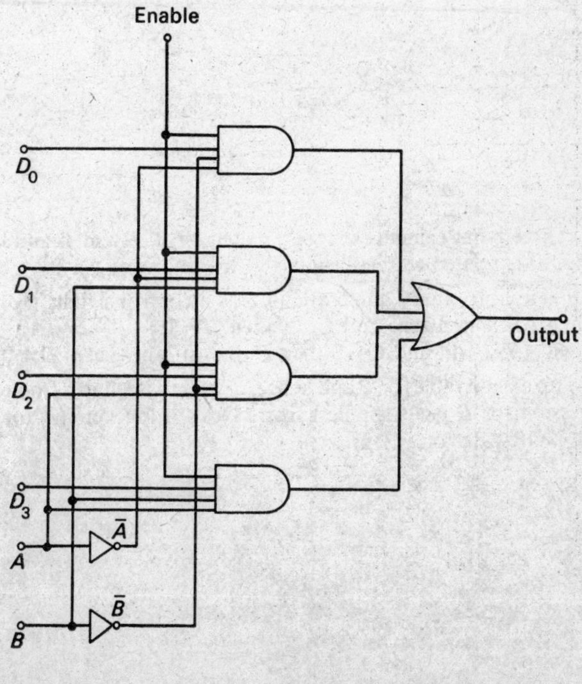

The diagram shows a logic circuit called a *multiplexer*. Inputs to the circuit are D_0, D_1, D_2 and D_3. By examining the logic gate actions, describe what happens when bits are presented to the terminals marked A, B, and ENABLE. Why are multiplexers important in computer systems? **(3–7)**

2. A decimal digit in the range 0 through 9 is represented by 4 binary signals W, X, Y, Z in a standard binary-coded decimal form. Give a Boolean expression for S, which represents the forbidden combinations of W, X, Y, Z which would represent the integers 10 through 15, stating clearly which binary signal represents the least significant digit. Simplify the expression for S, if possible, and draw an efficient logic circuit consisting of NOR-gates only which would detect a forbidden combination. **(8–9)**

3. By using truth tables prove the results:

$$X_{\text{v}}(\bar{X}.Y) = X_{\text{v}}Y$$
$$(X.Y)_{\text{v}}(X.\bar{Y}) = X \qquad \textbf{(11)}$$

4. Simplify the logic circuits below: **(12)**

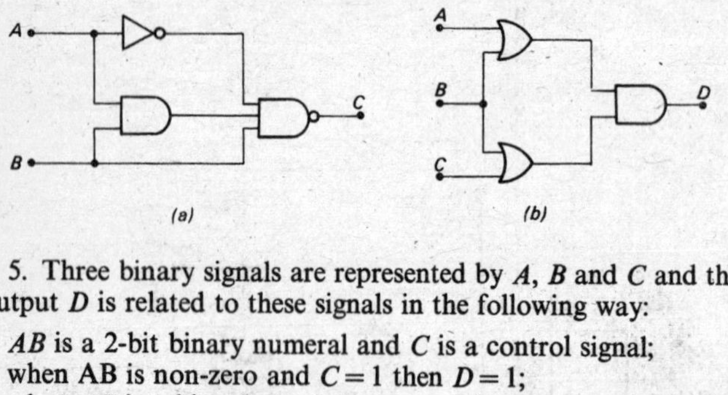

(a) (b)

5. Three binary signals are represented by *A*, *B* and *C* and the output *D* is related to these signals in the following way:

AB is a 2-bit binary numeral and *C* is a control signal;
when AB is non-zero and $C = 1$ then $D = 1$;
when *AB* is odd and $C = 0$ then $D = 1$ (in other cases $D = 0$);

Draw up a truth table for *D* and hence, or otherwise, find a Boolean expression for *D* in its simplest form. Draw a logic circuit for *D* using NOR-gates only. **(15)**

CHAPTER V

Two-state Devices and Sequential Circuits

FLIP-FLOPS AND THEIR USES

1. The basic flip-flop. A very interesting and important device results from the special combination of the two NOR-gates shown in Fig. 21. Here the output of one gate is fed back to the input of the other producing a state which is inherently *stable*. The circuit is shown in one of its *two* stable states. The application of a 1 at the input labelled R (*reset*) will make no difference to this particular state, as can be easily verified by referring to the truth table for the NOR-function (Fig. 5). However, the application of a 1 to the input labelled S (*set*) changes the A output to logic 0. This is then propagated to the right-hand gate input which results in $\bar{A} = 1$, which in turn is propagated to the left-hand gate giving a new stable state.

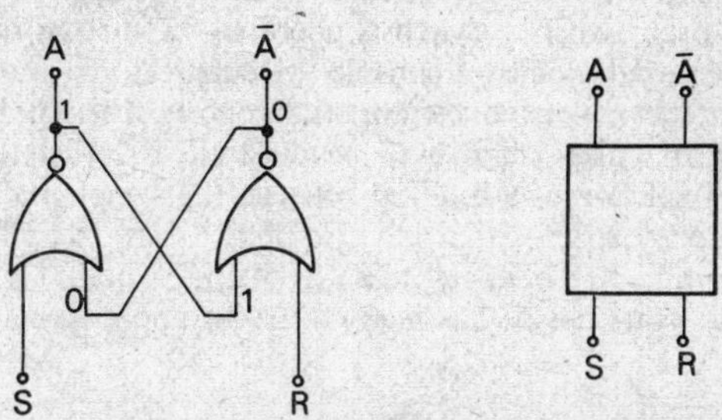

FIG. 21 *The basic flip-flop (the SR-flip-flop or latch).*

2. Provision of memory. It should be clear that this arrangement provides a *memory* facility, something which was absent from the purely combinational logic circuits considered in IV. This new feature has arisen because of the existence of *negative feedback*. This term is well known to physicists and engineers and describes an arrangement in which the output signal from a device (such as an amplifier) is fed back to the input in such a way that *stability* results. Examination of Fig. 21 will reveal that the device can "remember" which input was the one last fed with a 1 signal. This primitive but vital device is termed a *basic flip-flop* or *bistable multivibrator*.

The flip-flop provides storage for a single bit of information and, at the present state of the art, a fast flip-flop can be set in around 10 nanoseconds. Processing requires the transmission of information from point to point within the CPU. Intermediate storage is almost always required. Using cores (*see* 88–90) or other devices for this temporary memory would slow down computers considerably. The flip-flop supplies high-speed storage in all the computer sub-systems.

3. Action and application of basic flip-flop. Figure 21 also contains a simple box-symbol for the basic flip-flop which is used in this book. This symbol is used in Fig. 22 which shows in stage-by-stage form how the flip-flop is first set and then reset by application of a 1 at the S-input followed by application of a 1 at the R-input. It will be noticed that a 1 need be applied only *once* to set the flip-flop. A subsequent string of 1s applied to the S-input will make no difference to the state of the device. This property is frequently utilised in the avoidance of "contact bounce". The latter will often occur when a switch is operated to start an operation from the computer control console. Mechanical vibration of the switch contacts may produce more than one electrical pulse. Such a plurality of pulses might well produce effects other than that intended. Inclusion of a flip-flop between the switch and the rest of the circuitry ensures that a *single* pulse is produced from the random number of bounce pulses from the switch. This simple type of two-state device has many different applications in com-

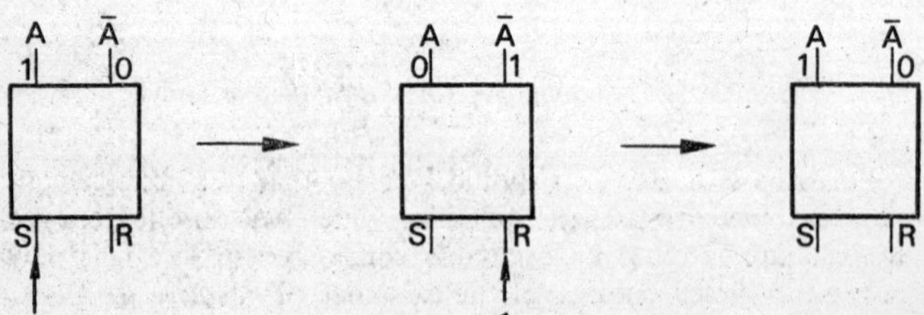

FIG. 22 *Action of the basic flip-flop.*

puter circuits, but by itself is incapable of providing the most important functions of counting and shifting.

4. The logical flip-flop. Addition of a small amount of combinational circuitry to the basic flip-flop produces a device of much greater general application. The necessary addition consists of two specially designed AND-gates connected in the manner depicted in Fig. 23. The AND-gates constitute what is known as a *steering circuit*, the purpose of which is to "steer" signals applied at the *trigger-pulse input*, T, to one side or other of the basic flip-flop.

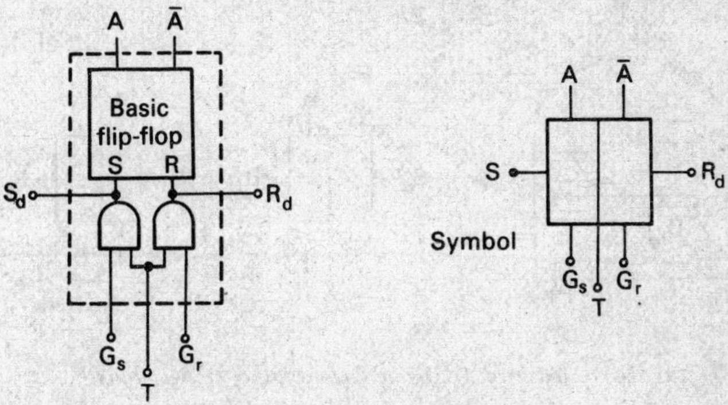

FIG. 23 *The logical flip-flop.*

The resulting device (general symbol shown in Fig. 23) is termed the *logical flip-flop* and has two outputs and five inputs. The direct connections to S- and R-inputs are now termed S_d (set direct) and R_d (reset direct) respectively. The AND-gate inputs are termed G_s (gate set) and G_r (gate reset). The electronics of these special capacitive AND-gates is shown in Fig. 24 and their function is essentially two-fold.

(*a*) They shape incoming trigger pulses from rectangular form to a "spike".

(*b*) They provide the pulse-steering facility.

Refer to Fig. 24. Suppose the G_s-input is at the 0 level. A negative-going rectangular pulse at T is differentiated by the capacitor to produce a negative and positive spike. The diode D_2 only passes the positive spike. When the G_s-input is at the 1 level, D_2 is effectively biassed off, and so no spikes reach the output of the gate. A pulse applied to the T-input causes a positive spike to go to the transistor whose corresponding gate input is at the 0 level. These positive spikes will turn the particular transistor *off*. If the reader studies the two right-hand diagrams of Fig. 24, he will see that *pulses applied to the T-input will only change the state of the flip-flop if on one side both gate and output terminals are initially at the same logic level*. It should be clear that we now have a much more useful device—one which will flip or not depending on the logic levels present at its gate inputs.

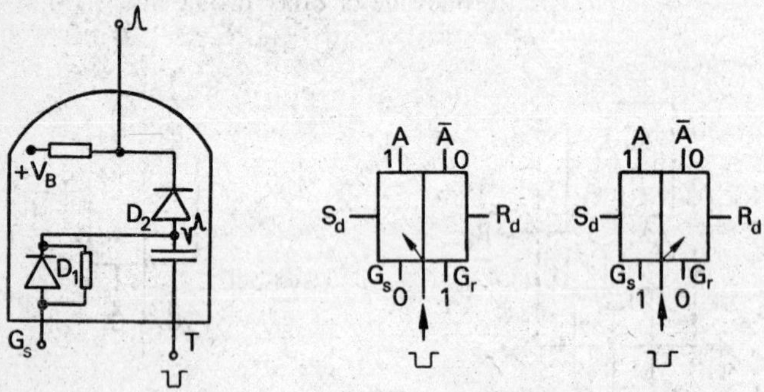

FIG. 24 *Capacitive AND-gate and operation of logical flip-flop.*

5. Internal gating. An important and interesting way of using the logical flip-flop is the *internally gated mode* in which the gate inputs are connected to the corresponding output terminals. This configuration is depicted in Fig. 25. Following the rule of behaviour derived above, it will be seen that, in this mode, the flip-flop will

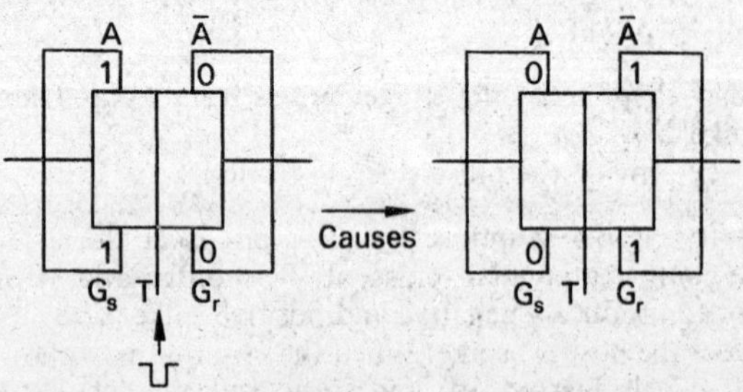

FIG. 25 *Internal gating (the T-flip-flop).*

change its state every time a trigger pulse is applied to it. If a number of internally gated flip-flops are connected in a chain, we obtain a simple binary counter.

6. The serial up-counter. A chain of this sort is shown in Fig. 26 and is called a four-stage serial up-counter. Each flip-flop in the counter is internally gated and the A output of each stage is connected to the T-input of the following stage. Application of trigger pulses to the right-most stage results in a pure binary counting sequence, part of which is seen in Fig. 27. Notice that the device is only properly an *up*-counter if the $\bar{A}$-outputs are examined; examination of the A-outputs results in a *down*-count from 1111 (decimal 15). With reference to Fig. 27 it will be noticed that a given stage will only flip on receiving a negative-going trigger pulse from the preceding stage. This occurs when the A-output of the preceding stage changes from a 0 to a 1 but not the other way around. Such pulses are shown on the third and bottom lines of Fig. 27.

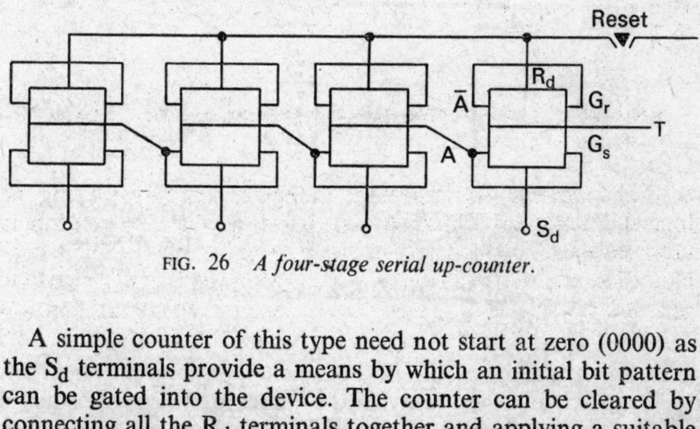

FIG. 26 *A four-stage serial up-counter.*

A simple counter of this type need not start at zero (0000) as the S_d terminals provide a means by which an initial bit pattern can be gated into the device. The counter can be cleared by connecting all the R_d terminals together and applying a suitable *reset* pulse.

7. Ripple-through and synchronous counters. The counter just described is often referred to as a *ripple-through* counter, the name deriving from the fact that changes at the right-hand end of the counter have to ripple through to the left-hand end. These events must clearly take time, making this kind of counter slower in action than the more sophisticated and faster *synchronous* counter. The latter type will not be described here but a brief comparison can be made. In the synchronous counter the design permits all the flip-flops to change simultaneously when the count goes from 1111 to 0000, whereas in the ripple-through type a relatively long time must elapse for the change from 1111 to 0000 to pass through the counter. Binary counters of both types are nowadays available on single integrated circuits (IC chips) measuring around 6 mm by 20 mm.

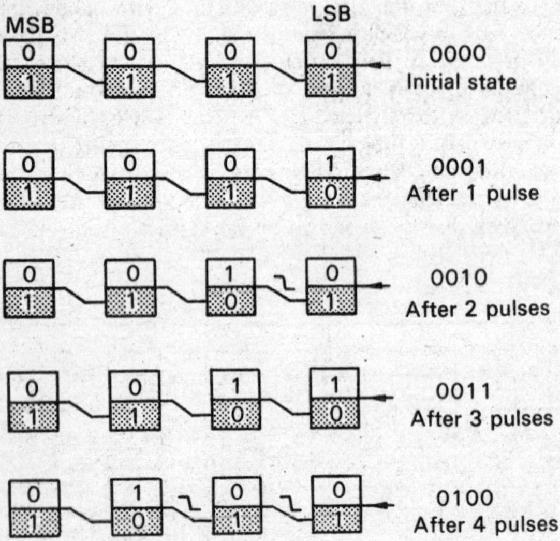

FIG. 27 *Action of a four-stage counter.*

8. External gating. A flip-flop is said to be *externally* gated if its G_s and G_r levels are determined by other logic elements external to the flip-flop. If the gate inputs of a flip-flop are cross-linked to the A- and $\bar{A}$-outputs of a preceding flip-flop and the pattern repeated to form a chain, we have the beginnings of a very important device—the shift register.

9. The shift register. Such a device is depicted in Fig. 28 where it will be noticed that, in addition to the cross-linking between stages, there is a common connection for all the T-inputs. An arbitrary bit pattern can be gated into the flip-flops via the S_d inputs. Subsequent application of pulses at the common

T-input causes the whole pattern to be shifted along from right to left. Here, then, we have a means of *storing* a string of bits and of moving the string *intact* in a serial manner; hence the name—shift register.

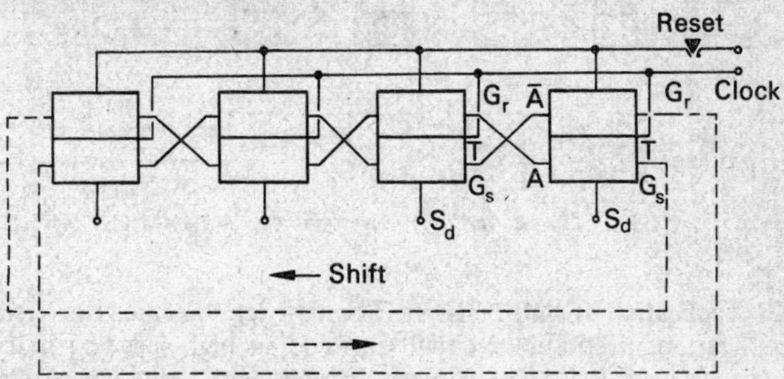

FIG. 28 *A serial storage/shift register.*

10. Cyclic shift register. The G_r and G_s inputs of the right-most stage in Fig. 28 would possibly be connected to some other part of the computer, thus permitting information to be fed into the register from the right by the action of a stream of clock pulses applied to the T-inputs. Another way is to gate a pattern into the register in parallel fashion, using the S_d inputs. The dotted lines in Fig. 28 show a way of connecting the flip-flops into what is effectively an endless chain, thus obtaining a *cyclic* shift register.

11. The operation of the shift register. This can be followed by assuming some initial state of the register and asking what happens to each flip-flop on the arrival of a shift pulse at the T-inputs. We must apply the rule that a given flip-flop will only change its state if the output and corresponding gate input are initially at the same logic level. The reader is advised to follow the operations shown in Figs. 29 and 30. Figure 29 shows a four-stage *non-cyclic* shift register. This is obtained by connecting the gate inputs of the right-most flip-flop to *fixed* logic levels of 1 at G_r and 0 at G_s. The initial contents of the register (looking at $\bar{A}$ outputs) is the pattern 0011 which is shifted left by two clock pulses to become 1100. In Fig. 30 we have the cyclic configuration already described. Initial contents in this case are 1100. Two shift pulses cause an anticlockwise rotation of the contents to yield 0011.

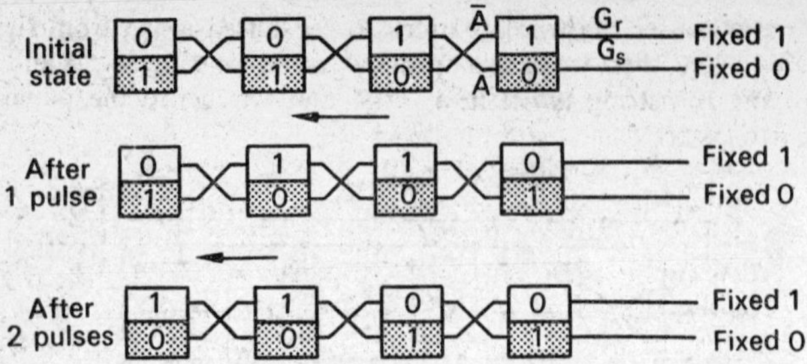

FIG. 29 *Action of a non-cyclic shift register.*

12. Application of shift registers. The shift register finds universal application in computer circuits, providing high-speed memory facilities, serial–parallel conversion and arithmetic operations based on multiplication and division by powers of 2. Like the counter, shift registers are commonly available on single integrated circuit chips, some providing quite sophisticated additional facilities such as logic gates which permit both right and left shifts in the same register.

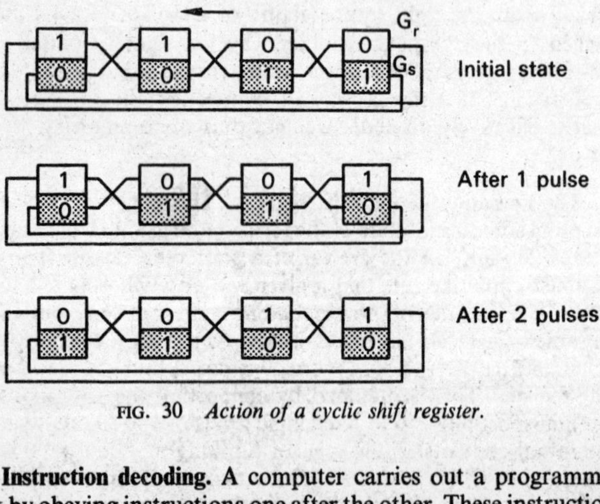

FIG. 30 *Action of a cyclic shift register.*

13. Instruction decoding. A computer carries out a programmed task by obeying instructions one after the other. These instructions constitute a stored program held in the computer's memory and have to be fed into the machine along with relevant data before a particular problem can be solved. Each stored instruction will contain coded information concerning the type of operation to be carried out, where to find the data to be operated upon and also where the results of the operation are to be placed. A possible instruction format is described later in VIII.

Although instructions can be held in great number in memory, they can only be obeyed one at a time on being transferred to a special shift register, called the *instruction register*. This register has connections to a set of interconnected gates, which are arranged to *decode* the pattern of bits which makes up the instruction and which generate appropriate *control signals*.

Let us examine a simple example. Suppose our computer uses the following code for the four basic arithmetic operations:

00 add
01 subtract
10 multiply
11 divide

Two adjacent flip-flops in the instruction register could be allocated to holding the two bits which together denote the type of arithmetic operation to be carried out. Figure 31 shows a possible arrange-

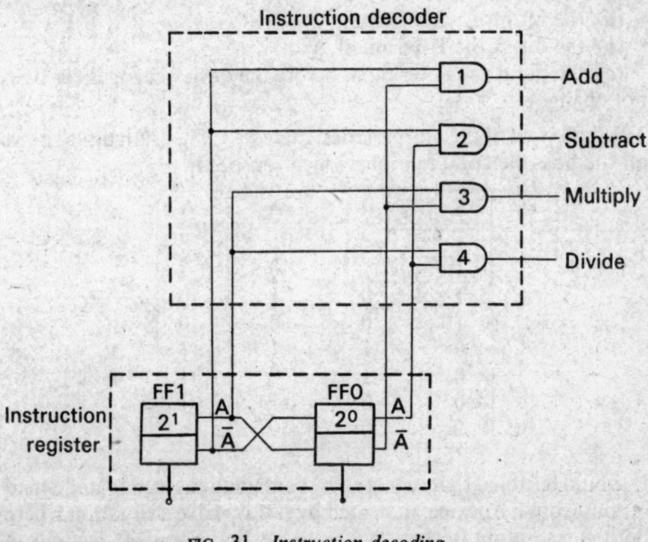

FIG. 31 *Instruction decoding.*

ment for decoding. Both A and Ā outputs of the flip-flops are used to feed the *instruction decoder*, the latter consisting of four AND-gates the outputs of which constitute the control signals generated by instructions placed in the instruction register. Suppose the operation code 01 is placed in the register. This will cause the Ā-output of FF1 to become a 1 and the A-output of FF0 to become a 1, with the result that AND-gate 2 will have two 1 signals so that this gate will be the only one of the four with an output signal. The latter signal is then used to initiate *subtraction* in the arithmetic unit of the machine.

14. The SR-flip-flop and its truth table. We have already examined the basic flip-flop, the logical flip-flop and described a number of applications. Many variations of these devices exist in practice and there is a great deal of variation in the names by which they are known. It is therefore important to specify the properties of a given flip-flop uniquely, this being most easily achieved by means of a truth table.

As an example consider the basic flip-flop. This device is also known by the name *SR-flip-flop* or *latch*. If we regard the A terminal as the output, it is clear that the state of the output depends on three things:

(*a*) the bit at the S terminal,
(*b*) the bit at the R terminal, and
(*c*) the bit at the A terminal before the device changes (or does not change) its state.

The final state of the output is designated A′. The truth table shows all the possible combinations which can occur.

S	R	A	A′
1	1	1	?
1	1	0	?
1	0	1	0
1	0	0	0
0	1	1	1
0	1	0	1
0	0	1	1
0	0	0	0

It should be noted that two of these combinations lead to undefined output from the device, indicated by ?. If we have a situation where both gates output 0, then each gate has both inputs 0, leading to a 1 output from both gates. Similarly, if both gates output a 1 then both have inputs of 1, leading to an output of 0 from both gates. Thus either of these conditions is unstable, and in practice the circuit will collapse to an unpredictable stable state. A more complex device called a J-K flip-flop (not described here) overcomes this problem by changing the state of the output whenever *both* S and R terminals are energised.

15. The T-flip-flop and its truth table. Internal gating of the logical flip-flop has been seen to provide a very useful facility, particularly in the counter. This type of flip-flop changes state every time a trigger pulse is applied; it is often called a T-flip-flop or *toggle*. The truth table for the T-flip-flop is as:

T	A	A′
1	1	0
1	0	1
0	1	1
0	0	0

16. The D-flip-flop and its truth table. An interesting and important modification of the logical flip-flop is shown in Fig. 32 where one

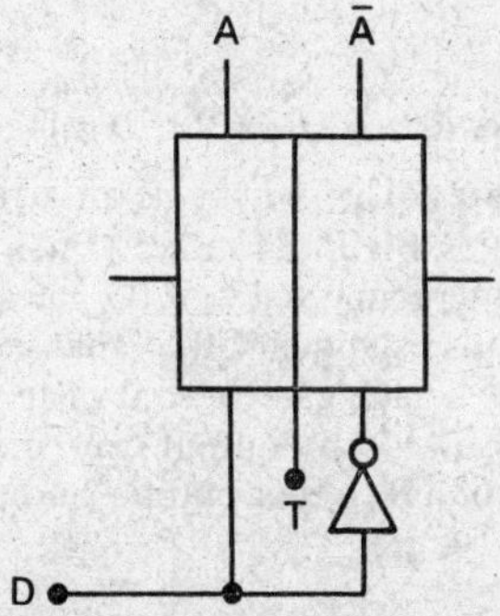

FIG. 32 *The D-flip-flop.*

of the gated inputs has an included inverter, input being the terminal D and output being taken from the Ā terminal. The reader should verify for himself that the device operates as a *delay* i.e., any bit present at D will subsequently appear at Ā *one trigger pulse later*. The truth table is shown as:

D	$\bar{A}$	$\bar{A}'$
1	1	1
1	0	1
0	1	0
0	0	0

(This type of flip-flop will find application in the serial adder described in VI.)

USE OF NAND-GATES

17. NAND-based devices. Two-state devices were introduced in this chapter by linking NOR-gates. However, it is quite possible to base sequential circuitry on the NAND-gate instead. Figure 33 shows two cross-coupled NAND-gates arranged to form a basic flip-flop. A 0 applied to the S terminal will cause the device to change to its other stable state (as can be verified by consulting the truth table for NAND). The reader should compare this arrangement with the NOR-based flip-flop which requires a 1 bit to be applied rather than a 0 bit.

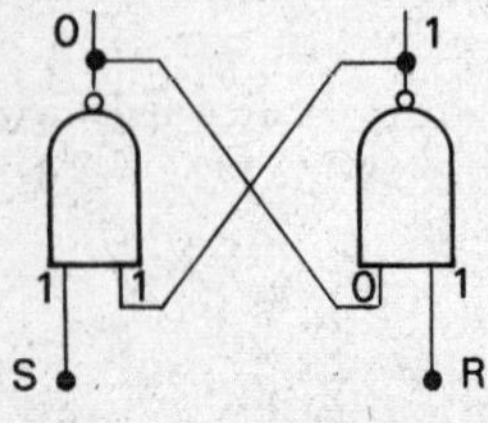

FIG. 33 *Basic SR-flip-flop, constructed from NAND-gates.*

18. A device with many stable states. The *polyflop* is an arrangement with three or more stable states. Figure 34 shows a three-state polyflop constructed from three interconnected NAND-gates. The circuit has been drawn with circular symmetry to emphasise the fundamental principal, which is that each gate must have an input from all other outputs except its own. Any output can be set to 0 by the momentary application of a 0 to that output. Successive states of the arrangement in Fig. 34 are:

A	B	C	
1	0	1	Apply 0 to A
0	1	1	Apply 0 to B
1	0	1	Apply 0 to C
1	1	0	Apply 0 to A
0	1	1	

Thus the three possible states are 101, 011, and 110.

Though seldom used in computer systems, polyflops can be regarded as generalised basic flip-flops.

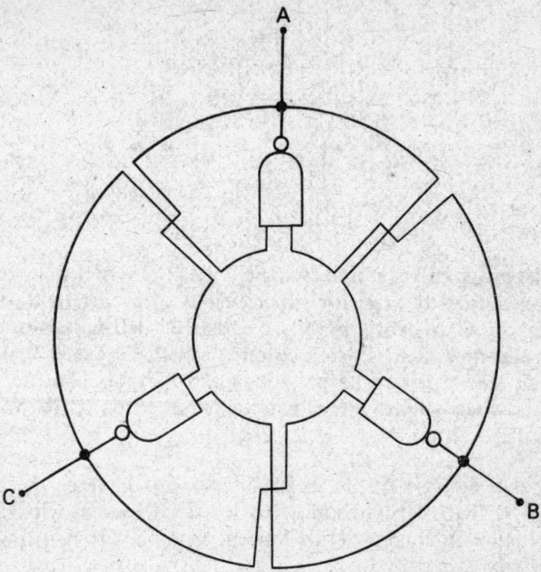

FIG. 34 *Polyflop circuit.*

19. A device with only one stable state. Certain pieces of computer hardware require that a brief pulse shall initiate a logic state which is to last for only a predetermined length of time. Such a state is described as a *quasi-stable* state. An arrangement which behaves in this way is called a *monoflop* (or monostable) and is illustrated in Fig. 35, where the device is shown in its stable state. The right-hand terminal of the right-most NAND-gate is maintained at logic 1 and a capacitor-resistor combination (C,R) provide the quasi-stable behaviour. A logic 0 of brief duration applied to S drives the output of the left-hand NAND-gate to logic 1. This level is communicated via C to the left-hand terminal of the right-most NAND-gate so that the output of this gate goes to 0, together with the right-hand terminal of the left-most NAND-gate. Thus, the whole circuit has achieved a new (quasi-stable) state. At the beginning of this state the top end of the resistor is at logic 1

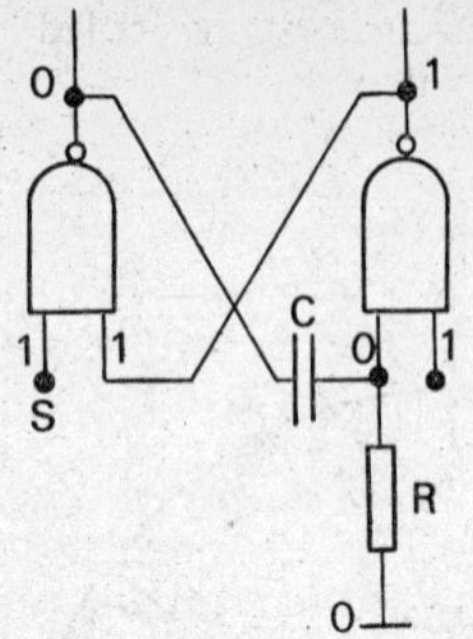

FIG. 35 *Monoflop.*

while the lower end is at a fixed logic 0. Hence there is a potential difference across the resistor which results in a current through R to charge C. When C is fully charged the left-hand terminal of the right-most NAND-gate becomes 0 with the result that the whole device reverts to its previous (stable) state. The time for which the quasi-stable state is maintained depends on the values of C and R.

20. Astable devices. At the beginning of this chapter the term *negative feedback* was introduced to described systems with *stable* states. Figure 36 illustrates this concept as applied to two coupled

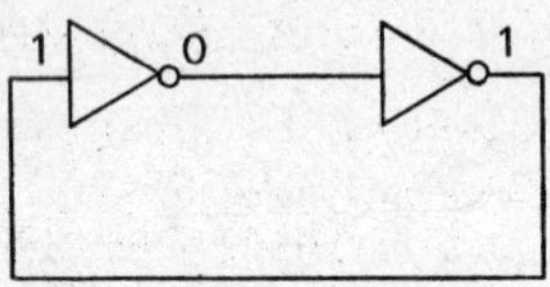

FIG. 36

inverters; the system is a stable one. This stability is destroyed if a third inverter is included in the feedback loop, as in Fig. 37. If the reader assumes a given logic level (say 1) at the output of one of the inverters, and then follows the action of the other inverters, he will be quickly led to the conclusion that the arrange-

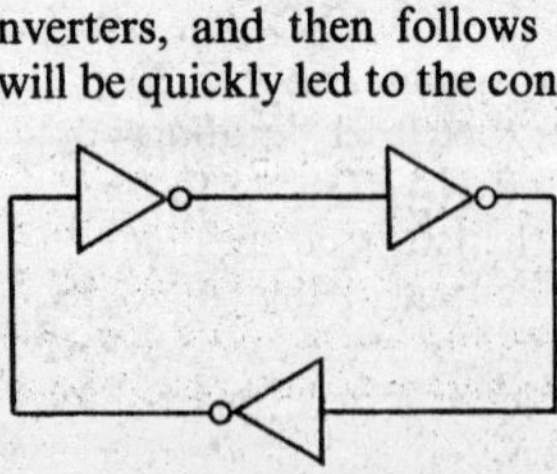

FIG. 37

ment has no stable state; in fact it *oscillates*. Such a device is said to be *astable* and the kind of feedback which makes it so is called *positive feedback*. If an output is taken from any point in the circuit of Fig. 37 it will consist of a very-high-frequency sequence of 1s and 0s.

An oscillator of this kind is a fundamental requirement of any computer system, as all the operations in the machine must be synchronised by such a *pulse generator*, or *clock* as it is usually called. A more useful clock is obtained by a symmetrical development of the monoflop. This is shown in Fig. 38 and is seen to contain capacitor-resistor combinations which determine the frequency of the clock pulses. An oscillator of this type is called an *astable multivibrator*.

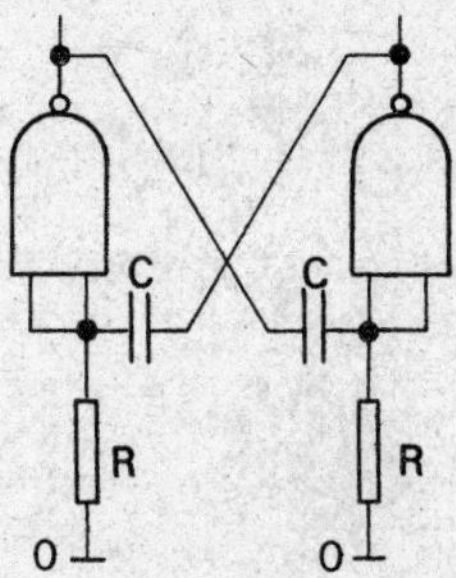

FIG. 38 *Astable multivibrator.*

PROGRESS TEST 5

1. Describe how (*a*) two NOR-gates, and (*b*) two NAND-gates, may be connected to form a device with two stable states. Name this device. What modifications would have to be made to the circuit to create:

(*a*) a monoflop;

(*b*) an astable multivibrator;

(*c*) a computer clock, i.e. an astable multivibrator which can be switched on and off by means of a control signal? (**1, 19, 20**)

2. Explain how a simple (ripple) up-counter can be constructed from a set of interconnected flip-flops. Draw diagrams to illustrate your answer. How can a *reverse* binary count be obtained from the device? (**6**)

3. Design a four-stage counter which counts up to ten (i.e. 0 through 9 followed by a reset to zero). Hint: some extra combinational logic is required. (**7**)

4. Distinguish briefly between synchronous and asynchronous counters. (**7**)

5. What do you understand by the term shift register? Show with diagrams how this important computer device may be constructed from two-state elements, and describe two ways in which data may be loaded into, and removed from a shift register (**9–11**)

6. The D-flip-flop provides a delay function in computer circuitry. Show how such a device is obtained by a simple modification of the logical flip-flop. What is the length of the delay produced, and what applications are there of this element in a CPU? (**16**)

CHAPTER VI

Computer Arithmetic

1. The fundamental arithmetic operations. Although a computer is capable of performing some very complex mathematical operations, nearly all of these can be broken down into quite simple arithmetic steps. The most important of these are the familiar processes of addition, subtraction, multiplication and division. Viewed fundamentally, even these can be seen as derived from a single operation and that is *addition*, since subtraction is negative addition, multiplication is repeated addition and division is repeated negative addition. So, all we require is an automatic device which will carry out the addition of binary numerals in the form of electrical pulses.

ADDITION AND SUBTRACTION

2. Binary addition. We consider the addition of the binary number N_2 to the binary number N_1. It is usual to refer to N_1 as the *augend* and to N_2 as the *addend*. The result of this addition is called the *sum*. As the binary system has a radix of 2, it follows that a *carry* of 1 will be generated whenever a 1 is added to a 1. Consider a couple of simple examples using 3-bit numbers.

$$\begin{array}{r} 101 = 5 \\ +\ 110 = 6 \\ \hline 1011 = 11 \\ \hline \end{array} \qquad \begin{array}{r} 100 = 4 \\ +\ 011 = 3 \\ \hline 111 = 7 \\ \hline \end{array}$$

Bits are added in pairs with only four possible cases arising. These are shown in truth-table form.

augend	*addend*	*sum*	*carry*
1	1	0	1
1	0	1	0
0	1	1	0
0	0	0	0

Inspection of this table reveals that the sum column is related to augend and addend columns according to the exclusive OR-relation discussed in IV, **7**, while the carry column is obtained by combining augend and addend according to the operation AND (IV, **6**). If A and B represent the bits to be added then sum, S, and carry, C, are given by:

$$S = A.\bar{B}_{\vee}\bar{A}.B$$
$$C = A.B$$

3. The half adder. Hence, the addition of a pair of bits may be carried out using a combination of EXCLUSIVE OR-gate (XOR-gate) and AND-gate. This combination, shown in Fig. 39, provides a sum bit and a carry bit and is known as a *half adder*. The half adder (symbol also given in Fig. 39) is aptly named however, as it does *not* take into account any *previous* carry which may have occurred. For example, in this addition

$$\begin{array}{r} 101 \\ +\ 111 \\ \hline 1100 \\ \hline \end{array}$$

the sum bit in the 2^1 column is dependent not only on the summends 0 and 1 but also on the 1 which has carried over from the 2^0 column.

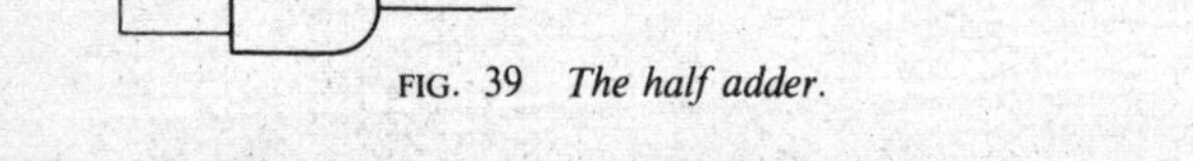

FIG. 39 *The half adder.*

4. The full adder. What we need is a three-input device, i.e. one which provides inputs for two summends and a previous carry bit. The device should generate a sum bit and a new carry bit. Eight possibilities arise when considering addition of this more general kind and these are given in truth-table form, where *A* and *B* are the summends, *K* is a previous carry, Σ is the sum and *D* is the new carry.

A	B	K	Σ	D
1	1	1	1	1
1	1	0	0	1
1	0	1	0	1
1	0	0	1	0
0	1	1	0	1
0	1	0	1	0
0	0	1	1	0
0	0	0	0	0

Examination of the truth-table reveals that the sum and carry are given by:

$$\Sigma = A.B.K_{\vee}A.\bar{B}.\bar{K}_{\vee}\bar{A}.B.\bar{K}_{\vee}\bar{A}.\bar{B}.K$$

$$D = A.B.K_{\vee}A.B.\bar{K}_{\vee}A.\bar{B}.K_{\vee}\bar{A}.B.K$$

A little Boolean algebra leads to an interesting restructuring of these expressions. Consider first the sum expression:

$$\begin{aligned}\Sigma &= A.B.K_{\vee}A.\bar{B}.\bar{K}._{\vee}\bar{A}.B.\bar{K}_{\vee}\bar{A}.\bar{B}.K\\ &= (A.B.K_{\vee}\bar{A}.\bar{B}.K)_{\vee}(\bar{A}.B.\bar{K}_{\vee}A.\bar{B}.\bar{K})\\ &= \underline{(A.B_{\vee}\bar{A}.\bar{B})}.K_{\vee}(\bar{A}.B_{\vee}A.\bar{B}).\bar{K}\\ &= (\bar{A}.B_{\vee}A.\bar{B}).K_{\vee}(\bar{A}.B_{\vee}A.\bar{B}).\bar{K}\end{aligned}$$

$$\text{i.e. } \Sigma = \bar{S}.K_{\vee}S.\bar{K}$$

The step between the last two lines is accomplished by applying the first of the two De Morgan theorems given in IV, **9**. Notice that we have now expressed the sum output as that which we would obtain if a half adder were fed with the logic variables S and K.

Now for the carry equation:

$$\begin{aligned}D &= A.B.K_{\vee}A.B.\bar{K}_{\vee}A.\bar{B}.K_{\vee}\bar{A}.B.K\\ &= (\bar{A}.B.K_{\vee}A.\bar{B}.K)_{\vee}(A.B.K_{\vee}A.B.\bar{K})\\ &= (\bar{A}.B_{\vee}A.\bar{B}).K_{\vee}A.B.(K_{\vee}\bar{K})\\ &= (\bar{A}.B_{\vee}A.\bar{B}).K_{\vee}A.B\end{aligned}$$

$$\text{i.e. } D = S.K_{\vee}A.B$$

The sum and new carry equations just derived show that a device which adds two bits and which incorporates a previous carry can be constructed from two half adders and an OR-gate. Such an arrangement is shown in Fig. 40. This device is called a *full adder*. Its symbol appears in Fig. 41.

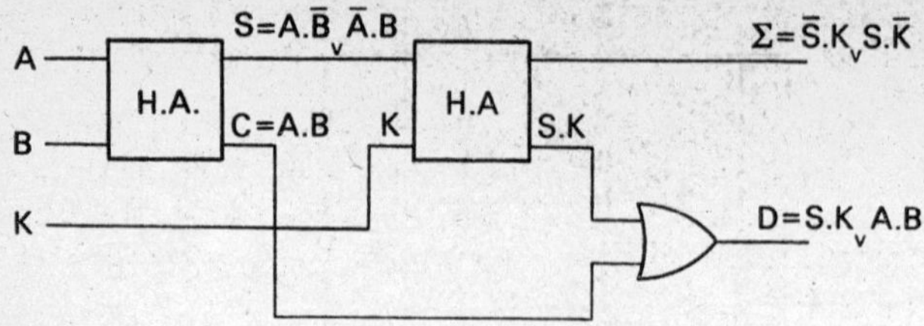

FIG. 40 *The full adder.*

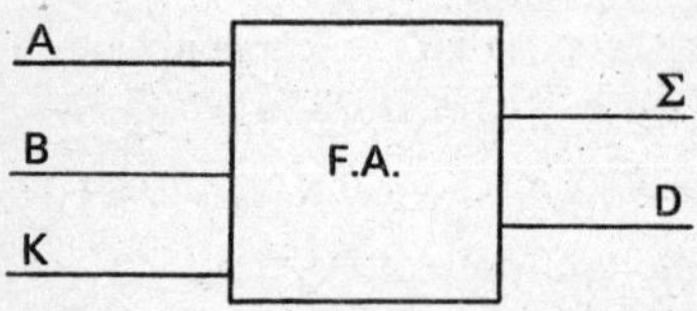

FIG. 41 *Full adder symbol.*

4. A serial adder. One way in which two binary numerals may be added is to add corresponding bits in pairs, starting at the least significant ends of the binary strings. This method is called *serial addition.* The full adder just described is presented with pairs of bits and will correctly produce the sum and new carry. There is, however, a small difficulty which has to be dealt with. This is the fact that, whenever two bits are added, the previous carry has to be referred to. Hence, we need some means of storing the carry which resulted from the addition of the previous pair of bits. This may easily be done by using a flip-flop to remember each new carry and subsequently present it to the K-input of the full adder. Figure 42 shows a full adder with a *carry flip-flop* connected between the D- and K-terminals, thus giving the desired *serial adder*. Augend

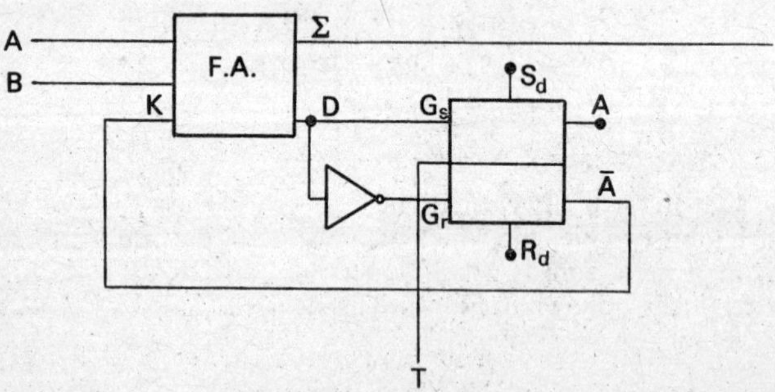

FIG. 42 *Serial adder.*

and addend binary strings can be clocked into the adder by means of a stream of clock pulses, the sum string appearing at the Σ-output.

It should be noticed that the carry flip-flop is fed with the same set of clock pulses as those used to feed the numbers into the adder. The reader should consult Fig. 43 which shows the detailed operation of the carry flip-flop and the necessity for the inverter feeding the G_r terminal.

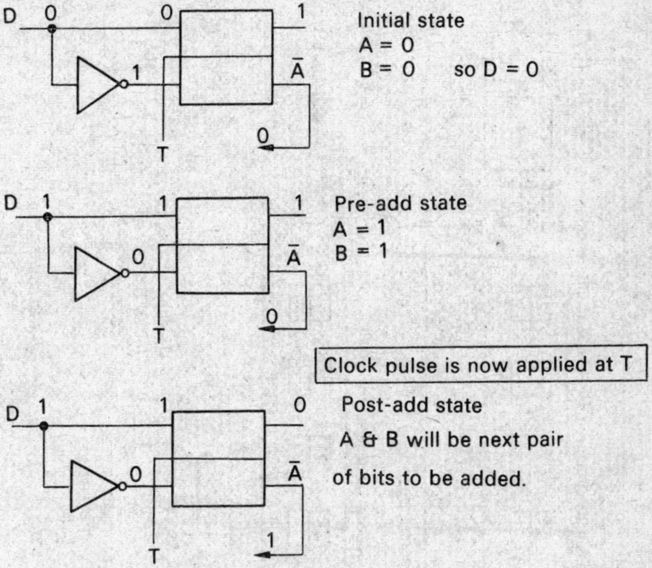

FIG. 43 *Action of the carry flip-flop.*

5. Addition and subtraction. We are now in a position where we can bring together a number of basic ideas to illustrate how the addition/subtraction process may actually be carried out. Figure 44 shows a primitive arrangement by means of which two 4-bit binary numerals can be added or subtracted at the touch of a button. The numerals represent signed integers in the range −8 through +7 (i.e. the twos complement system is used).

The augend (or minuend) is placed in the upper shift register called the *accumulator*. This may be done manually using the S_d inputs. Similarly, the addend (or subtrahend) is placed in the lower

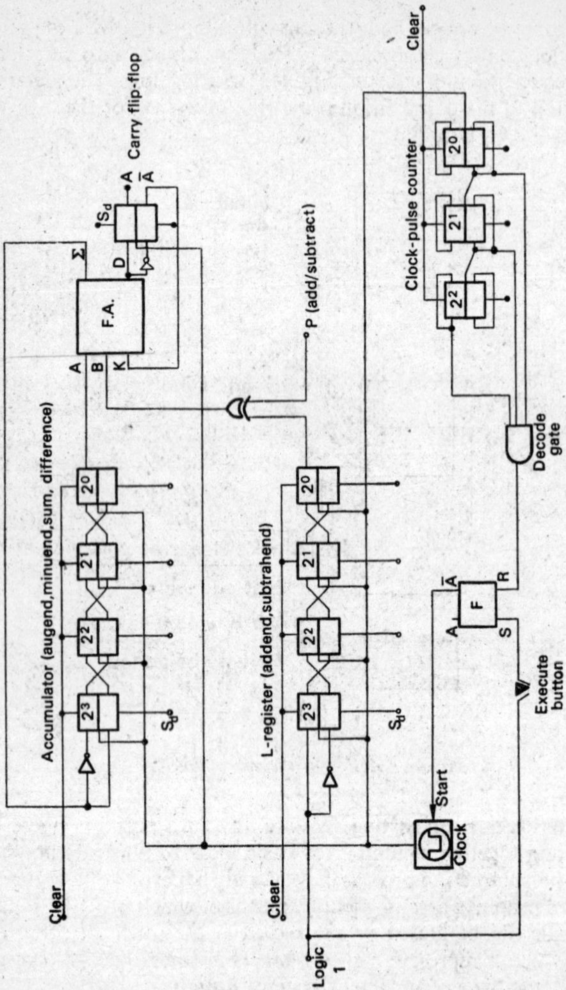

FIG. 44 *Adder/subtractor.*

shift register called the *L-register* (loading register). If addition is required, the terminal P is set to logic 0 and the carry flip-flop is set with its $\bar{A}$ output also at logic 0. For subtraction P is kept at logic 1 while the carry flip-flop is initialised at $\bar{A}=1$. When $P=1$ the *inverse* of the L-register contents is fed to the adder from the output of the XOR-gate. With the carry flip-flop initially at 1, this ensures that subtraction is performed by the addition of the twos complement of the L-register to the accumulator (remember—to form the twos complement we invert and add 1).

To initiate an addition (or subtraction) the *execute* button is depressed. This sets the flip-flop, F, to $\bar{A}=1$ which signal is sent to the clock, causing a stream of pulses to be sent simultaneously to the L-register, accumulator, carry flip-flop and the 3-stage counter on the lower right. Pair-wise addition of bits thus takes place as the numbers in L-register and accumulator are shifted rhythmically into the adder, the sum (or difference) being shifted at the same time back into the accumulator. Only 4 clock pulses are needed and this is where the counter comes in. On reaching a count of 4 (binary 100) the 2^2 $\bar{A}$-output $=1$, the 2^1 A-output $=1$ and the 2^0 A-output $=1$. These outputs are connected to an AND-gate so that after 4 pulses of the clock the gate produces a 1 output. This is sent to reset the flip-flop, F, which in turn, switches off the clock. The whole process is thus completed. The time taken for a single addition (or subtraction) can be made very small indeed, simply by increasing the clock-pulse frequency.

6. Practical cases of addition.

(*a*) *Addition of positive integers*

Accumulator: 0100 = +4
L-register : 0011 = +3
Result : 0111 = +7

A	L	C	RES
0	1	0	1
0	1	0	1
1	0	0	1
0	0	[0]	0
		[0]	

In this example A = bit from accumulator, L = bit from L-register, C = output of carry flip-flop and RES = resulting bit from Σ-output. The table shows the values of these bits after the application of each of the clock pulses.

Notice that the first bit in the C column is the *initial* output state of the carry flip-flop. This bit is set to 0 before addition and to 1 before subtraction. The last two bits of the C column (enclosed in a box) are the third and fourth *generated* carry bits. It is these two bits which may be used as a means of detecting *overflow* (the generation of out-of range numbers). If these bits are the *same* the generated result is in range (i.e. overflow has not occurred).

Let us see what happens when we try to add two integers the sum of which is out of the permitted range.

Accumulator: 0101 = +5
L-register 0011 = +3

A	L	C	RES
1	1	0	0
0	1	1	0
1	0	1	0
0	0	[1]	1
		[0]	

Here we have a case of *overflow*. The machine has given 1000 (decimal −8) instead of +8 which cannot be represented in 4 bits. Such a condition would be readily detected, however, as the last two carry bits are different when overflow occurs.

(*b*) *Addition of negative integers*

Accumulator: 1100 = −4
L-register : 1101 = −3
Result : 1001 = −7

A	L	C	RES
0	1	0	1
0	0	0	0
1	1	0	0
1	1	[1]	1
		[1]	

Overflow can arise with negative integers:

Accumulator: 1010 = −6
L-register : 1101 = −3

A	L	C	RES
0	1	0	1
1	0	0	1
0	1	0	1
1	1	[0]	0
		[1]	

The correct result of −9 cannot be represented, but again the overflow condition is easily detected.

(*c*) *Addition of mixed-sign integers*

Accumulator: 0100 = +4
L-register : 1101 = −3
Result : 0001 = +1

A	L	C	RES
0	1	0	1
0	0	0	0
1	1	0	0
0	1	1	0
		1	

And another example:

Accumulator: 1100 = −4
L-register : 0011 = +3
Result : 1111 = −1

A	L	C	RES
0	1	0	1
0	1	0	1
1	0	0	1
1	0	0	1
		0	

Note that overflow cannot occur during mixed integer addition; the result will always be in range.

7. Practical cases of subtraction. In this case $\bar{L}$ will represent the inverse of the contents of the L-register. Notice too that the carry flip-flop is initialised at 1 for subtraction.

(*a*) *Subtraction of positive integers*

Accumulator: 0100 = +4
L-register : 0011 = +3
Result : 0001 = +1

A	$\bar{L}$	C	RES
0	0	1	1
0	0	0	0
1	1	0	0
0	1	1	0
		1	

And the reverse:

Accumulator: 0011 = +3
L-register : 0100 = +4
Result : 1111 = −1

A	$\bar{L}$	C	RES
1	1	1	1
1	1	1	1
0	0	1	1
0	1	0	1
		0	

Overflow cannot occur in the subtraction of positive integers.

(*b*) *Subtraction of negative integers*

Accumulator: 1100 = −4
L-register : 1101 = −3
Result : 1111 = −1

A	$\bar{L}$	C	RES
0	0	1	1
0	1	0	1
1	0	0	1
1	0	0	1
		0	

And the reverse:

Accumulator: 1101 = −3
L-register : 1100 = −4
Result : 0001 = +1

A	$\bar{L}$	C	RES
1	1	1	1
0	1	1	0
1	0	1	0
1	0	1	0
		1	

Again overflow is not possible with subtraction of negative integers.

(*c*) *Subtraction of mixed-sign integers*

Accumulator: 0100 = +4
L-register : 1101 = −3
Result : 0111 = +7

A	$\bar{L}$	C	RES
0	0	1	1
0	1	0	1
1	0	0	1
0	0	0	0
		0	

And the reverse:

Accumulator: 1101 = −3
L-register : 0100 = +4
Result : 1001 = −7

A	$\bar{L}$	C	RES
1	1	1	1
0	1	1	0
1	0	1	0
1	1	1	1
		1	

And finally a case of overflow:

Accumulator: 1000 = −8
L-register : 0111 = +7

A	$\bar{L}$	C	RES
0	0	1	1
0	0	0	0
0	0	0	0
1	1	0	0
		1	

The correct result of −15 cannot be represented.

8. Detection of an overflow condition. A study of the above examples of addition and subtraction should convince the reader of the relative ease with which these processes can be rendered automatic. The rule for detecting an overflow condition should also now be apparent: *when an overflow occurs, the carry from the sign bit is different from the preceding carry* (only applies to twos complement *system*).

9. Parallel adder. An alternative device for the addition (and subtraction) of binary numerals is the *parallel adder*, in which the bits of the summends are taken all at the same time. Such a device is shown in Fig. 45 where the numerals $A_2A_1A_0$ and $B_2B_1B_0$ are to be added. The bit pattern representing the sum is obtained at the outputs $D_2\Sigma_2\Sigma_1\Sigma_0$. For addition the carry-in, P, is set to 0, while for parallel subtraction P is set to 1 and the *inverse* of the subtrahend is presented for addition to the minuend. Parallel adder/subtractors are speedy in operation but the processing of numbers containing many bits requires a great many full adders.

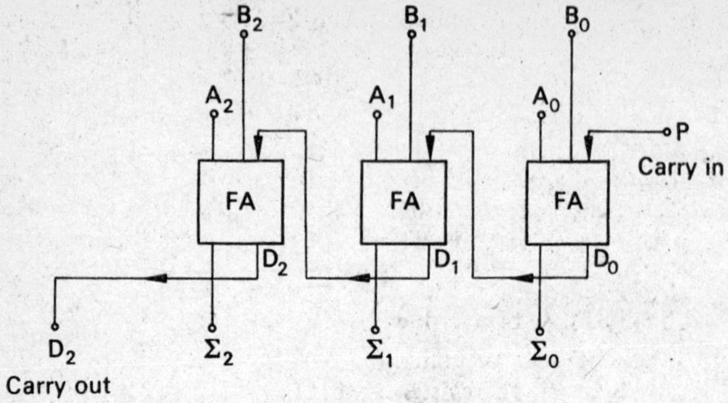

FIG. 45 *Parallel adder.*

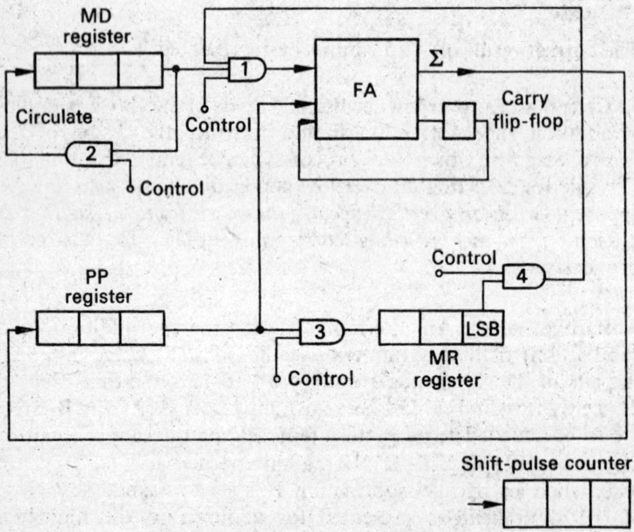

FIG. 46 *A serial binary multiplier.*

MULTIPLICATION AND DIVISION

10. Binary multiplication. We have already stated that multiplication is basically repeated addition. A computer could well be made to perform this process simply by adding the multiplicand a number of times equal to the value of the multiplier. Such a procedure would, however, be intolerably slow and wasteful of machine time. One method which has been successfully used is analogous to the ordinary manual method of multiplying two decimal integers. This method we all learned at school and consists in multiplying the multiplicand by each multiplier digit separately and then shifting the partial products.

Consider the binary multiplication of 7 by 5:

```
     111 = 7 (multiplicand)
     101 = 5 (multiplier)
  ------
     111 ⎫
    000  ⎬ partial products
   111   ⎭
  ------
  100011 = 35
```

Using computer circuits it is inconvenient to store each partial product and finally add, so each partial product is *accumulated* as it is generated. Further, it is easier in the machine version of this method to shift the accumulated partial product to the *right* rather than shift the multiplicand to the *left*. The process of binary multiplication is, in essence, extremely simple as it is based on the binary multiplication table:

$$1 \times 1 = 1$$
$$1 \times 0 = 0$$
$$0 \times 1 = 0$$
$$0 \times 0 = 0$$

11. Machine method of binary multiplication. Let us now repeat the multiplication of 7 by 5 using signed integers and following the machine method of accumulation and shifting right.

```
0111      = +7 (multiplicand—MD)
0101      = +5 (multiplier—MR)
------
0111      add MD
00111     shift partial product 1 place to right
00111     no MD added as MR bit = 0
000111    shift partial product 1 place to right
100011    add MD
```

	0100011	shift partial product 1 place to right
	0100011	no MD added as MR bit = 0
Product	00100011	shift partial product 1 place to right

We see that this method generates the correct product of +35 and that the product occupies *twice* as many bits as the original numerals. It should further be noticed that the accumulated partial product grows by one bit at each add and shift cycle and that one bit of the multiplier can, at the same time, be discarded.

12. A serial binary multiplier. A serial binary multiplier circuit is shown in Fig. 46, and is designed to multiply together two unsigned 3-bit numbers (a real circuit would be able to cope with much greater word lengths) which are initially loaded into the shift registers MD and MR. A third register (PP) is used for the partial product accumulation. Register PP is initially cleared. The least significant bit of MR register determines whether the multiplicand is added or not during each cycle of the multiplier. A binary counter is included, the function of which is to count the number of shifts which have taken place. The counter is designated SHC. A flowchart for the whole process is shown in Fig. 47 and the reader is advised to follow through the steps taken by the machine in forming the product of 7 (binary 111) and five (binary 101). This procedure is shown stage by stage in Fig. 48. Several points should be noted.

(*a*) When the LSB of MR is 1, MD is added to PP and the sum sent to PP.

(*b*) MD is contained in a cyclic shift register to preserve its contents.

(*c*) During shifting, gate 3 is opened so that the contents of PP and MR are shifted simultaneously, losing the LSB of MR in the process.

(*d*) The cycles are repeated until every bit of the multiplier has been inspected, at which point SHC contains a count equal to the number of bits in the multiplier. This count is decoded to terminate the cycling.

(*e*) At the end of the operation the most significant half of the product is found in PP, and the least significant half in MR.

More sophisticated methods for dealing with the multiplication of signed integers, and faster multiplication techniques are beyond the scope of this basic text.

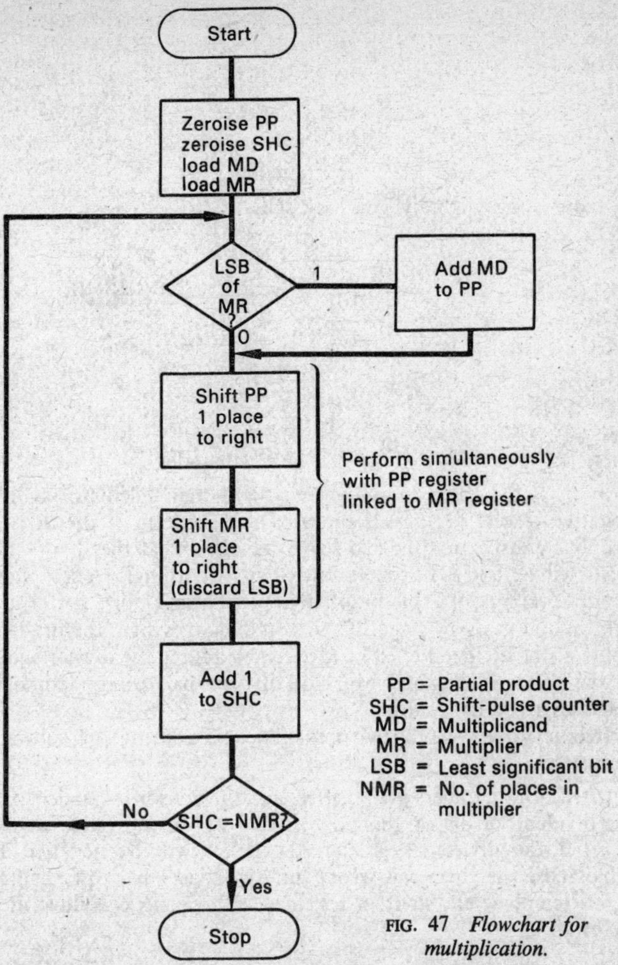

FIG. 47 *Flowchart for multiplication.*

13. Binary division. Division is the reverse of multiplication and is performed by the repeated subtraction of divisor (DR) from dividend (DD) to obtain the quotient. Machine division is carried out by subtraction and shifting the divisor downwards in significance.

Consider the division of the integer 145 by 13. The traditional long-division method goes as follows:

```
       11
  13 |145
      13
      --
       15
       13
       --
        2  remainder
```

In binary, the same division looks like this:

```
                1 011
  1 101 |10 010 001
          1 101
          -----
            101 00
             11 01
            ------
              1 111
              1 101
              -----
                 10  remainder
```

In both of the above long divisions the human calculator avoids negative results during his repeated subtractions of the divisor simply by inspection; he can see in advance what the sign of his result will be, and so he brings down digits accordingly. A computer cannot (yet?) adopt this intuitive approach and must perform a subtraction at every stage. If the result changes sign, the original value of the dividend must be *restored* by adding the divisor again in the same significance. Machine division using this method is thus described as *restoring*.

In binary division only two possibilities exist during each subtraction step.

(*a*) if both numbers are positive, and the divisor is smaller than the dividend or partial remainder, there will be a positive result.

(*b*) If the divisor is greater, the result will be negative, in which case the guess was wrong and the divisor has to be shifted right one place and another test made. This process is illustrated below.

```
      DD  0 010 010 001    = +145
  TC(DR)  1 001 1          = TC(+13)
          1 011 110 001    PR is negative—restore—QB = 0
      DD  0 010 010 001
   shift  1 100 11
          1 111 000 001    PR is negative—restore—QB = 0
```

DD	0 010 010 001	
shift	1 110 011	
	0 000 101 001	PR is positive—retain—QB = 1
PR	0 000 101 001	
shift	1 111 001 1	
	1 111 110 101	PR is negative—restore—QB = 0
previous PR	0 000 101 001	
shift	1 111 100 11	
	0 000 001 111	PR is positive—retain—QB = 1
PR	0 000 001 111	
shift	1 111 110 011	
	0 000 000 010	PR is positive—QB = 1
	remainder (+2)	quotient = 01011 (+11)

This shows how the restoring method is used to divide 145 by 13. Instead of subtraction the twos complement is added to the dividend (DD) or partial remainder (PR). TC(DR) denotes the twos comple-

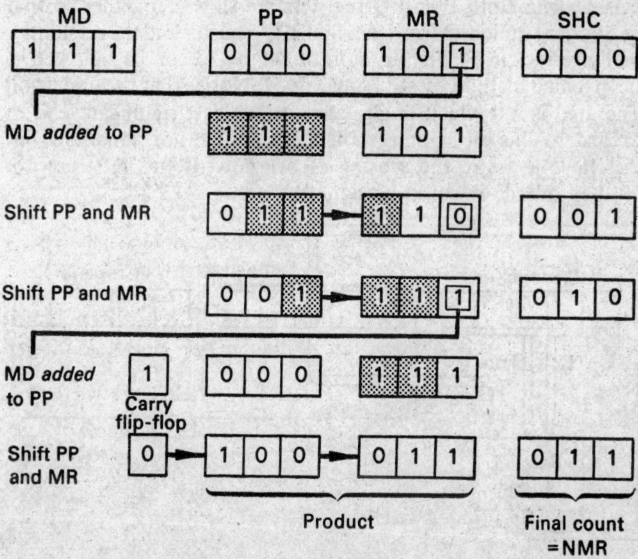

FIG. 48 *Stage by stage multiplication of 111 by 101.*

ment of the divisor. The procedure begins with alignment of the most significant bits (MSB) of divisor and dividend. If subtraction results in a negative partial remainder, a quotient bit (QB) of 0 is generated and the divisor is added back to return to the previous result. If the result is positive (0 in the SB), a quotient bit of 1 is generated and the following subtraction uses this result as partial remainder. Notice that the divisor complement is shifted one place right each time and that its sign bit is propagated too. The procedure comes to an end when the least significant bit (LSB) of divisor and partial remainder are aligned. The final result is the remainder.

14. A parallel binary divider. A parallel binary divider is shown in Fig. 49 and the associated flowchart in Fig. 50. The dividend, twice the length of the divisor, is first placed with its most significant half in register P, and its least significant half in register Q. After each subtraction of the divisor (stored in the DR-register) the sign-bit of P is examined and the appropriate 1 or 0 entered at the least significant end of the Q-register. If the sign-bit of P is a 1 the divisor is added to restore the previous result. In this machine method the dividend (decreasing by one bit at each step) is progressively shifted *left* instead of a progressive shift of the divisor *right*. Both P and Q registers are shifted together so that the quotient builds up from the right in Q-register and the remainder finally resides in P. The division of 145 by 13 can be followed in the machine method by studying Fig. 51. Notice that the first Q-bit generated is a 0 which finally rests in the least significant end of P-register. This bit belongs to neither quotient nor remainder but does have a use in the sensing of overflow. If this bit were not a 0 then overflow would be signalled.

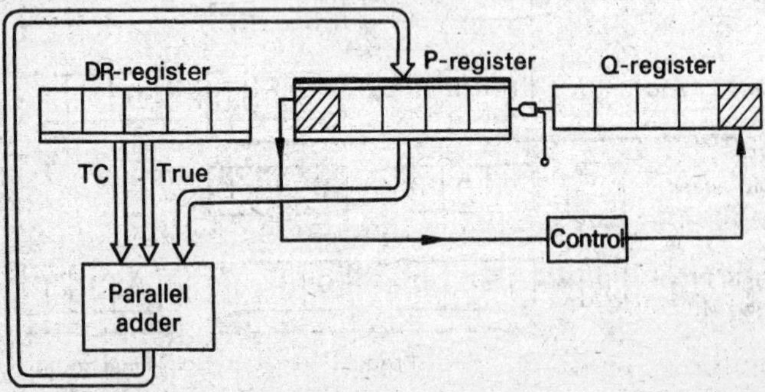

FIG. 49 *A parallel binary divider (restoring method).*

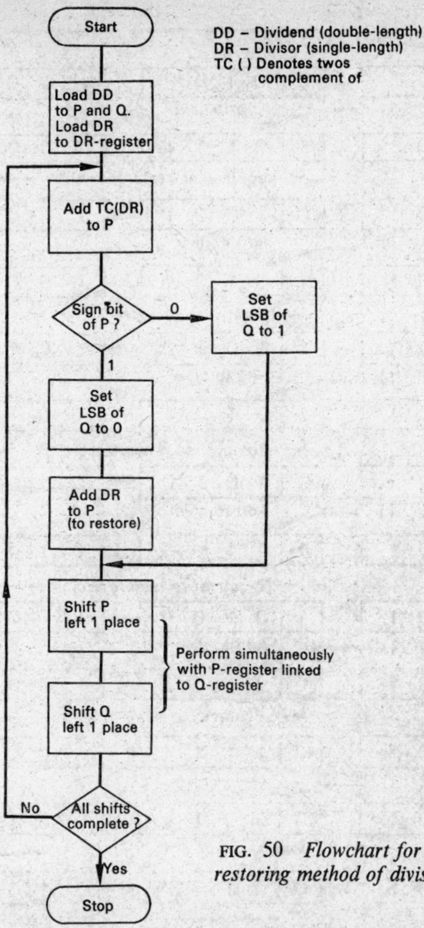

FIG. 50 *Flowchart for the restoring method of division.*

ADVANCED ARITHMETIC METHODS

15. Double-precision arithmetic. Suppose we wished to evaluate the cxpression

$$Z=\sqrt{(X^2-Y^2)}$$

with the values $X=0.157\ 2$

and $Y=0.152\ 1$

each number being to 4 decimal digits.

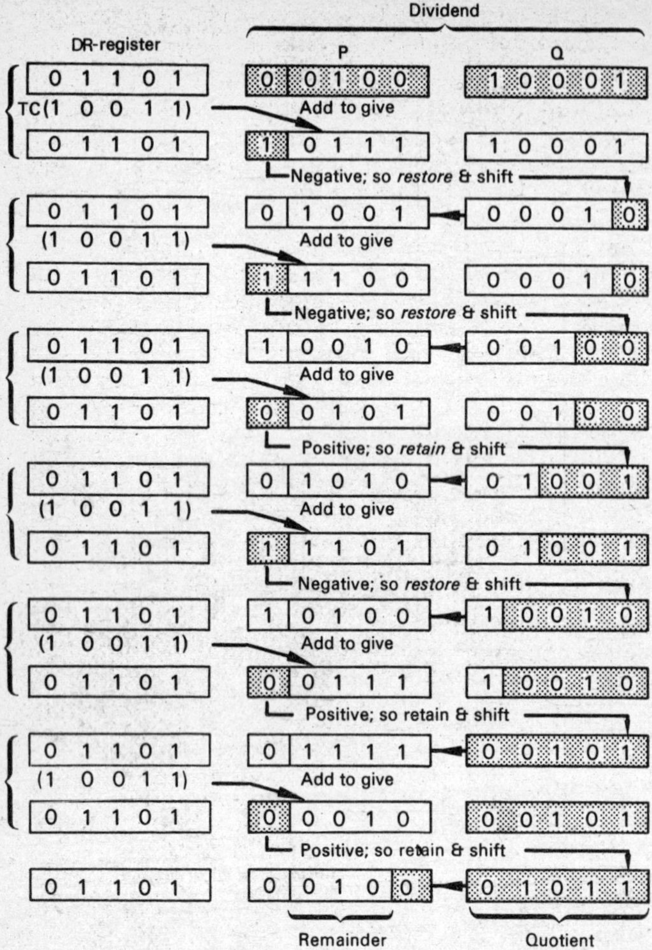

FIG. 51 *Machine division of 145 by 13 (restoring method).*

Manual calculation yields the values

$$X^2 = 0.024\ 711\ 84$$

and $$Y^2 = 0.023\ 134\ 41$$

The difference is $$X^2 - Y^2 = 0.001\ 577\ 43$$

In a machine only capable of representing 4 decimal digits (about 14 bits), this last result would appear as

$$X^2 - Y^2 = 0.0016$$

Now compare $\sqrt{0.001\ 577\ 43} = 0.039\ 7$
and $\sqrt{0.001\ 6} = 0.040\ 0$
These last two numbers differ by 0.75%, which may not seem very much, but in a long calculation errors of this size could mount up to serious proportions.

Many small modern machines use a word-length of only 16 bits and the above calculation performed on such a machine would indeed lead to the kind of errors indicated. However, this difficulty can be overcome by storing the data items in *double-precision* form. This is accomplished by storing each number in *two* words. This is shown in Fig. 52 where the numbers N1, N2, N3 etc. are stored from location 0 onwards. The most-significant half-word carries the sign bit of the number while the less-significant half-word always starts with a 0 bit. We see that a double-precision word in a 16-bit machine consists of 30 data bits plus one sign bit. Double-precision arithmetic operations are nowadays often available as part of the basic machine code; if not, special software has to be provided.

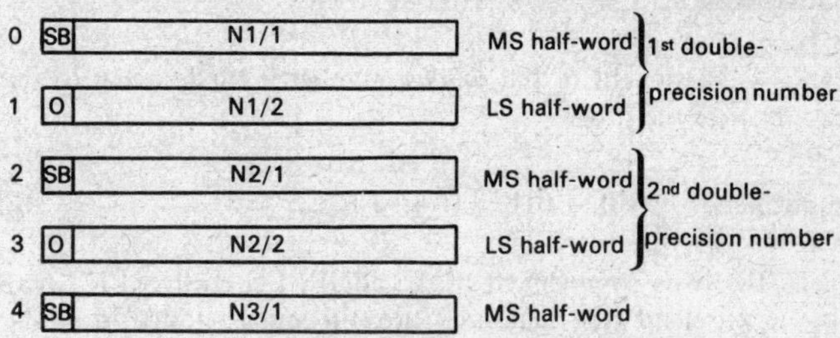

FIG. 52 *Storage of double-precision numbers.*

16. Floating-point arithmetic. The subject of floating-point arithmetic is a complex one and so only a brief examination of the ideas involved can be made here.

(*a*) *Addition.* In order to add two floating-point numerals it is first necessary to equalise the exponents of the augend and addend. This is done by incrementing the *smaller* of the two, so that there is only a loss of less-significant digits. As an example, consider two decimal numerals in floating-point form:

$$\begin{array}{r} 0.321\ 8\ \text{E}+6 \\ +\ 0.542\ 6\ \text{E}+8 \end{array}$$

In this format (often encountered in computer print-outs) the mantissa appears before the letter E and the signed exponent after it. Shifting the smaller number, we obtain:

$$\begin{array}{r} 0.003\ 2\ \text{E}{+}8 \\ +\ 0.542\ 6\ \text{E}{+}8 \\ \hline 0.545\ 8\ \text{E}{+}8 \end{array}$$

The 4-digit accuracy of the sum is consistent with the 4-digit accuracy of addend and augend.

(*b*) *Subtraction.* The process is essentially the same as addition except that the subtrahend is first converted to complementary form.

As an example consider two binary floating-point numerals:

	f	ε	
minuend	0.101	011	$= (1/2 + 1/8) \times 2^3 = 5$
subtrahend	0.110	010	$= (1/2 + 1/4) \times 2^2 = 3$

First, the exponent of the *smaller* number is made equal to the exponent of the other:

subtrahend	0.011	011	$= (1/4 + 1/8) \times 2^3 = 3$

Next, the twos complement of the adjusted subtrahend is *added* to the minuend (the mantissas are, of course, added—not the exponents):

minuend		0.101	011	
T(subtrahend)		1.101	011	
sum	1	0.010	011	$= \frac{1}{4} \times 2^3 = 2$
	↑ discard			

The result is finally normalised:

0.100	010	$=\frac{1}{2}\times 2^2 = 2$

(*c*) *Multiplication.* Given two binary floating-point numerals N_1 and N_2, the machine must evaluate the product.

Now,
$$N_1 = f_1 \times 2^{\varepsilon_1}$$
and
$$N_2 = f_2 \times 2^{\varepsilon_1}$$
The product is

$$p = N_1 \times N_2$$

and so

$$p = (f_1 \times f_2) \times 2^{(\varepsilon_1 + \varepsilon_2)}$$

We see that the arithmetic unit has to form the product of the mantissas and the sum of the exponents. Also, as in fixed-point multiplication, the product will contain *twice* the number of bits of the multiplier and multiplicand.

(*d*) *Division.* The quotient of the two numerals N_1 and N_2 is:

$$q = N_1/N_2$$

with N_2 a non-zero number.

Hence,

$$q = f_1/f_2 \times 2^{(\varepsilon_1 - \varepsilon_2)}$$

In this case the mantissas are divided and the difference of the exponents is formed by the arithmetic unit.

Many modern computers provide separate units for floating-point and fixed-point work. This means that floating-point and fixed-point operations can go on concurrently. In older machines floating-point arithmetic was implemented by specially written software.

PROGRESS TEST 6

1. Perform the following additions and check by converting the binary numerals to decimal:

(*a*) 11 101 + 10 110
(*b*) 1 110 110 + 111 111
(*c*) 1001.1 + 1011.01
(*d*) 0.101 + 0.111 **(2)**

2. Perform the following subtractions in binary and check by converting the binary numerals to decimal:

(*a*) 1011 − 1000
(*b*) 1101 − 1011
(*c*) 1011.1 − 111.1
(*d*) 1011.01 − 1011.1 **(2)**

3. A serial adder is supplied with two 16-bit numbers. Find the time taken to perform the addition at a clock frequency of 50 kHz (50 000 pulses per second). **(4)**

4. Write down the logic for the binary subtraction of one number from a larger one and devise a serial subtractor to use this logic. **(5, 6)**

5. Using a 4-bit integer computer to illustrate your answer, show how overflow can occur during both addition and subtraction processes. How is the overflow condition detected by the machine? **(6–8)**

6. Perform the following subtractions in binary numeration using twos complements:

(*a*) 1011 − 1101
(*b*) 111 − 1101 **(7)**

7. Estimate the maximum time taken to multiply two 16-bit numbers by

(*a*) repeated addition,
(*b*) the shift-and-add method,

at a clock frequency of 50 kHz. **(10–12)**

8. What is a floating-point numeral? What advantages result from its use? **(16)**

9. When used with floating-point numerals, what do the following terms mean:

(*a*) Fraction (*b*) Exponent (*c*) Normalised? **(16)**

10. A 16-bit word computer represents numbers in floating-point format. Each word uses a 12-bit mantissa and a 4-bit exponent. Twos complements are adopted for negative quantities. Show in a step-by-step manner how the machine would carry out the subtraction 7 − 2. **(16)**

CHAPTER VII

Computer Memories

MEMORY CONCEPTS

1. Introduction. As we saw in II, 4, a vital subsystem of the computer is that bearing the general name *memory* (or *store*). Memory is used for holding numbers, results of calculations, instructions, and other information. A modern computer system will, in general, contain a number of different types of memory device each suited to its particular purpose. Some of these types will be described below. An important point to bear in mind is the fact that memory technology is a fast-moving and competitive field, so that it is quite possible for new techniques and devices radically to alter the available hardware in a very short time.

2. Memory terminology. Some of the terms used in connection with memories are now defined.

(*a*) *Location.* Any place in memory capable of containing a unit of information; e.g. a *word* in a word-oriented memory, or a *character* in a character-oriented memory.

(*b*) *Address.* The position of a location in memory.

(*c*) *Read.* To obtain data *from* one type of memory and transfer it to another.

(*d*) *Write.* To transcribe data *into* one type of memory from another.

(*e*) *Volatility.* The property of some memories such that their contents are lost when power is removed.

(*f*) *Destructive read-out.* Memories have this property when the contents of a location are obliterated by the reading operation.

(*g*) *Capacity, C.* The number of words or characters that can be contained in a particular memory. The symbol K is commonly used in the computer world to represent 1024 (2^{10}). For example, one might speak of an 8K memory, i.e. one with a capacity of 8192 words. This notation should not be confused with the S.I. prefix kilo- (k) which of course stands for 1000 (10^3).

(*h*) *Propagation delay*, T_P. The time elapsed from the instant of executing an instruction calling for data from memory to the instant when the calling signal reaches the memory.

(*i*) *Latency (or waiting time)*, T_L. The time elapsed from the instant the calling signal arrives at memory to the instant when transfer of data from memory begins.

(*j*) *Read time*, T_R. The time elapsed from instant transfer from memory begins to the instant it is completed.

(*k*) *Access time*, T_A. The time taken to retrieve data from memory, measured from the instant of executing an instruction to call for the data to the instant when the data is stored in the specified location. It should be clear that

$$T_A = T_P + T_L + T_R$$

The relation between the various times associated with memory is shown in Fig. 53.

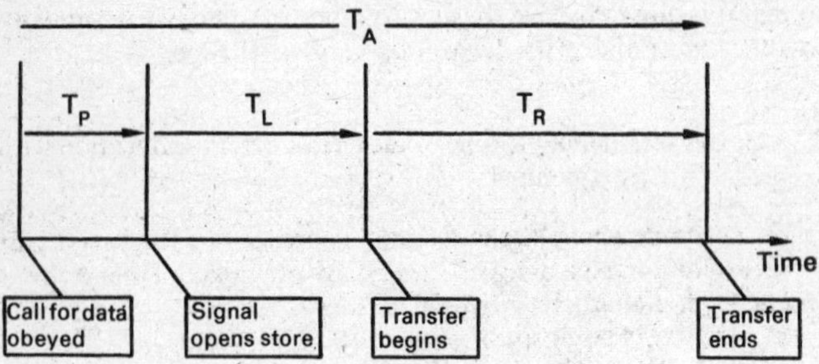

FIG. 53 *Relation between time invervals.*

3. Classification of computer memories. A broad view of different types of computer memory reveals a large variation in capacities and access times. Different memory types are used for different requirements in the same computer system. We shall now list four principal categories characterised by combination of capacity and access time.

(*a*) *Scratchpad Memory (or Kernel Store)*. This is a high-speed memory reserved for the storage of intermediate results in a calculation. At the time of writing the most common type of scratchpad memory is one which consists of semiconductor registers in integrated circuit form. Typical parameters: C$\not>$256 words; T_A: 10–200 nanoseconds.

(*b*) *Main Memory.* This type of memory must possess the optimum combination of large capacity and short access time. Its function is to hold the many individual instructions which go to make up a computer program and to make these instructions quickly available for decoding and subsequent execution. The pre-eminent technology used for main memory is that which utilises the ferrite magnetic core, but there are now very firm indications that the core store will be almost certainly superseded by recently developed semiconductor devices. Typical parameters: $C^{(max.)}$ 256 000 words; T_A: 200 ns – 5μs.

(*c*) *Mass Memory.* This sort of memory is characterised by its much larger capacity and longer access time. It is used for the retention of whole files of information. The most important type of mass memory today is the magnetic disk. Typical parameters: $C^{(max.)}10^9$ bytes; $T_A^{(max)}$: 500 mns.

(*d*) *External Memory.* Finally we must mention this limiting case. Information in the form of computer programs and other alpha-numeric data may be stored in limitless quantities on punched cards, paper tape and magnetic tape external to the computer. In this case, C may be theoretically infinite, while T_A could, in practice, be many minutes (for example, while a sequential search is made by the machine through a large reel in a magnetic tape unit).

4. Store access classification. Computer memories can also be divided into two main types on the basis of the kind of access possible.

(*a*) *Random-access memories* are those designed to give a constant (or almost constant) access time for any location addressed and regardless of the location previously addressed. Such memories are also referred to as direct-access (or even, less accurately, immediate-access) memories. The ferrite core store is a typical example of this kind of device while the magnetic disk, although providing random access, shows some greater variability in access time due to the effect of (rotational) latency.

(*b*) *Sequential-access memories* are those in which data can only be accessed in the sequence in which it is stored; i.e. an item can only be processed after all the preceding items have been accessed. An example of this type of memory device is the magnetic tape store.

MAGNETIC MEMORIES

We shall now examine a number of computer memory devices all of which rely on magnetic phenomena of one sort or another.

5. The ferrite-core memory. Developed in the 1950s, this memory device consists of a three-dimensional array of ferrite cores. Each core is a tiny toroid (with internal diameters sometimes as small as 0.3 mm) made of a ferrite (a material consisting of iron oxide to which small quantities of transition metal oxides have been added). An externally applied magnetic field can change the direction of magnetisation of a core from one stable state to another. It is this property which enables the core to store a 1 or a 0 depending on the direction of magnetisation (*see* Fig. 54).

A wire threaded through a core may carry an electric current the magnetic field of which will determine the magnetic flux density in the core. The singular property of ferrite is that it has a very nearly rectangular hysteresis loop (graph of flux density in core plotted against magnetising current). Such a loop is shown in Fig. 55, where it can be seen that to change the state of magnetisation

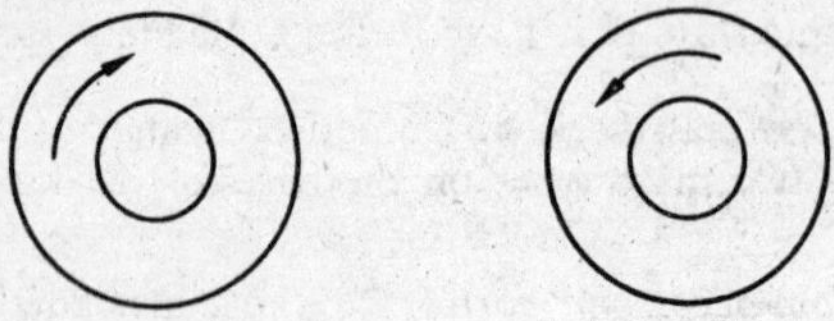

FIG. 54 *Bit representation in a ferrite core.*

from a 1 to a 0 requires a certain minimum magnetising current, I_m, in the threaded wire. Similarly, to change from 0 to 1 requires current, $-I_m$, in the wire.

In a core memory *two* wires, called the x- and y-wires pass through each core, so that the magnetising field is provided by the sum of the fields of the current in these wires. Current pulses sent along the x- and y-wires are used to address a particular core. The magnitude of these pulses is only $\frac{1}{2}I_m$, which alone is insufficient to affect a core. Two pulses of this magnitude, applied

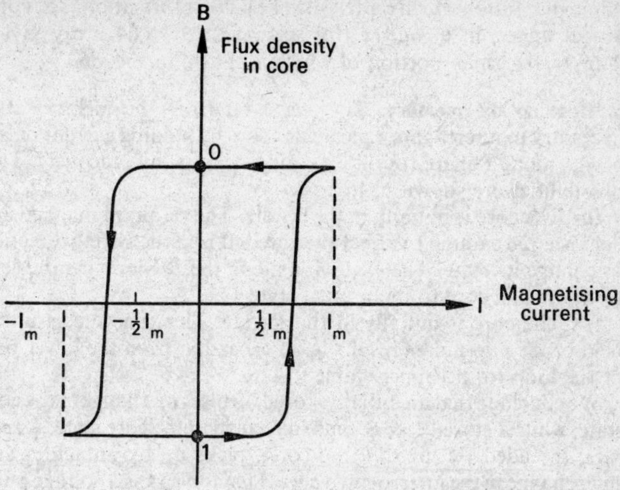

FIG. 55 *Ferrite core hysteresis loop.*

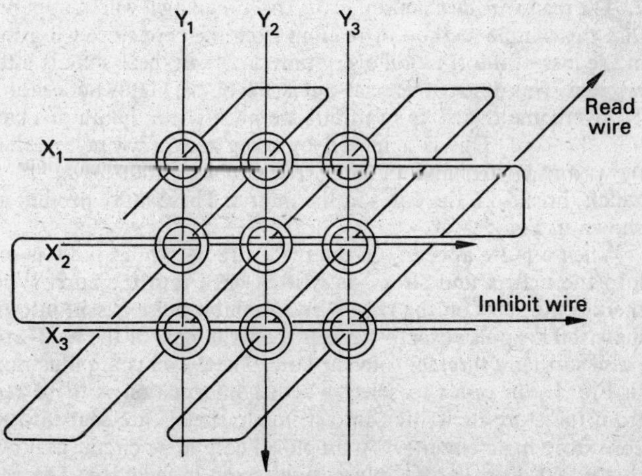

FIG. 56 *Two-dimensional core array.*

simultaneously, will create a field strong enough to change the state of magnetisation which represents one bit of information. The cores are arranged in a *matrix* (for example a 64×64 array giving 4069 bits) a small portion of which is shown in Fig. 56.

6. Reading the memory. To *read* a bit from the memory it is necessary to interrogate a particular core by sending current pulses of $\frac{1}{2}I_m$ along the appropriate x- and y-wires simultaneously. Two possibilities are shown in Fig. 57.

(*a*) The core is initially in the 0 state. The resultant magnetising field is large enough to affect the core but is in the wrong direction to change its state. The excursion along the B/I-loop can be seen to return the core to its original state.

(*b*) The core is initially in the 1 state. This time the resultant field of the two pulses results in an excursion from the lower part of the loop to the upper stable 0 state.

We conclude that an initially stored 0 causes no change in the core state, while a stored 1 *does* cause a change in the core state. A *read wire*; threaded through *all* the cores, picks up by induction any such change in the interrogated core. This appears as a voltage pulse if the core had stored a 1 and no pulse at all if the core had stored a 0.

7. The read-wire mechanism. From the foregoing it will be apparent that this simple method of reading from the core store will result in the loss of information every time a core in the 1 state is interrogated. This destructive read-out is, of course, highly undesirable. To overcome this state of affairs we must write the output back into the core. This is achieved by using *read-write* pulses along the x- and y-wires and an *inhibit* pulse along a fourth *inhibit wire* which threads *all* the cores in the matrix. These pulse profiles are shown in Fig. 58.

When a pulse appears on the read wire no inhibit pulse is sent into the matrix and so a 1 is written back into the core. When there is no pulse on the read wire an inhibit pulse is sent into the matrix. This pulse exactly cancels the write part of the read-write pulse so that a 0 remains in the core. These events are illustrated in Fig. 59. In order to select whether information is to be read from the store or written into it, mode signals are sent into the core store logic circuitry. A simplified core logic circuit is shown in Fig. 60. For clarity only a single core is included. The *read gate* and *write gate* are presented with signals to select the appropriate mode. By studying this diagram and the flowchart of Fig. 62

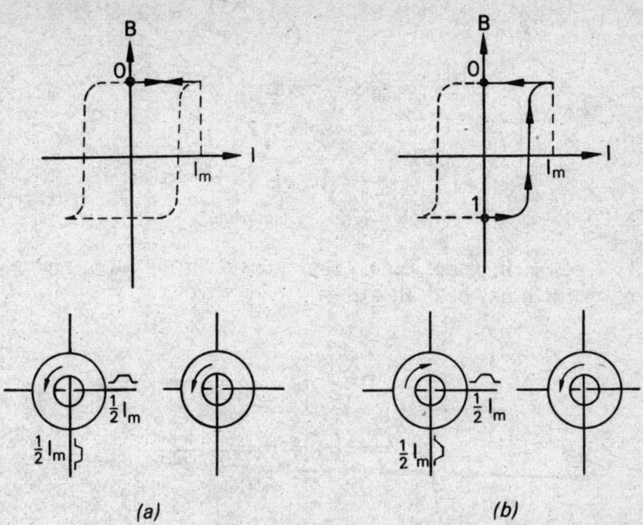

FIG. 57 *Effects of core interrogation.*

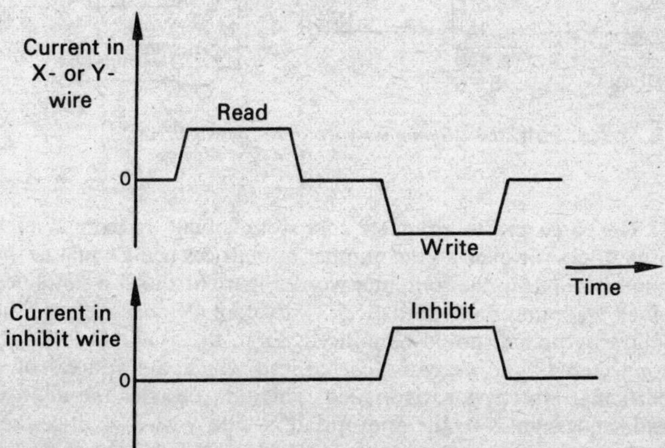

FIG. 58 *Core store current-pulse profiles.*

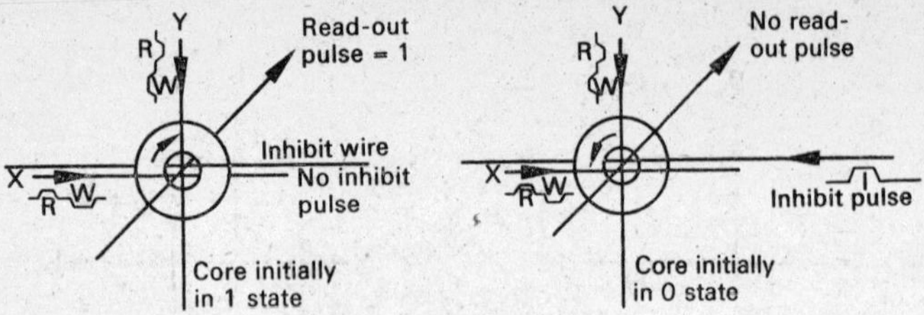

FIG. 59 *Action of inhibit pulse.*

it will be seen how the various possibilities occurring during reading and writing may be dealt with.

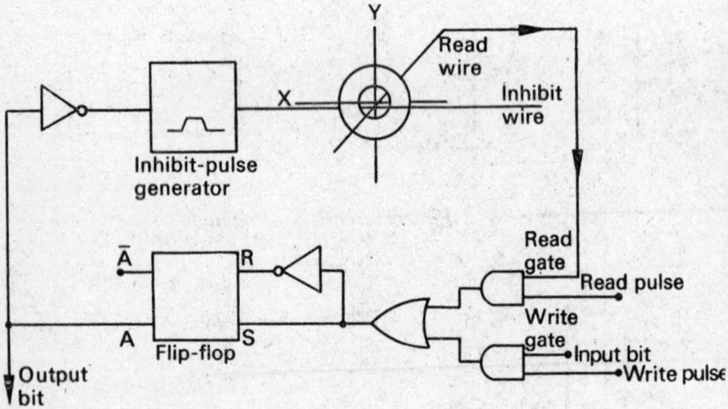

FIG. 60 *Simplified core store control circuit.*

8. The core store. A complete core store is built up from a stack of matrices (or planes), the number of matrices being equal to the number of bits in the computer word. Figure 61 shows a simplified block diagram of a hypothetical 3-wire core memory system. The following points should be noticed. First, the x- and y-wires are connected to the *address selector* into which the address of a particular stored word is loaded. This unit decodes the address and sends signals to the appropriate x- and y-wires. Notice that the x- and y-wires are common to each matrix so that a pair of read-write pulses reads (or writes) a whole word simultaneously. The read-wires from each matrix are connected to the flip-flops

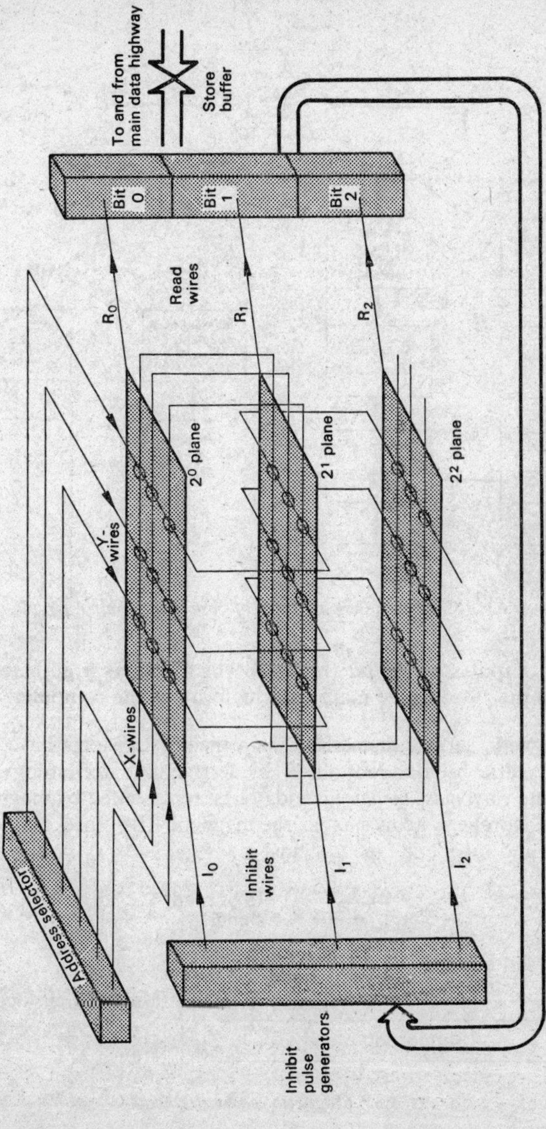

FIG. 61 *Three-wire core memory system.*

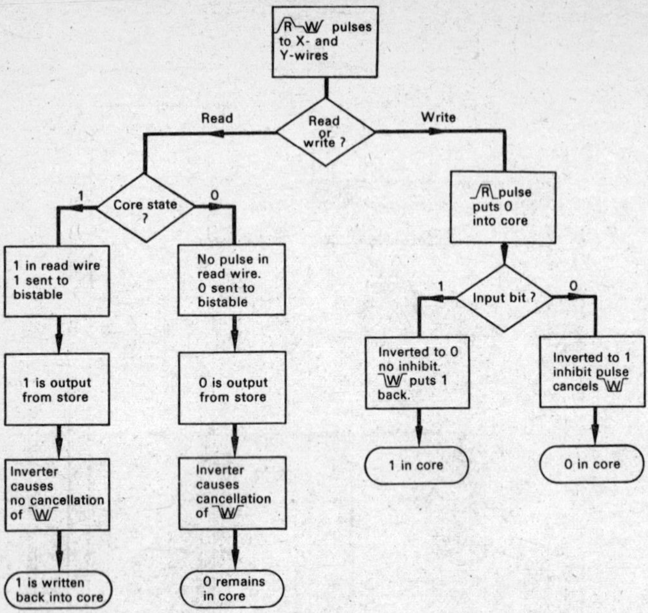

FIG. 62 *Flowchart showing logic of core store control circuit.*

in the output *store buffer* (*register*) which acts as a go-between linking the store to the main data highway of the computer.

9. Magnetic surface memories. Main memory systems have, for many years, been monopolised by ferrite core technology. In the same way, *mass memory* is today best represented by magnetic surface storage systems such as the magnetic disk store, magnetic drums and magnetic tape systems.

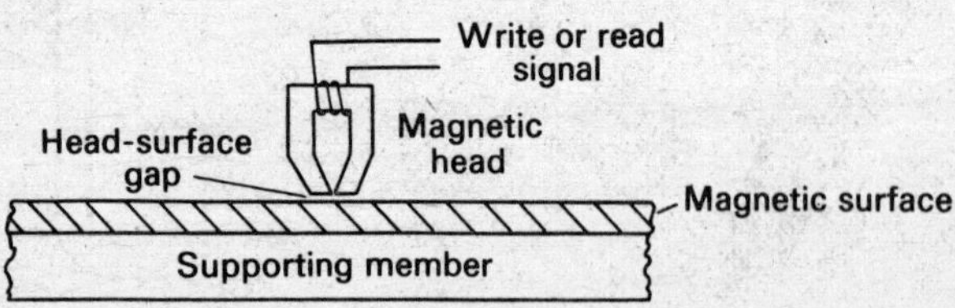

FIG. 63 *Magnetic read-write head.*

The principle of these systems is reminiscent of that utilised in the domestic tape recorder, but pulses representing bit patterns are recorded instead of complex waveforms. The fundamental arrangement of the recording surface and read/write head is shown in Fig. 63. The recording medium moves under the head at constant speed during both reading and writing operations. During writing, current pulses sent into the head winding produce a fringing field in the head gap. This field penetrates the magnetic material and causes magnetic dipoles to be recorded on the moving surface. During reading, motion of surface-recorded dipoles past the head induces small voltage pulses in the head winding which can then be amplified and subsequently interpreted.

Different methods of recording are possible, the main ones being the RTZ (return to zero), the NRTZ (non-return to zero) and *phase recording* techniques. These are compared in Fig. 64.

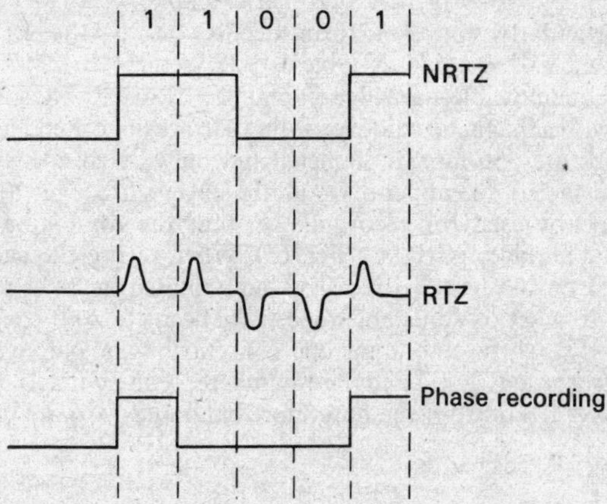

FIG. 64 *Methods of magnetic recording.*

(*a*) In RTZ mode, each successive 1 generates a positive pulse and each successive 0 generates a negative pulse. RTZ is *self-synchronising* in the sense that we know when a bit is passing under the head as we observe a pulse, positive or negative, when it does. However, RTZ requires magnetic patterns to be recorded which change polarity twice as often as a better method—NRTZ.

(*b*) In NRTZ, when a 1 follows a 1 or a 0 follows a 0, no change of state can be detected on output. This technique is *not* self-synchronising, in that a string of bits of the same value generates only one pulse at the beginning. Consequently, a separate timing track has to be recorded in parallel with the data track to let us know when to look for a pulse. It should be noted that we pack twice as much data into a centimetre of magnetic material using NRTZ as using RTZ recording techniques.

(*c*) A variation of NRTZ is called phase recording. In this variation, we change the present state to its opposite when we wish to record a 1 and leave it the same when we wish to record a 0.

In modern high-density recording, the packing density may be hundreds of bits per centimetre of magnetic material. Some specific magnetic surface memories will now be described.

10. Magnetic disk stores. Disk stores are available in a wide range of sizes from single-disk memories storing about 1 million 16-bit words on one disk, to large mass memory multiple-disk stores holding up to 1000 megabits. As an example, we shall examine one particularly common form of disk store—the EDS, or *exchangeable disk store*. A typical EDS is the ICL 2802 which utilises a removable cartridge containing 6 disks. Each disk is coated with a magnetic oxide recording surface deposited on metal. The disks are 356 mm in diameter and only 1.3 mm thick. The upper surface of the upper disk and the lower surface of the lower disk are not used for recording, so that the total number of recording surfaces is 10 (*see* Fig. 65). When in use the cartridge is placed on a vertical drive shaft and rotated at 2400 rev/min relative to a set of adjustable read/write heads.

Each disk surface contains 200 concentric bands along which data is recorded. The bands are numbered consecutively from 0 upwards starting from the outermost band and working inwards

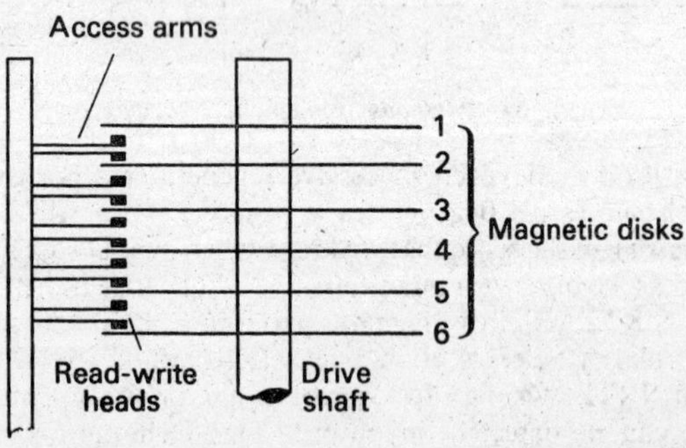

FIG. 65 *A typical exchangeable disk store (EDS).*

(*see* Fig. 66). Each band is divided into 8 equal *data blocks*, each separated from its neighbour by an *interblock* gap. This gap also contains a short *identifier block* that describes the data block preceding it. The whole disk surface consists of 8 sectors, each made up of 200 blocks. Each block holds 512 six-bit bytes. This number of bytes per block is constant for all blocks and is achieved by increasing the number of bits per unit length of band towards the centre of the disk.

The total capacity of our disk cartridge can now be calculated.

1 cartridge = 10 surfaces
1 surface = 8 sectors
1 sector = 200 blocks
1 block = 512 bytes

so,

$$C = 10 \times 8 \times 200 \times 512$$
$$= 8\ 192\ 000 \text{ bytes}$$

We see that the *nominal* capacity of the cartridge is 8 megabytes.

A disk cartridge can be mounted on its *transport deck* very quickly and easily. When not in use the cartridge is kept in an individual plastic dust-proof container.

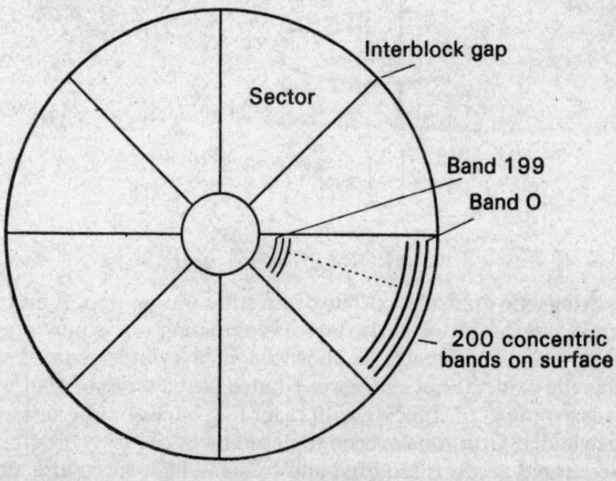

FIG. 66 *Organisation of a disk surface.*

11. The read/write head assembly. This comprises 10 heads mounted on metal *access arms*. The arms are arranged in pairs, providing one head for the bottom surface of a disk and one for the top of the next disk. In operation, all the arms move simultaneously extending in pairs between adjacent disks. Each head consists of two separate units—a read/write unit and an erase unit. The heads do not actually touch the disk surfaces but plane on a viscous film of air only 3 micrometres thick.

When a band has been selected and the head assembly is in position, data can be transferred to or from one band per surface. Once initiated, data transfer will continue block by block without further program instructions until the transfer is terminated. Each head is activated in turn so that data is recorded serially on the corresponding band of each disk. The area defined by these successive bands is referred to as a *cylinder* and can be regarded for programming purposes as a continuous area of cartridge (*see* Fig. 67). The entire area is accessible without further head movement as the heads are always positioned over the respective band on each disk surface.

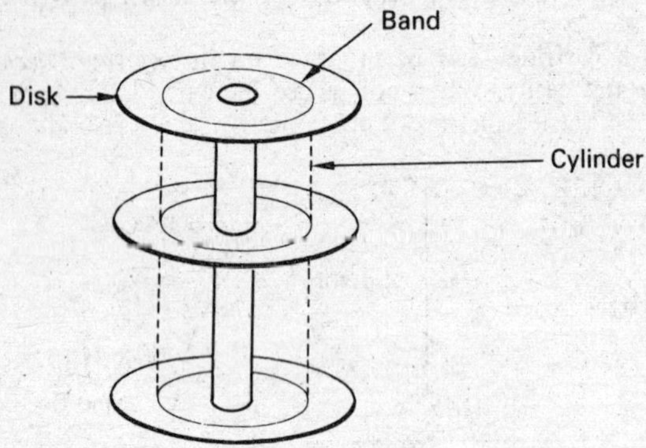

FIG. 67 *The cylinder concept.*

12. Magnetic drum stores. The drum store was an important mass memory device in the early days of computing but is now rapidly fading out of existence. It consisted of a cylinder coated with magnetic oxide; the cylinder was rotated past a series of read/write heads arranged to coincide with recording bands on the surface of the cylinder. Drums have been replaced by large mass core storage where rapid access is required and by small high-speed disk stores where medium access speed is needed with medium to large capacity.

13. Magnetic tape stores. Magnetic tape is the commonest form of *backing store* and external memory used in computer installations. The tape consists of a continuous strip of polyester plastic coated with magnetic oxide on which data may be recorded. Such tapes are typically about 13 mm wide and around 700 m long. They are wound on to reels approximately 27 cm in diameter.

A *magnetic tape deck* is used to transfer data between tape and computer. The deck consists basically of a drive system (Fig. 68) capable of rotating two tape reels at very high speed so that tape is wound from one reel to the other. During transportation between reels, the tape passes a set of read/write heads.

In one system, information is recorded in seven parallel tracks which run the length of the tape. Of these seven, six tracks are used for data, while the other is a parity track. Information *across* the tape thus consists of a *stripe* made up of one parity bit and six data bits. This is shown in Fig. 69. The stripes (parity–checked six-bit bytes) are grouped into blocks of typically 400 bytes to the block. Further, since data cannot be written or read properly unless the tape is running at high speed (several metres per second), a gap is left between blocks to avoid recording during deceleration

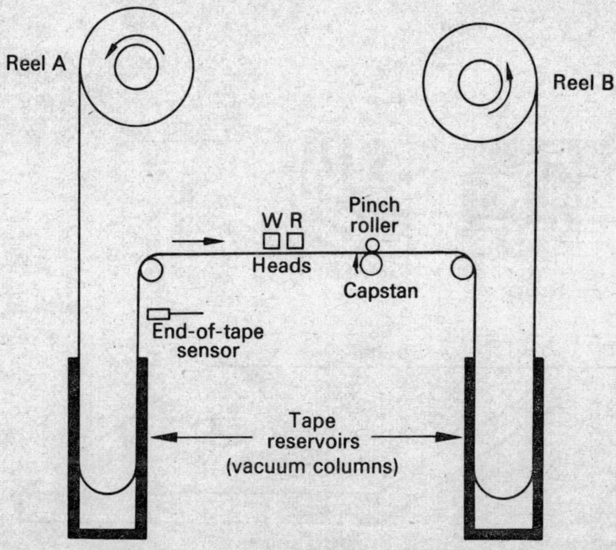

FIG. 68 *Magnetic-tape drive system.*

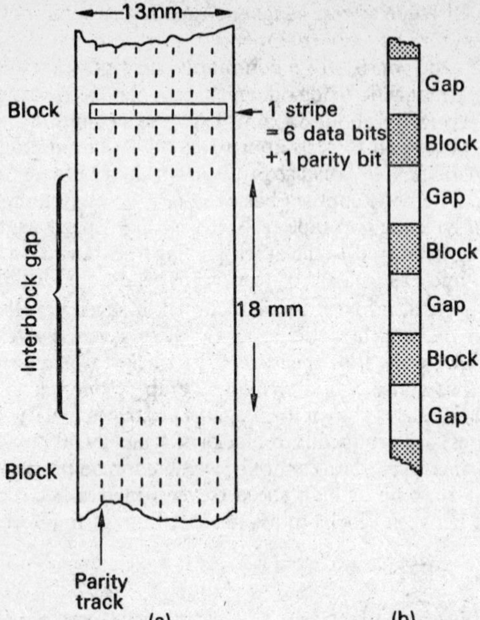

FIG. 69 *Magnetic tape.*

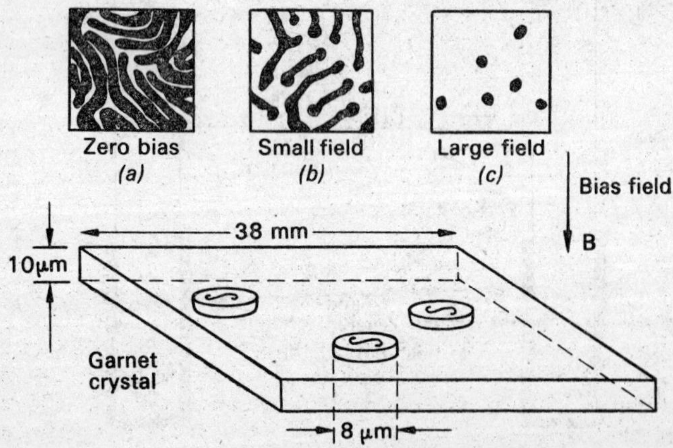

FIG. 70 *Formation of magnetic bubbles.*

and acceleration of the tape. Odd parity is used, since then the stripes are clocked automatically, i.e. each stripe has at least one reversal of magnetisation to define its position. Recording is in NRTZ mode. Recording densities used in magnetic tape systems vary typically in the range 8 bits/mm to 32 bits/mm.

The rate at which data can be transferred in a tape transport may be calculated from the equation:

$$R = Ndv$$

where R = the bit transfer rate (bits per second),
N = the number of data tracks,
d = the recording density (bits per metre),
and v = the tape speed (metres per second).

e.g.

$N = 6$
$d = 32$ bits/mm $= 32 \times 10^3$ bits/m
$v = 3$ m/s

So,

$$R = 6 \times (32 \times 10^3) \times 3$$
$$= 576\,000 \text{ bits/s}$$

This corresponds to 96 kilobytes per second.

A typical tape reel can hold something in the order of 10 megabytes of information, a figure which is in the same order as the magnetic disk cartridge described above. The most important limitation of tape is, however, that it is a sequential access medium producing variable access times which may run into minutes. Compare this with disk store access times of the order of 100 ms. An interesting feature seen in Fig. 68 is that tape drive systems incorporate separate heads for reading and writing. This is done so that data just written can be immediately read back for checking purposes.

14. Magnetic-bubble memories. In 1970 the Bell laboratories found that rare-earth garnet crystals of diameter 38 mm and no thicker than 10 micrometres could support *magnetic bubbles* only 8 micrometres in diameter for use in computer memories. These so-called bubbles are created in the garnet crystal by the application of a *bias magnetic field* normal to the thin crystalline layer. There is a critical field value when the normal magnetic regions called *domains* "snap" into stable cylindrical "bubble" domains (*see* Fig. 70). Magnetic bubbles may be thought of as short, cylindrical magnets afloat in a near-frictionless sea of reverse magnetisation. Bubbles, like magnets with like poles closest, repel one another. Bubble packing densities are around 1500 per square millimetre.

Controlled propagation of strings of bubbles may be achieved along tracks consisting of alternating I- and T-shaped permalloy overlays placed close to the surface of the crystal. A rotating in-plane magnetic field induces attractive and repulsive poles on these overlays. The diagram in Fig. 71 shows stages of propagation in which S-poles on the upper ends of bubbles attach themselves to induced N-poles in the overlay. Rotation of the field causes bubble "hopping" along the track.

Transfer gates consist of magnetic overlay strips positioned so that bubbles are deflected along alternate propagation routes according to the direction of overlay magnetisation, which is switched by current pulses through a conductor overlay. By means of these gates, continuously generated bubbles may be selectively admitted to a shift-register memory as a sequence corresponding to information to be stored.

In 1974, RCA laboratories developed a bubble read-out technique based on the *faraday effect.* Light from an LED (light-emitting diode) passes through the garnet crystal, through a sheet of polarising material and thence on to a photo-diode. Bubbles passing through the light beam cause rotation of the plane of polarisation with subsequent variations in the light intensity falling on the photo-diode. In this way, the stream of bits carried by the bubbles becomes a sequence of electrical pulses forming output from the bubble store.

Magnetic-bubble speeds of up to 9 km/s have been observed and bubble memories show great promise for microcomputers of the future.

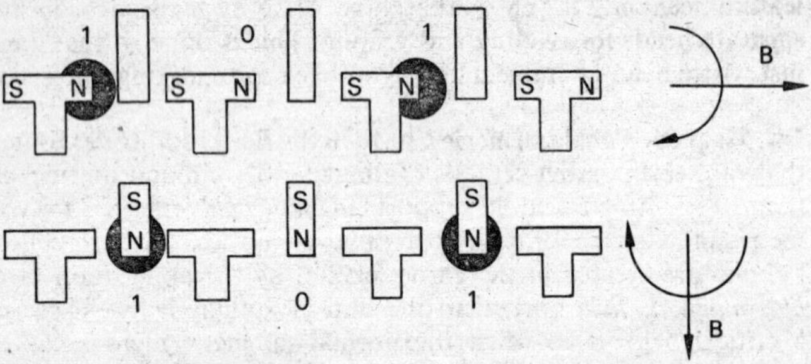

FIG. 71 *Controlled propagation of bubble strings.*

NON-MAGNETIC MEMORIES

15. Semiconductor memories. The very important integrated circuit packages have already been described in II, **11**. It will be recalled that many thousands of flip-flop elements may be contained on a very small chip of silicon. These semiconductor memories are not only of large capacity and small size but may also be considerably faster than ferrite core stores. There are two main types of semiconductor memory. First, there is the read and write *random-access memory*, or RAM, which can be used as a direct replacement for core store, but its contents are volatile, so that it must be refreshed every 2 ms or so. The contents of *read-only memory*, or ROM, are non-volatile but cannot be altered during the operation of the computer.

A semiconductor memory with potential access times in the order of nanoseconds has been developed by Bell Telephone Laboratories. Each memory cell consists of a metal-semiconductor diode with a guard ring connected in series with a diffused p–n junction diode. Each interconnected cell occupies an area 0.1 mm square which implies a packing density of 100 bits/mm^2.

In 1976, IBM's Thomas J. Watson Research Centre announced a field-effect transistor memory array with a considerably greater packing density. The array uses FETs and is capable of storing 8 kilobits of information with a density of 7600 bits/mm^2.

16. Holographic memories. The very small wavelength of visible light (400–700 nm) implies that information can be recorded on film at very high densities. Using modern emulsions it becomes possible to record data photographically at densities exceeding 10^6 bits/mm^2. This would allow the contents of the Concise Oxford English Dictionary to be stored in digital form in an area of one square centimetre. The problem with realising this by conventional imaging techniques is that very expensive optics would be required, necessitating lenses able to resolve bits about 1 micrometre in size.

Holographic (rather than photographic) storage of data overcomes this problem. A hologram is an interference pattern recorded on a photo-sensitive plate by mixing laser light from a reference beam and laser light scattered from the object bearing the information to be recorded. The data in the hologram is effectively "smeared" over the whole of the plate and so precision optics is not required in the reading and writing processes. Precise positioning of the hologram is also unnecessary and a degree of redundancy is built into the system so that dust and scratches on the emulsion have little or no effect on the recorded information.

Data in the reconstructed image are arranged as an array of dots—one dot for each bit. Information may be read out by directing a laser beam on to the hologram so that the reconstructed image falls on to a photodiode array. In 1973 the Plessey company announced a prototype store with a 200 ns access time to any one of 1024 holograms. The data could be read out at 5 Mbits/s. Figure 72 shows a typical holographic random-access memory.

Because of the very high potential capacities of holographic memories—comparable with present-day mass memory—there should eventually be no need to transfer data from mass- to main memory at all. At present the main limitation is that information in a holographic store is fixed or can only be changed on a very long time scale. Hence this type of store is presently of value for

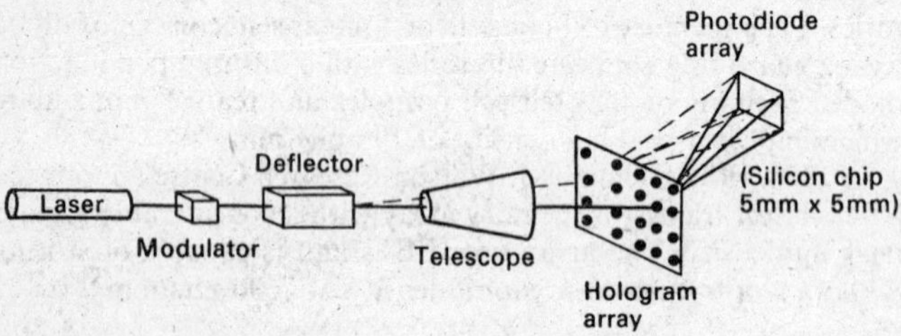

FIG. 72 *Holographic random-access memory.*

storing large amounts of *fixed* information such as machine instructions.

PROGRESS TEST 7

1. Distinguish the terms latency and access time. **(2)**

2. How many words are there in a 16-K memory? In a 64-K memory? **(2)**

3. Computer memories may be classified according to their capacity. Explain this classification and give examples of hardware used and the associated access times. **(3)**

4. What is a random-access memory? **(4)**

5. A core store has a capacity of 4096 words, each 24 bits long. What is the number of (*a*) cores; (*b*) matrices; (*c*) read wires; (*d*) inhibit wires? **(5–8)**

6. What is the function of a store buffer register? **(8)**

7. Explain the terms RTZ and NRTZ as used in connection with magnetic-surface memories. What is phase recording? **(9)**

8. Explain what is meant by a cylinder of records on a magnetic disk file, and indicate the reasons for using this arrangement. **(11)**

CHAPTER VIII

Data Flow in the Computer; How Instructions are Obeyed

PUTTING THE BITS TOGETHER

1. A hypothetical machine. The previous chapters have examined some of the subsystems which are prerequisites for the construction of an integral computing system. We must now see how it is possible for these subsystems to be interlinked in a manner which facilitates the carrying out of a sequence of instructions and the movement of associated data.

Figure 73 depicts a highly simplified hypothetical computer. It consists of the following important units:

(*a*) *A main store* which can retain several K of 16-bit words each of which may represent a single machine instruction, a signed number, or two 8-bit characters.

(*b*) *An address register* which is used to hold the address of a specified word in main store.

(*c*) *A buffer register* the function of which is to act as a general purpose data transfer register in which numbers can be stored to be added or subtracted from other numbers in the accumulator.

(*d*) *A program counter* which enables the computer to proceed through a program from one instruction to the next. Except in the case of jump instructions, the next instruction is found by incrementing the address of the previous instruction by 1. The address register sometimes contains the address of an instruction and sometimes the address of an operand, so the address of the present instruction must be preserved so that it can be incremented appropriately, while the address register is in use for other purposes. This is done in the program counter into which the present instruction is transferred before being destroyed in the address register. The program counter can count in binary as well as store an address, so that incrementing can be performed by means of pulses from the clock unit.

(*e*) *An instruction register* which holds the instruction currently to be obeyed. This register is connected to the function decoder in order that the bits which represent the desired function will produce appropriate signals to call into action those parts of the arithmetic unit necessary for executing the function.

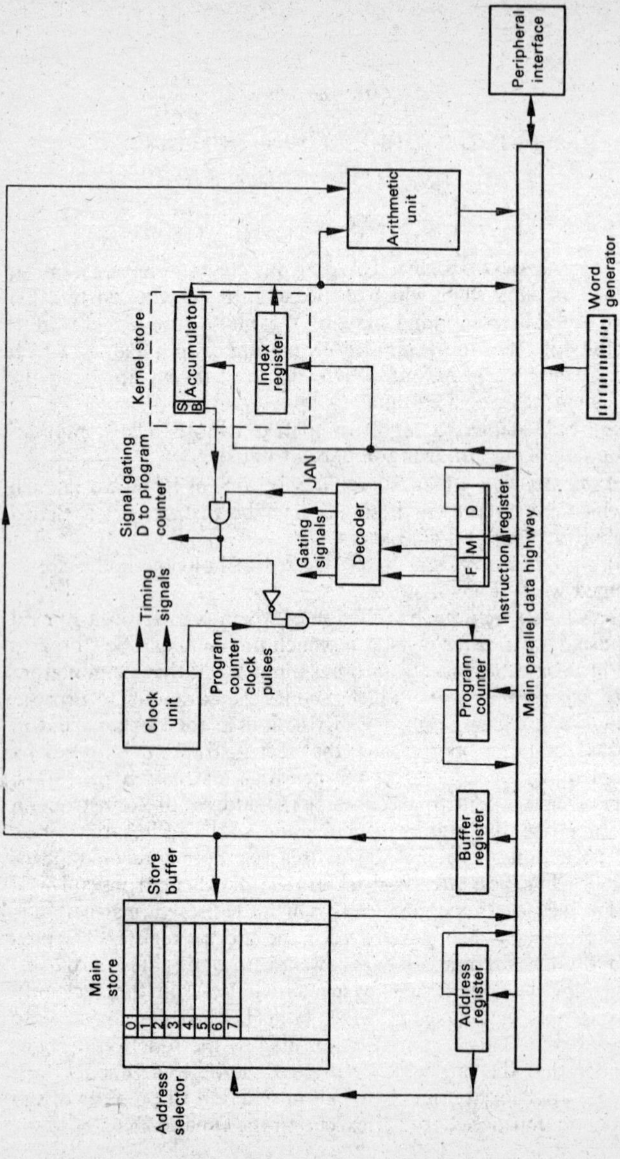

FIG. 73 *ASS—a hypothetical computer.*

(*f*) *A kernel store* consisting of two registers. These are the *accumulator*, which is referenced in nearly all the available machine instructions and which is used to hold the result of an arithmetic or other operation, and the *index register*, which has important uses in address modification and conditional transfers.

(*g*) *An arithmetic unit* which is used to perform basic arithmetic operations and the various logical functions.

(*h*) *A peripheral interface* which enables information into and out of the machine to be connected to a range of input and output devices, such as electric typewriters or VDUs.

(*i*) *A clock unit* which generates streams of precisely synchronised pulses and distributes them to various parts of the machine. These pulses are used to shift information from one register to another, to increment the program counter, to operate carry flip-flops, to open and close gates at the right time and, in general, to provide the whole system with a kind of heart-beat.

2. Channelling the bits. Although only one example is shown in Fig. 73, each line of information flow (whether serial or parallel) contains *control gates*, by means of which the streams of bits may be directed to the correct destinations. Such gating may be performed by means of AND-gates through which the information may or may not be allowed to pass.

Figure 74 shows how gating may be accomplished. In (*a*) information may be diverted from the source X to either C or D. A logic 1 at A results in flow to C, while a 1 at B causes the information to be routed to D. Of course, if 1s are presented simultaneously at A and B, then the same bit pattern will appear at both C and D. The reader should verify for himself that the AND-operation will produce these results. In (*b*) a 1 at I acts as an *inhibit* signal which *prevents* information flow from X to Y.

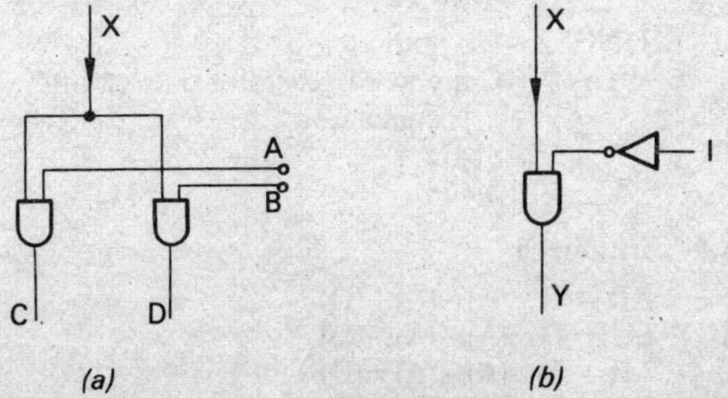

FIG. 74 *Gating information.*

3. The data highway. This consists of a 16-bit parallel gating system for routing information between registers, main store and the arithmetic unit. Only a single word may be on the highway at any one time although several registers may have information simultaneously gated into them. The input and output devices are linked via the peripheral interface into the data highway also.

GETTING THE BITS TO WORK

Any word in the machine is simply a set of 16 bits. This set may, however, be interpreted in a number of ways. First, a word may be used to represent a computer instruction, and secondly, it may represent data such as numbers or characters. We shall examine some possible word structures below.

4. Instruction format. Our hypothetical computer will use instructions of the form:

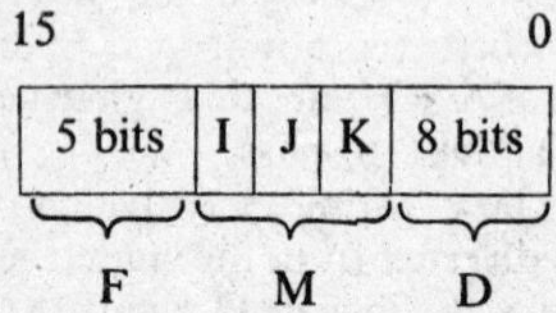

The left-most five bits constitute a *function field*, F, which may be used to specify a maximum of 32 different functions. These functions are listed below together with a *mnemonic*—a group of 3 letters which uniquely identify the particular instruction.

Group 0

000 00	DNO	Do nothing
000 01	WGA	Copy word-generator pattern into accumulator
000 10	—	Spare
000 11	—	Spare

Group 1 Arithmetic

001 00	ADD D	(A)←(A)+(D)
001 01	SUB D	(A)←(A)−(D)
001 10	MLT D	(A)←(A)×(D)
001 11	DIV D	(A)←(A) / (D)

Group 2 Shifting & Logic

010 00	SAR D	Shift (A) RIGHT D places (a logical shift)
010 01	SAL D	Shift (A) LEFT D places (a logical shift)
010 10	AND D	(A)←(A) . (D) (collate)
010 11	NEQ D	(A)←(A)≢(D) (not-equivalent)

Group 3 Load & Store

011 00	LDA D	(A)←(D) (load the accumulator)
011 01	STA D	(D)←(A) (store the accumulator)
011 10	LDI D	(I)←(D) (load the index register)
011 11	STI D	(D)←(I) (store the index register)

Group 4 Input & Output

100 00	ICP D	Input an 8-bit character from peripheral D to LSE[1] of accumulator
100 01	OCP D	Output an 8-bit character to peripheral D from MSE of accumulator
100 10	INP D*	Input a number from peripheral D to accumulator
100 11	ONP D*	Output a number to peripheral D from accumulator

Group 5 Conditional Transfers (Accumulator Test)

101 00	JAZ D	Jump to instruction in location D if (A) = 0
100 01	JAN	Jump to instruction in location D if (A) < 0
101 10	JAP	Jump to instruction in locationD if (A) > 0
101 11	JAF D	Jump to instruction in location D if accumulator has overflowed

Group 6 Conditional transfers (Index Register Test)

110 00	JIZ D	Jump if (I) = 0
110 01	JIN D	Jump if (I) < 0
110 10	JIP D	Jump if (I) > 0
110 11	JIF D	Jump if index register has overflowed

Group 7 Miscellaneous

111 00	JUN D	Jump unconditionally to instruction in location D
111 01	INC D	Increment the index register (by +1 if D unspecified)
110 10	ABS	(A)←positive magnitude of (A) irrespective of sign of (A)
111 11	—	Spare

[1] LSE = Least Significant End.

The following points should be noted.

(*a*) brackets denote "the contents of"; e.g. (A) means the contents of the accumulator.

(*b*) the back-arrow ←, is used to mean "is assigned"; e.g. (A)←(D) means set the contents of the accumulator equal to the contents of address D.

(*c*) the left-most 3 bits of the function define the particular *group* of functions to which the instruction belongs. This facilitates logical organisation of the decoding circuitry.

(*d*) the starred (*) functions in group 4 are strictly not primitive machine code (as the rest are). Indeed many computers would require a specific piece of *software* (program) for their implementation. Such functions are called *macros*.

5. Displacement and modifier fields. Bits 0–7 constitute a *displacement field*, D, which is used to specify either an *address* or an *integer*. The exact interpretation of this field depends on the state of the *modifier field*, M. The latter consists of bits 8, 9 and 10 called *tag bits*, K, J, and I respectively. A number of cases arise:

(*a*) When I = J = K = 0, we have the case of *direct addressing* which means that D represents any main store address in the range 0 through 255. For example, the instruction

01100 000 00001101

would be interpreted as

LOAD THE ACCUMULATOR WITH THE CONTENTS OF LOCATION 13

In the case of the shift instructions SAR and SAL, the displacement is taken to be an integer. For example,

01000 000 00000011

would mean

SHIFT THE ACCUMULATOR CONTENTS TO THE RIGHT THREE PLACES

(*b*) When the I-bit = 1, we have the case of *indexing*—a facility which effectively extends the range of main store addresses specifiable by a given instruction. Whenever the I-bit is set, the contents of the index register are *first* added to the displacement D, thus giving an address which may be well outside the usual range of

0 through 255. For example, if the index register contained the number

0000 0011 0110 0000 (decimal 864)

and the computer encountered the instruction

00100 100 00100100 (mnemonic ADDI 36)

then 36 would be added to 864 giving the address 900. Hence, the instruction actually carried out would be

SET THE ACCUMULATOR CONTENTS TO THE PREVIOUS ACCUMULATOR CONTENTS PLUS THE CONTENTS OF MAIN STORE LOCATION 900

By this time the reader will have noticed how cumbersome it becomes when instructions have to be written out in full binary form. The mnemonic equivalent of the last instruction is enclosed in brackets above. The convention here will be to express the mnemonic displacement in decimal and to include the tag-bit letter (I, J, or K) after the function code only if the particular tag-bit is set (i.e. = 1).

(*c*) When the J-bit = 1, we have the case of *relative addressing*. In this case the effective address is found by adding the displacement D to the address of the instruction that has just been accessed. Here, D is regarded as a signed integer in the range −128 through +127 (twos complements are assumed).

(*d*) When *both* I and J are set, we have *indirect addressing*. In this case the effective address is that *contained* in the location whose address is given by the displacement D. This facility extends the range of addressable locations considerably. For example, if location 255 contained the number 65 535, then the menemonic instruction

LDAIJ 255

would have the meaning

LOAD THE ACCUMULATOR WITH THE CONTENTS OF LOCATION 65 535

(*e*) When the K-bit is set, the displacement D is taken as a *literal*. This means that the D field is interpreted as a *signed integer* rather than an address. The integer lies in the range −128 to +127. For example,

00110 001 00001000 (MLTK 8)

has the effect of multiplying the accumulator contents by the number eight. (An instruction with the same effect would be

01001 000 00000011—why?) Here is a summary of the possible M-field patterns.

I	J	K	
0	0	0	direct addressing
0	0	1	literal
0	1	0	relative addressing
1	0	0	indexing
1	1	0	indirect addressing

6. Integer format. Integers will be held in the machine according to the format below:

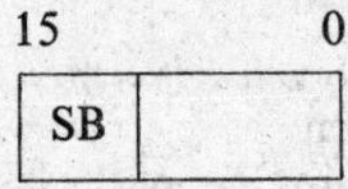

Bit-15 is the sign bit and the *twos complement* system will be used. It follows that the possible range of integer representation is

$$-32\,768 \leqslant \text{integer} \leqslant +32\,767$$

7. Fraction format. The 16-bit word may also be interpreted as a binary fraction with the format:

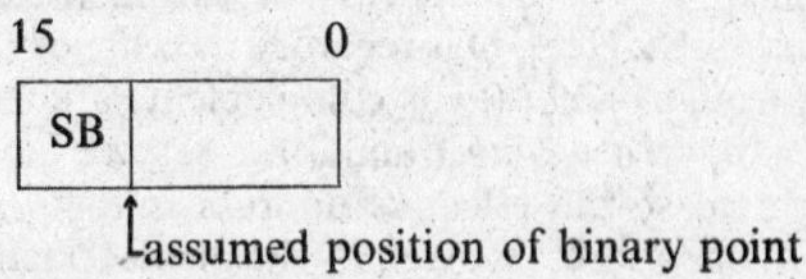

In twos complement the possible range is

$$-1 \leqslant \text{fraction} \leqslant 1 - 2^{-15}$$

$$\text{i.e. } -1 \leqslant \text{fraction} \leqslant +0.9999695\ldots$$

8. Floating-point format. Floating-point numerals will take the form:

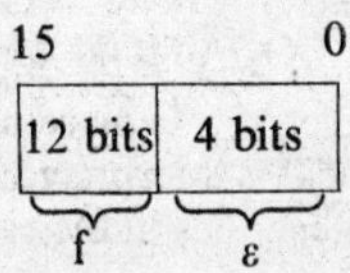

f is a signed fraction
ε is a signed exponent

Numbers are stored so as to represent the form

$$N = f \times 2^{\varepsilon}$$

9. Character format. The 16-bit word may also be used to store two 8-bit characters, thus:

15	0
8 bits	8 bits
character	character

10. Control cycling. Having defined a hypothetical machine (let us call it ASS—*A Simple System*) and its associated instruction set (a machine code which we shall name LOCO—for *Low-level Code*), we must now see how such a system could carry out some specific task.

The task to be performed is defined by a set of stored instructions known as a *program* which we shall assume is already held in main store locations 0 through 6. Suppose the task is as follows:

ADD TOGETHER THE TWO NUMBERS IN LOCATIONS 7 AND 8. IF THEIR SUM IS NEGATIVE, PLACE THE SUM IN LOCATION 10, OTHERWISE PLACE THE SUM IN LOCATION 9

Location	Contents	Mnemonic	
0	01100 000 00000111	LDA 7	LOCO PROGRAM
1	00100 000 00001000	ADD 8	
2	10101 000 00000101	JAN 5	
3	01101 000 00001001	STA 9	
4	11100 000 00000100	JUN 4	
5	01101 000 00001010	STA 10	
6	11100 000 00000110	JUN 6	
7	00000 000 00000010	+2	DATA
8	11111 111 11111001	−7	
9	–		
10	–		

FIG. 75

Figure 75 shows how the first 11 main store locations might look prior to the program's execution.

In order to understand how ASS is able to carry out the above program it is important to realise that the control subsystem alternates between two cycles, FETCH and EXECUTE. The timing of these cycles is carried out by the clock unit which sends precisely synchronised signals to the various subsystems.

(*a*) *Fetch cycle.*

(*i*) send program counter (PC) contents to address register (AR).

(*ii*) open gates between instruction register (IR) and main store location holding instruction specified by AR.

(*iii*) transfer specified instruction to IR.

(*iv*) begin execute cycle.

(*b*) *Execute cycle.*

(*i*) decode F-and M-fields.

(*ii*) is F a jump instruction?

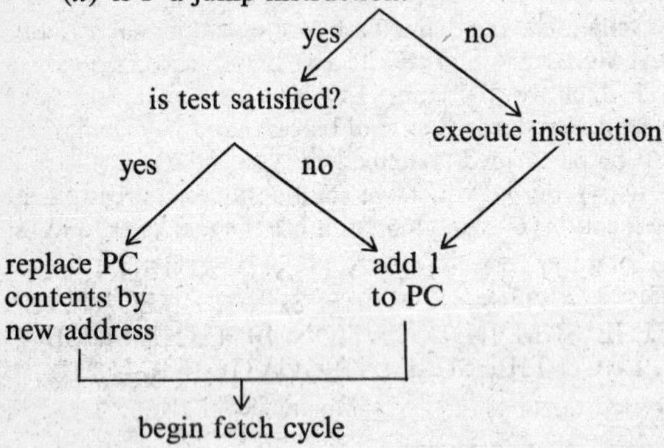

11. Program operation. We are now in a position to follow the program through in a step-by-step fashion. It is assumed that the PC has been initially set to zero.

FETCH: PC → AR; transfer [LDA 7] from loc. 0 to IR.
EXEC. : LDA decoded; +2 placed in accumulator; PC incremented to 1.
FETCH: PC → AR; transfer [ADD 8] from loc. 1 to IR.
EXEC. : ADD decoded; −7 added to accumulator; PC incremented to 2.
FETCH: PC → AR; transfer [JAN 5] from loc. 2 to IR.
EXEC. : JAN decoded; SB of accumulator found = 1; PC *set* to 5.
FETCH: PC → AR; transfer [STA 10] from loc. 5 to IR.
EXEC. : STA decoded; sum (−5) placed in loc. 10; PC incremented to 6.
FETCH: PC → AR; transfer [JUN 6] from loc. 6 to IR. ←
EXEC. : JUN decoded; PC *set* to 6.

The following points should be noted.

(*a*) Instructions are normally extracted from store and obeyed in *sequential* fashion.

(*b*) Jump instructions (such as JAN) make *conditional transfer* possible. It is this facility which provides the computer with the ability to make *decisions* which depend on some previously calculated result.

(*c*) Numbers and instructions are both held in store as patterns of bits and as such are indistinguishable. For example, the contents of location 1 above can be regarded as the LOCO instruction ADD 8 *or* as the positive integer 8200.

(*d*) The reader will have noticed that no special LOCO instruction was provided to command the machine to *stop*. However, there are two points in the above program where the control system would find itself going endlessly through the *same* fetch-execute cycle, thus effectively terminating any further useful activity. Such an instruction, where a jump instruction transfers control to itself, is called a *dynamic* (or *loop*) *stop*.

PROGRESS TEST 8

1. Give examples of registers to be found in a typical computer system and briefly describe the function of each. (**1**)

2. Explain how control gates are used to control the flow of information within a central processor. (**2**)

3. What are the principal types of instruction found in the low-level instruction set of a digital computer? You should illustrate your answer by referring to an imaginary code such as LOCO. (**4**)

4. Determine the effect of the following sequence of LOCO instructions:

0	INP		9	LDA	21
1	STA	20	10	SUBK	1
2	INP		11	STA	21
3	STA	21	12	JAP	6
4	LDAK	1	13	LDA	22
5	STA	22	14	ONP	
6	LDA	22	15	JUN	15
7	MLT	20			
8	STA	22			

(**4**)

5. With reference to a 16-bit word describe four different types of word format. (**4–9**)

6. What do you understand by the term modifier field? (**5**)

7. Distinguish carefully between direct addressing, relative addressing, and indirect addressing. Illustrate your answer using the LOCO language. (**5**)

8. Explain the term control cycling. (**10**)

9. What is a loop stop? (**11**)

CHAPTER IX

The Man-Machine Interface; Peripheral Sub-Systems

PERIPHERALS JOIN THE PROCESSOR

1. Peripheral interface. The ASS computer described in the last chapter was depicted as a collection of various interconnected subsystems, connections being provided by a parallel data highway. One subsystem vital to the operation of the whole machine is the *peripheral interface*. This is a hardware system which provides input and output channels for the connection of various peripheral devices. A peripheral is the name given to any input/output device enabling man to communicate with the central processor. Many different types of peripheral are in use today and the principal peripherals are shown schematically in Fig. 76. Each peripheral is coupled to the processor via a standard multiway connector plug which carries all wiring for the necessary control signals and data flowing between the processor and the peripheral. In this way a processor can be fitted with a large number of different peripherals according to the number of channels provided on the processor itself. This allows for the later expansion of the total system with minimal alteration of the hardware.

2. Input/output instructions. Individual peripherals may be selected by the use of specific input/output instructions in machine code. For example, in LOCO we might have more realistic forms of the input/output instructions, ICP and OCP, as follows.

D-field value	*Peripheral*
0	Tape reader
1	Tape punch
2	Card reader
3	Card punch
4	On-line teletype
	and so on

Thus, the instruction OCP 1 would send the most significant 8 bits of the accumulator to the tape punch where an 8-bit character

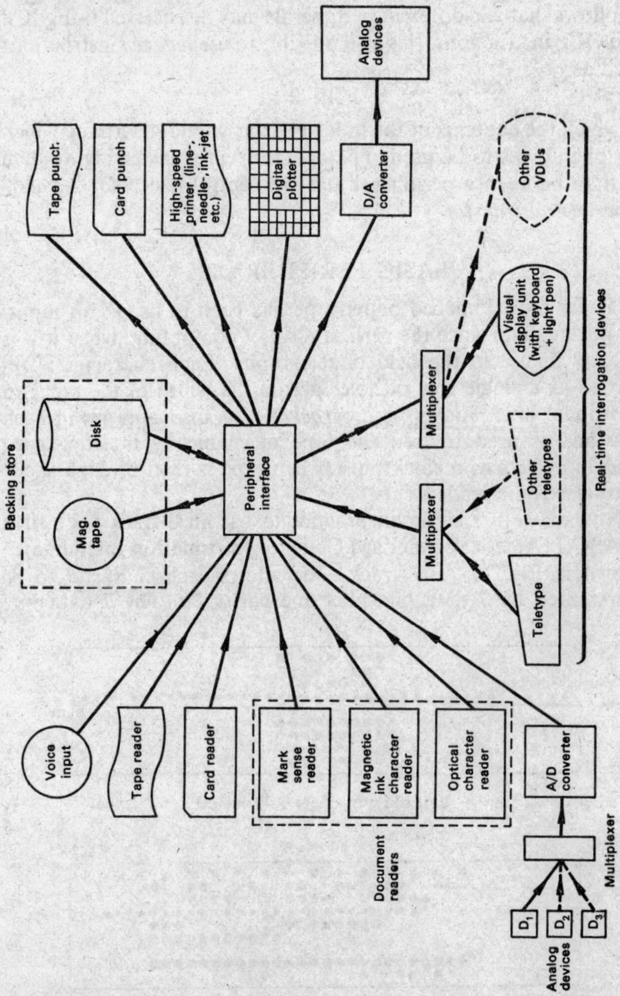

FIG. 76 *Computer peripherals.*

would be punched on paper tape. The instruction ICP 2 would transfer a character from card reader to accumulator.

If the 8 bits of the D-field are interpreted as an *unsigned* integer, it follows that 256 different peripherals may be accessed using ICP and OCP instructions. It is also possible to use *indexed* instructions such as

ICPI 0

in which the contents of the index register would determine which peripheral was to be used. The operation of transferring an item of data between a peripheral and the central processor is called a *peripheral transfer*.

BASIC PERIPHERALS

3. Paper tape. Punched paper tape has been in use as an input/output medium since the earliest days of computing, when it was already in use in the field of telegraphy. Each character is recorded as a single row of holes across the width of the tape; an additional hole, known as a *sprocket hole*, also appears in each row and is used to feed the tape mechanically in slow-speed readers or acts as a clock pulse when tape is read by high-speed opto-electronic readers.

Nowadays it is common practice to use an 8-track code such as ASCII (American Standard Code for Information Interchange) shown in Fig. 76. An 8-track code allows each character to be represented by 7 data bits plus one *parity bit*. The 7 data bits

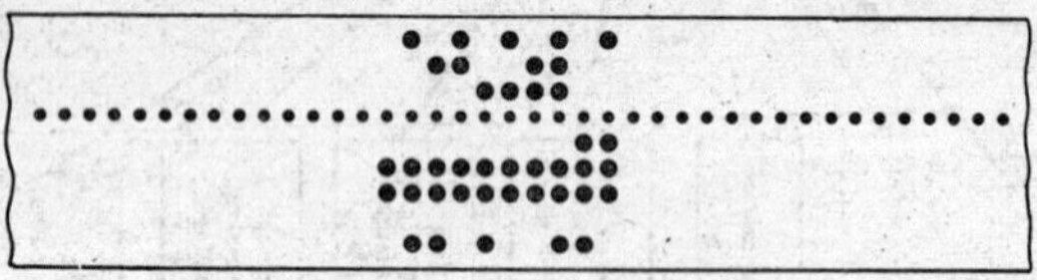

Left to right: digits 0 through 9

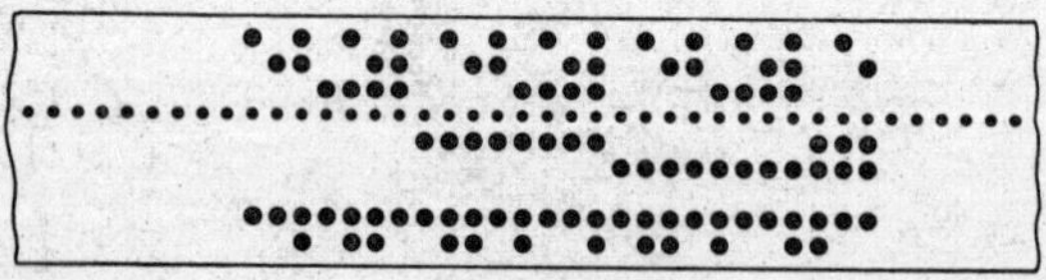

Left to right: letters A through Z

FIG. 77 *Paper tape with ASCII characters (even parity).*

provide sufficient unique combinations to represent 128 alphanumeric characters and symbols. The paper tape in Fig. 77 shows ASCII characters representing digits 0 through to 9 and the letters A through Z. The eighth (parity) bit is used for the detection of errors which may occur during punching or reading. On an *even-parity* system the parity bit is set equal to 0 or 1 so that the total number of 1s in the character is always even. For example, assuming an error has arisen in one bit only, the ASCII character 1 101 0110 would result in an error signal (as there are five 1s) and would *not* pass as a letter V, the correct code for which is 0 101 0110.

Typical paper tape is approximately 25 mm wide and comes in reels about 300 metres long. Individual character rows are punched into the tape with a density of 400 to the metre.

4. Paper-tape reader. A schematic diagram of a paper-tape reader is shown in Fig. 78, where tape is fed from the reel on the right to an opto-electronic read-head. The head consists of a lamp under which the tape moves at high speed (up to 2.5 metres per second). Below the lamp is an array of photo-diodes, one for each bit position in the character. A hole in the tape allows light to fall

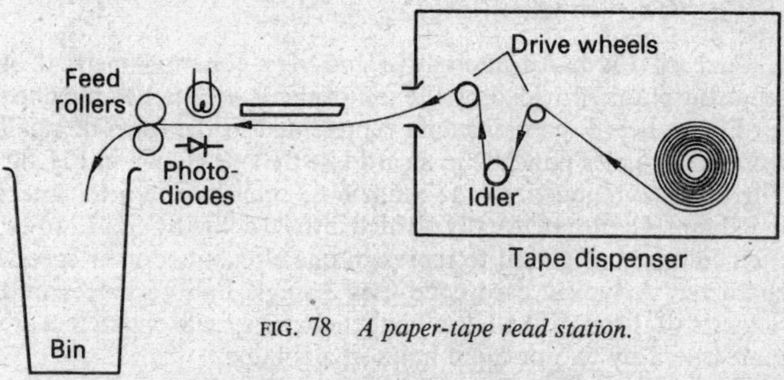

FIG. 78 *A paper-tape read station.*

on a photo-diode which then produces an electrical pulse; the absence of a hole in the tape results in light being prevented from falling on a diode and so no pulse is obtained. The pattern of pulses corresponding to one tape character is usually sent to a small buffer register, where parity is checked prior to transfer to the accumulator. Paper tape is a compact medium and relatively cheap to produce. Readers can operate at speeds of up to 1000 characters per second.

5. Paper-tape punch. A typical tape *punch* is shown in Fig. 79. As an *output* medium paper tape is useful for small volumes of data which can be printed off-line on a teleprinter. Paper tape can also be produced for subsequent transmission over a data link or can provide a numerical list for controlling an automatic machine tool. Tape-punch speeds vary from 25 to 300 characters per second.

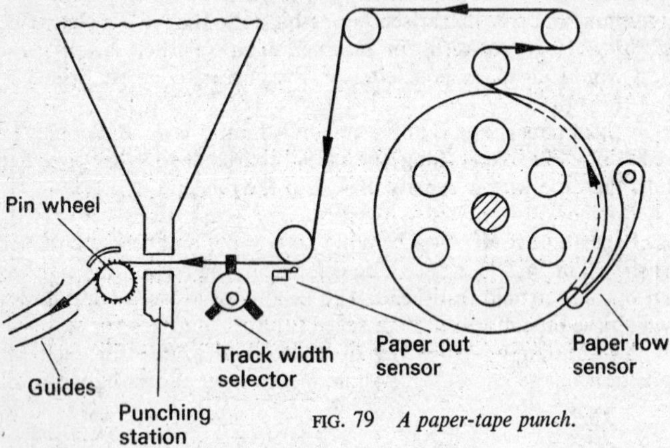

FIG. 79 *A paper-tape punch.*

6. Punched Card. An alternative and very common method of input/output is provided by the use of the *punchcard*. A punched card (punchcard) contains data represented in the form of small rectangular holes punched in a card like the one shown in Fig. 80. The most common size is 187 mm × 83 mm, having a thickness of 0.2 mm. Cards are usually divided into 80 columns and 12 rows, each column being used to represent one alphanumeric or special character. A typical card code uses a single hole to represent a numeric (0 through 9) while alphabetics and special characters are represented by two or more holes in a column.

Card rows are divided into two *punching areas* known as *curtates*. The *upper curtate* (or zone Z) consists of the top three rows on the card, the top row being number 10, the next down 11, and the third down is 0. The *lower curtate* (or numeric area N) consists of rows 0 through 9. It should be noted that the two punching areas overlap in that they both share row 0. One of the top corners of the standard card is cut off. This is to ensure that cards cannot be inserted into a reader the wrong way up or the wrong way round.

Normally, each punchcard holds a separate item of information, i.e. one set of data, or one language instruction. For this reason the punchcard is often called a *unit record.* If it is not possible to record one item on one card, use is made of continuation cards, a continuation symbol being punched either at the end of one card or at the beginning of the next. A group of columns on a card forms a *field*, different fields consisting of different numbers of columns depending on the amount of information to be conveyed. For example, a *numeric field* of 4 columns could be used to represent decimal integers from 0 through 9999.

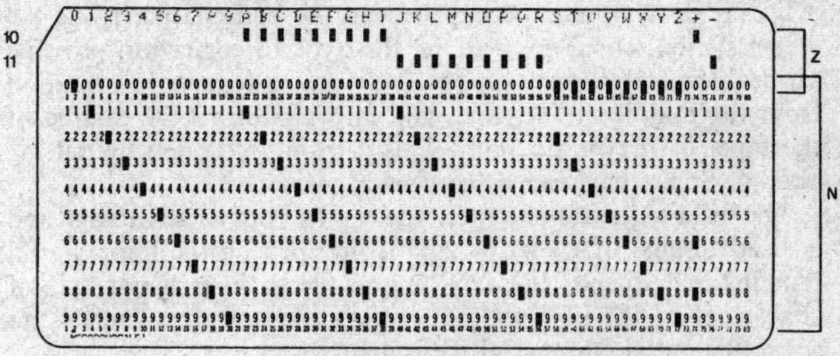

FIG. 80 *80-column punched card.*

7. The keypunch. Punchcards are prepared by means of a keyboard operated machine called a *keypunch.* The operator depresses keys on the keyboard to cause holes to be punched, column by column, into the card. Blank cards are placed in a *card hopper* from where they are fed along a track, through the punch and into a *stacker*. Most keypunches include a simple print unit for printing characters along the top edge of the card.

8. Card reader. Direct input from cards to computer is performed by means of a *card reader*. In a typical system up to 3000 cards may be loaded into the hopper of the reader and then read opto-electronically at speeds ranging from 300 to 2000 cards per minute. The direction of card feeding is parallel to the columns, all 80 columns being read simultaneously. It should be apparent that conversion from the card code to the machine's internal code has to be carried out somehow. The details of this are fairly complex but the process is often performed by means of logic circuitry in the card reader itself.

In other systems a *card image* (i.e. a pulse pattern corresponding to the holes in the card) is processed by a special program loaded into the processor. The hypothetical LOCO instruction, ICP 2, is clearly very inefficient as many more bits than 8 may, in practice, be transferred from card to computer in a single peripheral transfer. At the same time it should be clear that there are obvious advantages in programming a system in which the CPU regards all the peripherals as equivalent.

9. Tapes v. cards. A disadvantage of paper tape arises when corrections have to be made. If an error is detected after a character has been punched into the tape, it can be removed by means of a DELETE symbol superimposed on the bad character. As the delete symbol consists of all 1s, this type of correction presents no problems. However, suppose we want to remove information from the middle of the tape, add information to the middle of the tape, or maybe do both. This can only be done by cutting and sticking, which can be somewhat messy.

The fixed sequence of paper tape can be both an advantage and a disadvantage. If a reel of tape is dropped on the floor, it still remains in sequence but it is impossible to interchange sets of characters on the tape without cutting and splicing. There is no separable individual record with tape.

Tape is not so fast for the computer to use as the punchcard, while preparation of tape and cards is comparable.

10. High-speed printers. Printed output from a computer is very commonly required. This may be accomplished by means of relatively slow teletype machines which print one character at a time and which are often quite adequate for scientific applications but intolerably slow for commercial requirements. For this reason the *line printer* was developed. These high-speed peripherals print a whole line at a time and have two basic versions; the *barrel printer* and the *chain printer*.

A schematic diagram of a barrel printer appears in Fig. 81. The main part is a rotating stainless steel barrel on which the characters are etched in relief. The complete character set (usually 64 characters) is reproduced in a band around the circumference of the barrel and there are as many bands (character sets) as there are print positions (often 120) along a line. The paper is at rest during printing. The barrel is rotated at high speed, each character being presented to the print line in turn. When the row of Bs (for example) is in the print position, solenoid hammers are simultaneously actuated in all positions where a letter B is needed; next the row of Cs moves into position and these are printed. This process continues until a complete line is built up in the space of one revolution of the barrel. In one type of machine, the barrel makes two revolutions to every line of print, one for printing, the other for advancing the paper (with this arrangement it is possible to print at twice the normal speed if a restricted character set is used, the paper being advanced while the unused characters are opposite the hammers). Other types have a blank sector on the drum to allow time for the paper to be advanced.

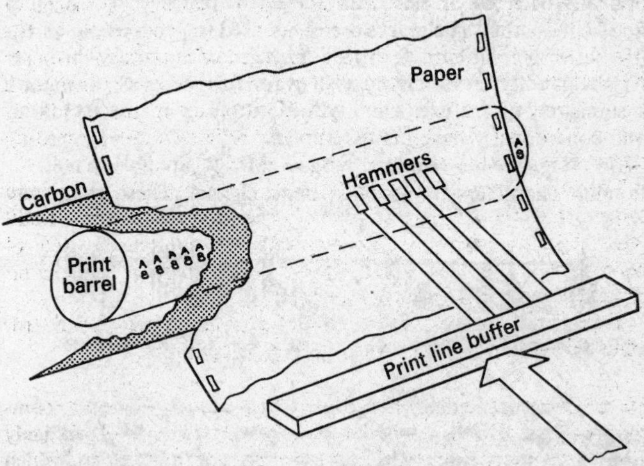

FIG. 81 *Barrel printer.*

An important feature of the line printer (barrel or chain) is the *print line buffer*. This is a memory contained within the printer which is used to hold one line of print. This device ensures that more efficient use is made of processing time. In the time to print one line (around 50 ms) the CPU could perform thousands of operations. By transferring a whole line of characters from the CPU to the print buffer (rather than single characters) the printer can then take over control of the printing operation, extracting characters from the buffer as required. This leaves the CPU free to build up the next output record while printing is taking place. Typical speeds for a barrel printer are 600 or more lines per minute. Disadvantages result from slight maladjustment of the hammers causing some to operate early and others late. This can produce print misalignment and/or vertical smudging of the print.

ADVANCED PERIPHERALS

11. Document readers. Transformation of data on documents on to paper tape or cards is both expensive and time-consuming; hence, a good deal of research has been carried out with the aim of devising equipment which can read original documents. The resulting devices are of three main types:

(*a*) *Mark sensors* can accept forms on which data has been entered by means of a set of pencil marks. The marks are either optically detected or electrically detected (pencil lead is a fairly good conductor). The marks are either used to produce punchings (if the form is in card form) or may generate pulses which are passed directly into a digital system for further processing. Such systems rely on the user's ability to position the marks accurately and consequently have limited appeal.

(*b*) *Magnetic-ink character readers* (MICR) are able to read the familiar characters found on a bank cheque. These characters,

FIG. 82 *E13B characters.*

FIG. 83 *CMC7 characters.*

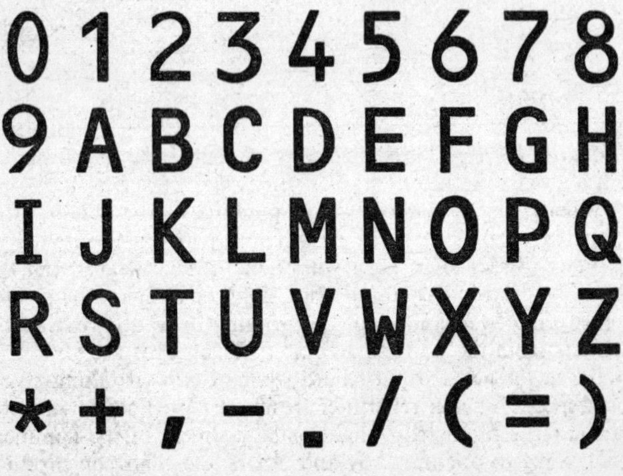

FIG. 84 *OCR character set.*

printed in magnetic ink (containing a ferromagnetic substance but not itself magnetised), are read by a detector and produce an internally coded representation in the machine. The type face used is known as E13B and is shown in Fig. 82. The rather odd shape of the characters is a compromise between familiarity to the human eye and legibility to the reading device. Another system is in common use on the continent of Europe; this is designated CMC7 and uses characters consisting of bars of different widths (Fig. 83).

(*c*) *Optical character readers* (OCR) read characters by analysis of their configuration. The character is scanned by a spot of light and the variations in brightness are transformed into an electric pulse pattern that is specific to the particular character and serves to identify it. One of the problems with this system is that certain characters are easy to confuse with others, e.g. O and Q. A special computer type face has been developed which, although almost exactly like standard type face, eliminates close similarities between characters (Fig. 84).

12. Digital plotters. The digital (incremental) plotter produces computer output directly in graphical form. A pen is traversed on a slide and writes on paper fed over the surface of a rotatable drum (Fig. 85). The pen can be raised and lowered on signals from the computer while other signals activate stepping motors to produce unit steps in either traverse or rotation. Steps in traverse and

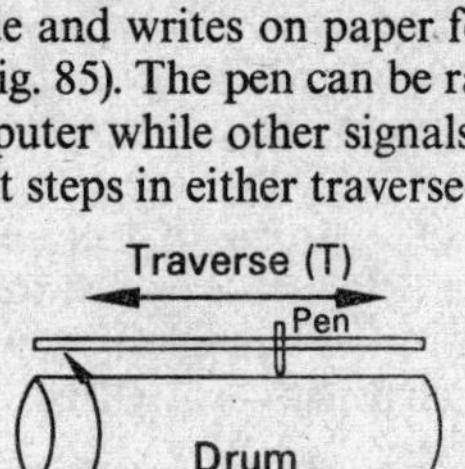

FIG. 85 *Digital plotter.*

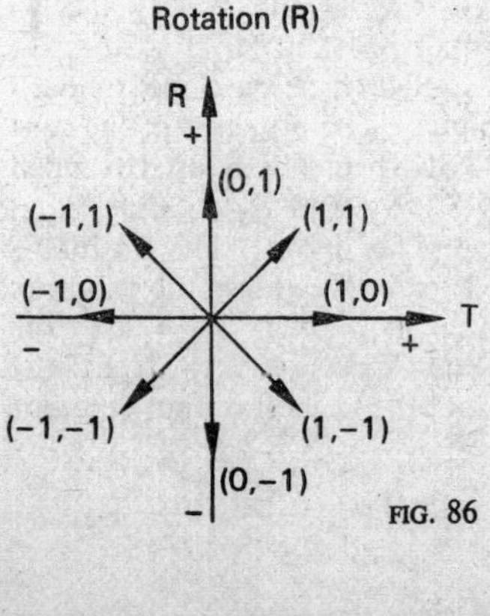

FIG. 86 *Vector generation by digital plotter.*

rotation may be either 1 or 0, thus generating eight basic vectors, each of which may be signalled with or without the pen in the lowered position. Figure 86 shows how these vectors are generated. Each plotter increment is usually in the order of 0.2 mm so that even quite simple pictures and graphs require many thousands of plotter steps.

13. Interdomain conversions. The digital computer operates in the *digital domain* i.e. all its operations are carried out in terms of discrete signals—the now familiar 1s and 0s. Many devices in the external world however, operate in the *analog domain*—they function in terms of continuously variable quantities. The output of many measuring instruments takes the form of an electrical potential difference, e.g. that from thermocouple thermometers or medical monitoring equipment. It is therefore necessary to be able to convert information from one domain to the other. Devices used for such interdomain conversions are termed A/D (analog to digital) and D/A (digital to analog) converters. We shall examine these in turn.

14. Digital-to-analog conversion. The heart of the modern D/A converter is the d.c. amplifier—a device with a very high voltage gain (voltage gain is the ratio of input to output voltage), typically in the order of 10^6. The addition of a feedback resistor, R_f, and input resistors R_1, R_2 and R_3 results in one kind of *operational amplifier*. Figure 87 shows such an amplifier arranged to function as a D/A converter. Texts on operational amplifiers show that the output voltage of this kind of arrangement is given by

$$V_0 = -(G_1V_1 + G_2V_2 + G_3V_3)$$

where $G_1 = R_f/R_1$, $G_2 = R_f/R_2$, $G_3 = R_f/R_3$ and V_1, V_2 and V_3 are the voltages applied to the input resistors R_1, R_2, and R_3. In the D/A converter all the input voltages have the same standard value, V_R (called the reference voltage). The principle of the conversion process is that the input pattern of bits is used to open or close a set of logic switches S_1, S_2, and S_3 so that V_R is communicated (or not) to the amplifier inputs. The positional values of the input bits is allowed for by weighting the values of the input resistors. For example $R_1 = 1\text{k}\Omega$, $R_2 = 2\text{k}\Omega$ and $R_3 = 4\text{k}\Omega$. Also, let $R_f = 1\text{k}\Omega$, and $V_R = -4$ volt. It follows that $G_1 = 1$, $G_2 = \frac{1}{2}$, and $G_3 = \frac{1}{4}$ and the general output equation becomes:

$$V_0 = 4(G_1 + G_2 + G_3)$$

Suppose now that the input bit pattern is 011 (binary 3). This would cause switches S_2 and S_3 to close, while S_1 would remain open. Hence,

$$V_0 = 4(0 + \tfrac{1}{2} + \tfrac{1}{4}) = 3\ \text{V}$$

With an input of 101 (binary 5), S_1 and S_3 would close and S_2 would remain open, so that

$$V_0 = 4(1 + 0 + \tfrac{1}{4}) = 5\ \text{V}$$

Thus, the device converts directly from a digital form to an equivalent analog output in the form of a voltage.

D/A converters are available in integrated-circuit form and are relatively cheap, a 12-bit converter costing only a few pounds. They will generate outputs accurate to at least 1 part in 4000 in a few microseconds. One application is the driving of a CRT (cathode-ray tube) graphics display in which ditigal information from the computer specifies position coordinates on the screen of a television-type screen. The D/A converters transform this information into voltages which are used to deflect the electron beam which draws pictures at very high speeds.

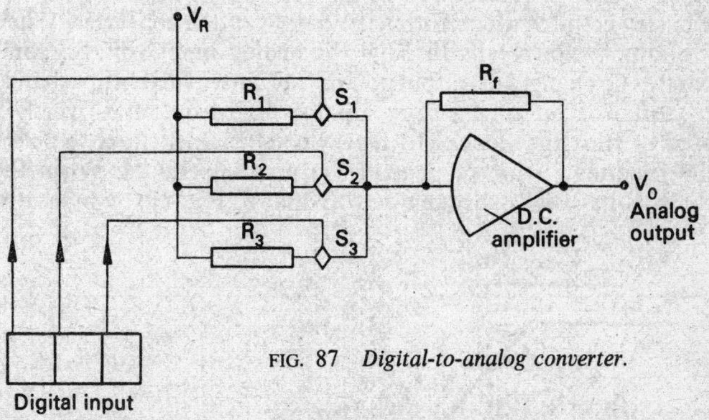

FIG. 87 *Digital-to-analog converter.*

15. Analog-to-digital conversion. In this case we have a voltage which is to be digitised. A typical A/D converter which achieves this is shown in Fig. 88 in which the basic elements are two *comparators*. A comparator is an operational amplifier arranged so that the output voltage changes polarity when the two inputs become equal. The conversion process is as follows:

A pulse is sent to an electronic device called a ramp generator which produces a steadily falling voltage (*see* Fig. 88). This same

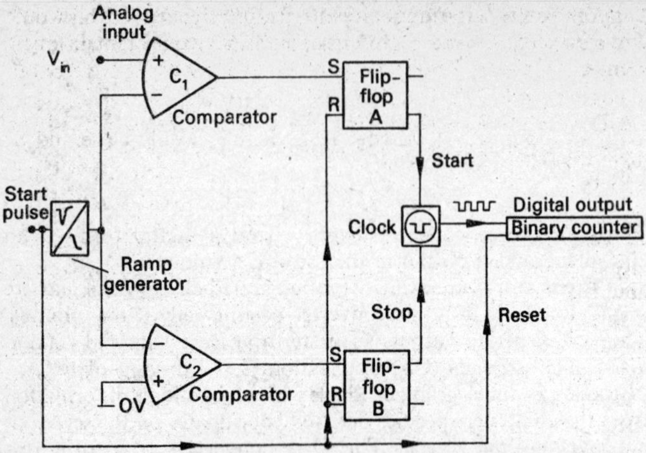

FIG. 88 *Analog-to-digital converter.*

pulse is used to reset the two flip-flops A, and B, and to zeroise a binary counter which forms the output of the converter. When the ramp voltage falls through the analog input voltage, comparator C_1 changes its output polarity abruptly. This abrupt change constitutes a pulse which sets flip-flop A, the output of which is used to start the clock. The binary counter then starts to count the resulting stream of pulses for a time interval Δt. When the ramp voltage falls through zero (point Y, Fig. 89), comparator

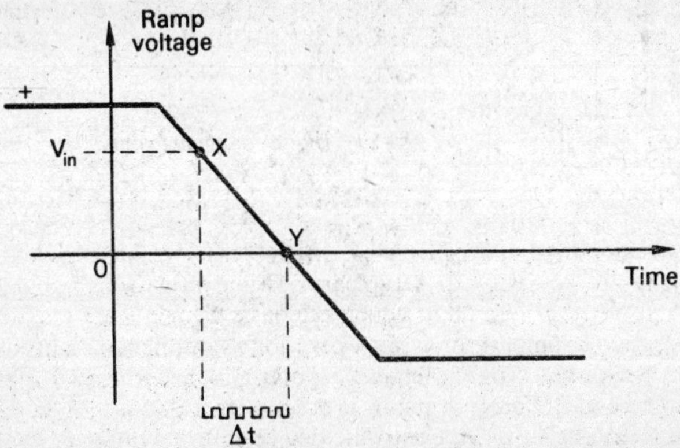

FIG. 89 *Ramp voltage in analog-to-digital converter.*

C_2 abruptly changes output polarity causing flip-flop B to set and send a stop signal to the clock. The resulting number in the binary counter will clearly be proportional to Δt and hence to the input analog voltage.

A/D converters are slower than D/A devices, but can produce 12-bit precision in about 20 microseconds for a cost of only a few pounds.

16. Real-time interrogation devices. Systems in which computer output is required immediately, or almost immediately, after the input has been presented, are called *real-time* systems. An example of this type of system is the use of the computer to record and update aircraft seat reservations. The computer is first of all *interrogated* to see if there is a seat available on a particular flight. If so, and the customer accepts it, a ticket is issued and the vacancy deleted from the system. There are two principal types of interrogation devices.

(*a*) *On-line typewriters* (terminals) from which interrogating messages may be sent to the computer by means of a keyboard resembling that of an ordinary typewriter. Response from the computer takes the form of lines of print output on to a paper roll. These devices may either be directly linked to the peripheral interface, or may be located at some considerable distance (even hundreds or thousands of kilometres) from the computer installation. Such remote terminals are connected to the computer via a *data link* using a radio transmission channel or the public telephone system. Digital signals from the keyboard are converted into a form suitable for the data link by means of a unit called a *modem* (MODulator-DEModulator).

(*b*) *Visual-display units* (VDUs) which are far superior to the on-line typewriter as far as *editing* is concerned. Correcting or updating of information stored in the computer is far more convenient using these devices which are based on the use of a CRT display able to handle alphanumeric characters. The response of a VDU is almost instantaneous (cf. the typewriter terminal at a typical 10 characters per second). Information is sent to the computer via an associated keyboard and response takes the form of displayed characters on a screen, a typical display consisting of 13 lines each 40 characters long. CRT displays used for the presentation of diagrams are often fitted with a so-called *light pen*, a name which is somewhat misleading. This is a hand-held light-sensitive device (either a photo-diode or a flexible light-guide connected to a photo-multiplier) which detects the position of a CRT spot. Displays with light pens have many applications. A diagram, generated from stored data, can be amended or added to, merely by touching the screen with the light pen. VDUs do not, of course, produce *hard copy* (i.e. a permanent record), although some commercially available units allow the attachment of a hard copy device to overcome this deficiency.

Interrogation devices transfer data at a relatively low rate, and it would be wasteful to allocate a separate computer channel to each device. Consequently, several devices are normally attached to the same channel through a unit called a *multiplexer*. This unit scans the peripheral devices attached to it to determine whether any requires attention. Each active peripheral is connected in turn to the peripheral interface long enough for one item of data (usually one character plus a code to identify the particular peripheral) to be transferred.

PROGRESS TEST 9

1. Describe a coded form of data on (*a*) punchcards, (*b*) paper tape. **(3, 6)**

2. On the basis of one 8-bit byte per character, compare the storage densities in bits/cm^2 of: (*a*) 8-track paper tape, (*b*) 80-column punchcards—one column per character, (*c*) a page of this book, as a possible input to an OCR, (*d*) 9-track magnetic tape—12 mm wide and 32 bits/mm. **(3, 6, 11, VII, 13)**

3. What is the speed in characters per second of:

(*a*) A card reader operating at 1200 cards per minute;

(*b*) a line printer operating at 1000 lines per minute and printing 24 alphabetic characters on a line of 120 print positions? **(8, 10)**

4. Compare and contrast the advantages and disadvantages of paper tape and punched cards as input/output media. **(9)**

5. What do you understand by the term print line buffer used in connection with the line printer? **(10)**

6. Describe three types of peripheral device other than those using cards or paper tape. In each case give an indication of the speed with which information is transferred and the physical principles of operation of the device **(10, 11, 12, 16)**

7. Describe the operation and typical application of: (*a*) MICR, (*b*) OCR. **(11)**

8. Show with the aid of a diagram, how logic switches may be coupled to an operational amplifier to provide a simple means of digital-to-analog conversion. **(14)**

CHAPTER X

The Development of Computer Languages

LOW-LEVEL PROGRAMMING

1. Machine codes. In VIII we saw that our hypothetical machine was enabled to carry out a specified task automatically by obeying a set of *instructions* stored in the computer memory. Such a set of instructions is called a *program* and the art of preparing instructions for computer execution is called *programming*.

Each instruction stored in the ASS computer (as with all computers) consists of a string of bits grouped into *function*, *modifier* and *displacement* fields. For example in location 12 we might have an indexed addition instruction. This could be written down on paper as follows:

ADDRESS	INSTRUCTION
1100	00100 100 00001000

the left-most four bits being the address (location 12), the next five bits the ADD function, the following 3 bits denote INDEXING (i.e. addition of index register contents to displacement prior to execution) and the remaining 8 bits give the address of the number to be added. This long collection of bits specifies the instruction completely but is hardly a convenient form for the human programmer to handle. An improvement might be to write

ADDRESS	INSTRUCTION
12	4 4 8

which is a little easier on the eye. The instruction [4 4 8] is an example of a *machine code* instruction and in the early days of computing every computer program consisted of instructions of this kind. Such instructions are in decimal notation and would be punched on tape or cards directly in this form. The price paid for this easier form of programming is that the machine has to be pre-programmed with instructions which can translate the decimal machine code into internal binary form.

2. Store directive. The program which translates the decimal machine code would also render it unnecessary to specify the address of every instruction to be stored in the machine. This is done by the inclusion of a *store directive* at the head of the machine code program. The short program on page 115 might be read into the machine as in Fig. 90.

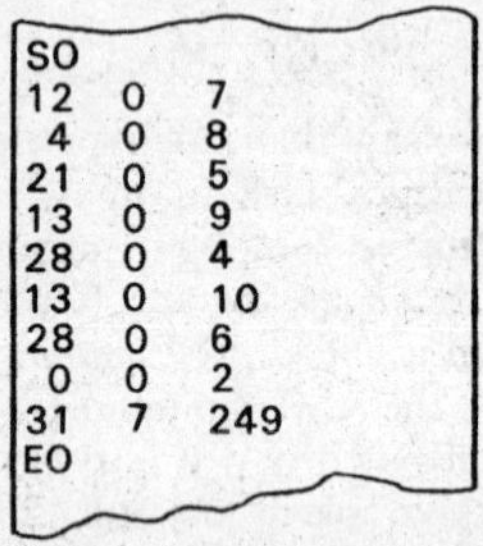

FIG. 90

The store directive, SO, at the head of the program instructs the machine code translator to store the instructions consecutively from location 0 onwards. The terminating directive E0 tells the machine to start execution with the instruction in location 0. Notice that the last two instructions in the above program are not really instructions at all, but are written as though they were. Such instructions, in fact representing the numbers +2 and −7, are termed *quasi instructions*. The directives S0, and E0 are sometimes called *pseudo instructions* as, although they are interpreted by the machine code translator, they take no part in the subsequent running of the program.

3. Mnemonic forms. Although perfectly good programs can be written in the above purely decimal form, it still requires some effort on the part of the programmer to remember that 12 means LOAD THE ACCUMULATOR, that 28 means JUMP, and so on. A further improvement to aid the programmer can be made by using a *mnemonic-cum-decimal* form of each instruction. Mnemonic (aid to memory) forms of LOCO instructions have already been introduced in VIII, where we wrote, for example, LDA 7 and JUN 6, instead of the decimal machine-code forms 12 0 7 and 28 0 6. It is perfectly possible to write, and subsequently punch, programs in this mnemonic form, and many of our programming examples will be set down in this manner.

4. Symbolic addresses. Consider now an instruction such as

MLT 67

The location 67 will presumably contain a number with which to multiply the contents of the accumulator. It is probably completely immaterial, however, that this number has been stored in location 67—any other location (not containing a program word) would do just as well for this data storage. Thus, it is of great value to be able to use *symbolic addresses* in a program; these permit the alphabetic naming of storage locations within the machine. So, our next improvement to the programmer's lot would be to enable him to write:

MLT A

i.e. multiply the accumulator contents by the contents of the location A.

A facility of this kind would also include the symbolic *labelling* of instructions to which jumps are made in other parts of a program (*see* Fig. 91).

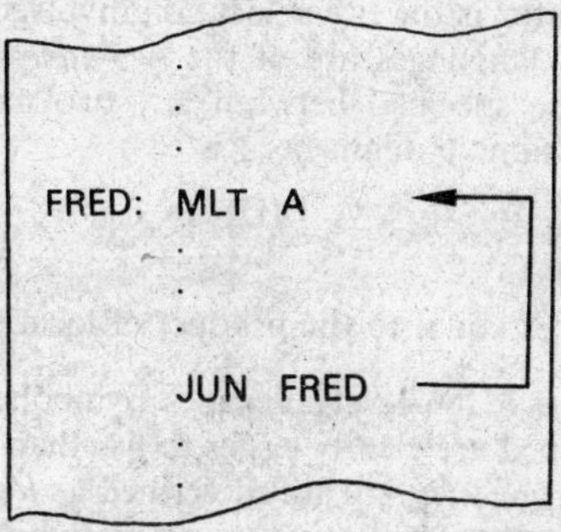

FIG. 91

5. Assembly language. Programs written in this kind of mnemonic form, where there is a one-to-one relationship between each mnemonic instruction and its corresponding binary machine-code form, are said to be written in *assembly language*. The use of such symbolic languages greatly facilitates the writing of computer programs, but in order to run them on a machine it is necessary for the computer to first of all be loaded with a special program called an *assembler*. The job of an assembler is to take a program written in an assembly language as data and to produce as the result a binary program which will be executed by the machine. The original program, written in assembly language, is referred to as the *source program*, while the resulting binary machine-code program is called the *object program*. The process of *machine-code assembly* can be represented thus:

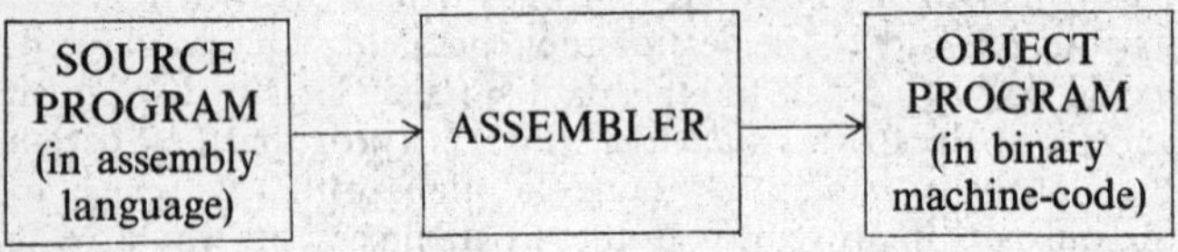

e.g.

FRED: MLT A might become 1100 | 00110 000 01000011

6. Single-address and two-address codes. It should be noted that the examples already given were in a *single-address* code. This means that only one address is specified in a particular instruction, as the accumulator is the other location involved by implication. Some assembly languages are of the *two-address* type, enabling operations to be specified between any two named main store locations. An example might be:

A MLT B

which would mean

set location A equal to the product of locations A and B.

7. Disadvantages of low-level languages. Symbolic languages of the type just described are clearly easier to use than the fundamental machine codes but they are still described as *low-level* languages in that the computation of quite simple mathematical expressions has to be broken down into a not inconsiderable number of elementary steps. A further feature of these low-level languages is that they are very largely *machine-dependent*; i.e. we cannot expect the assembly languages of two different machines to be the same, as machines differ in design and have different instruction formats (although there may be some compatibility between machines of the same series, e.g. ICL 1901, 1902, . . . etc.). To generalise, we may say that low-level languages are *machine-oriented*.

HIGH-LEVEL PROGRAMMING

8. Problem-oriented languages. Suppose we wished to evaluate the expression

$$R = N_1.N_2 + N_3.N_4$$

for given values of the variables N_1, N_2, N_3 and N_4. This could be done using our ASS computer and the low-level language LOCO as follows. First we should require that the variables are represented by numbered locations in the machine. For example, N_1 could be stored in 31, N_2 in 32, N_3 in 33 and N_4 in 34, while the result R, could be placed in 30. A further location, say 35, is also needed for temporary storage. Here is the necessary program segment.

Instruction	*Effect*
LDA 31	$(A) \leftarrow N_1$
MLT 32	$(A) \leftarrow N_1 \times N_2$
STA 35	store $(N_1 \times N_2)$
LDA 33	$(A) \leftarrow N_3$
MLT 34	$(A) \leftarrow N_3 \times N_4$
ADD 35	$(A) \leftarrow (N_1 \times N_2) + (N_3 \times N_4)$
STA 30	$R \leftarrow (N_1 \times N_2) + (N_3 \times N_4)$

Notice that *seven* LOCO instructions are needed to evaluate R, and that the program itself bears no resemblance to the expression in algebraic form. It would be infinitely more convenient if the programmer could write a single instruction which ideally bore a good deal of similarity to the conventional algebraic notation. The instruction

```
LET R = N1*N2+N3*N4
```

is in fact perfectly possible in the *high-level* language known as BASIC (Beginners' All-purpose Symbolic Instruction Code). This language, pioneered by Kemeny and Kurtz at Dartmouth College in New Hampshire, is an example of a *problem-oriented* language. In other words, the programmer can instruct the computer in a language which is very closely allied to that which was used to express the original problem. The instructions in this kind of language offer no clue to the manner in which the machine goes about obeying them. Indeed, the computer-user very often has no interest in the machine at all; it is sufficient for him to know that a program written according to the rules of the particular problem-oriented language will work. Languages which create this kind of freedom are said to be *machine-independent* (in practice there is some deviation from this ideal but the concept is a useful one).

9. Compilation. A program written in a high-level language has to be translated into the fundamental binary machine-code instructions with which the computer hardware can deal. A *compiler* is a complex program which will accept a source program in a high-level language and translate it into the corresponding machine code program which will be eventually obeyed by the computer. In general:

a single high-level instruction corresponds to a number of machine code instructions.

Each high-level language will require a different compiler for each machine since the final object program depends on the particular machine being used, but the high-level language itself is *ideally independent* of any particular machine.

10. Definition of a high-level language. This may be broken down into two sets of rules.

(*a*) The rules of *syntax*, which tell us if a particular instruction is structurally correct.

(*b*) The rules of *semantics*, which tell us what a legally structured instruction means.

e.g. in BASIC, the instruction

LET E = A*(B + C*D)

is *syntactically* correct. The *semantic* rules tell us that we take the product of C and D, add B to the result and multiply this by A, the final value being assigned to the variable E.

However, the intstructions

LET E = A*(B + C*D)

and LET E = A*(B + *D)

each contain a *syntactic* error. The first has a missing right-hand bracket, while the second has two mathematical operators (+ and *) side by side.

11. The process of compiling a program written in a high-level language. This is briefly as follows.

(*a*) The compiler program is read into the machine.

(*b*) The compiler program is executed with the source program as data. During the execution the compiler usually makes two *passes*.

(*i*) In the first pass the compiler reads the source program, checks the syntax of each instruction, builds lists of symbols used and stores the instructions in a temporary area of the main store.

(*ii*) In the second pass the rules of semantics are applied to translate the syntactically checked instructions in the temporary area into a set of equivalent binary machine code instructions. It is this set which constitutes the final object program.

(*c*) When this is complete, the process of compilation is over and the object program is ready to be run.

12. Dumping. Once a source program has been fully tested it is often useful to output the compiled binary program to a suitable peripheral unit where it can be put on to paper tape, card, disk or a magnetic tape file for future use. Such a process is called *dumping* the object program. A dumped program, being in binary machine code, can be dealt with directly by the processor on subsequent occasions without having to go through the compilation every time.

13. Reverse Polish notation. How is it possible for a computer to correctly interpret a high-level instruction like the one already encountered?

LET R = N1*N2 + N3*N4

The semantic rules of BASIC tell us that this instruction means:

Fetch N1
and Fetch N2
Multiply them together and keep the result
Fetch N3
and Fetch N4
Multiply them together and keep this result
Add together the two stored results.

This seems to us quite a natural procedure, so why don't we write

N1 N2*N3 N4*+

The latter ordering of symbols follows exactly the natural procedure given above, but such an ordering is not the one normally adopted when using conventional algebra. If some means could be found for converting between the more conventional ordering of symbols and the one just given, the computer would have little trouble in following our instructions.

This new kind of ordering of symbols is called *reverse Polish notation* (RPN). It is called Polish notation in honour of its inventor—Lukasiewicz—and is reverse(d) since Lukasiewicz's ordering was exactly the opposite of the one adopted for computer application.

A very attractive feature of RPN is that it dispenses with the use of *brackets* altogether. For example, the expression

$$A+(B*C-D)*E$$

becomes

$$A\ B\ C*D-E*+$$

in RPN.

14. The push-down stack. The conversion of an algebraic expression into RPN can be carried out with the help of a *push-down stack*. Conceptually, a push-down stack is a box in which only the last item put in is accessible at any one time; items can be removed only in the opposite order to that in which they were inserted. (The term LIFO-stack is synonymous with push-down stack; the letters stand for Last In, First Out.) Stacks of this kind can be implemented in the actual hardware of the computer by using a set of linked shift registers. Alternatively, stacks may be simulated using conventional programming techniques. There are two basic commands which may be used to control the operation of a stack.

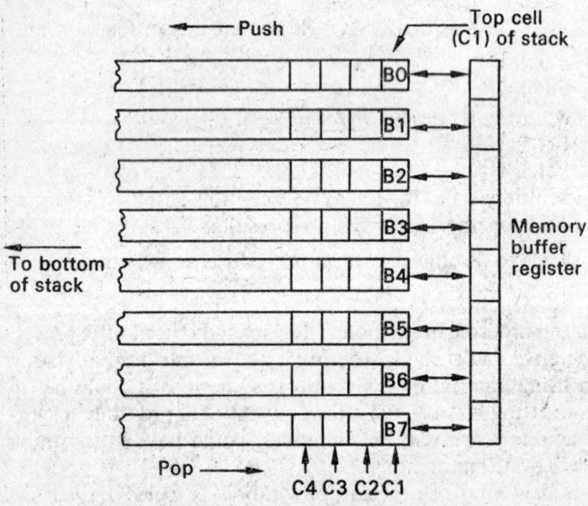

FIG. 92 *Push-down stack constructed from shift registers; each cell (vertical) holds one 8-bit byte.*

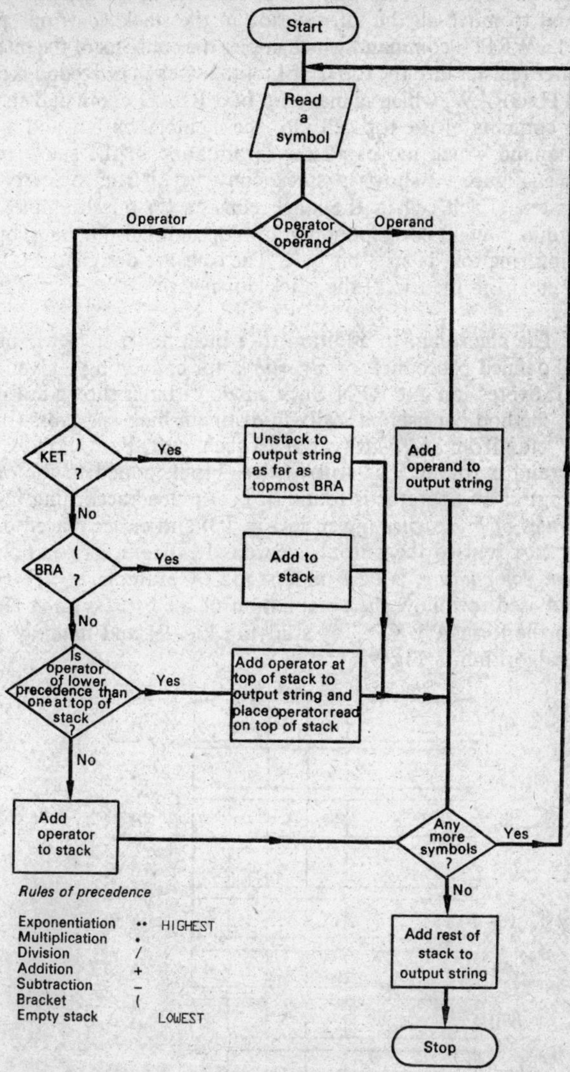

FIG. 93 *Algorithm for conversion of an algebraic expression to RPN.*

The first is called PLACE, which is made up of a PUSH command to move all the information in the stack *down* one place, and a WRITE command which copies the contents of the memory buffer register into the top CELL of the stack. The second is called WITHDRAW, which is made up of a READ command to copy the contents of the top cell into the memory buffer, and a POP command which moves all the information in the stack *up* one place. Figure 92 shows a stack constructed from a set of shift registers. Each cell in the stack consists (in our example) of a column of eight corresponding flip-flops so that one item, or unit of information, is an 8-bit byte. The cells are designated C1, C2, C3 etc. from the top of the stack downwards.

15. The algorithm. In addition to a push-down stack we need a well defined procedure, or *algorithm*, for converting a given algebraic expression into RPN. Such an algorithm is shown in Fig. 93. The method consists basically in distinguishing *operators* (+, −, *, /, etc.) from *operands* (variables such as A, F, R, B etc.). If an operand is found, it is sent to the output (added to the output string); if an operator is found, it is examined according to a set of *rules of precedence* (given in Fig. 93) and either placed on the stack or sent to the output accordingly. The process, known as *stack compilation*, is best understood by example, so the reader is advised to follow the compilation of the expression A/(B+C) into the form A B C+/ by studying Fig. 94 and making use of the algorithm in Fig. 93.

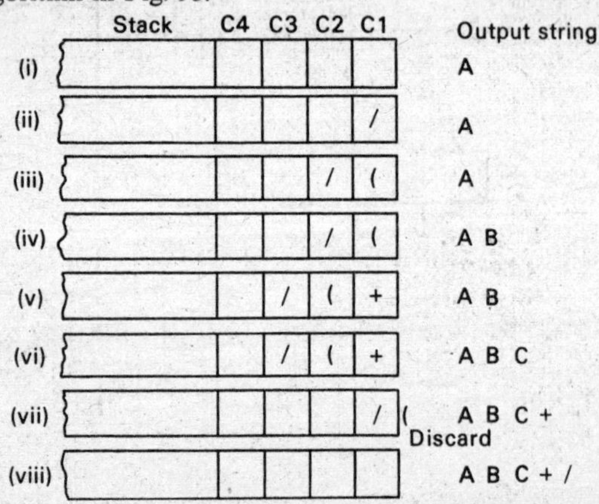

FIG. 94 *Stack compilation of A/(B+C).*

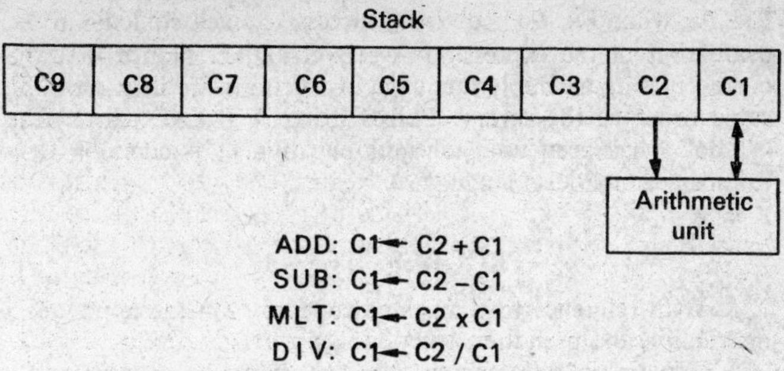

FIG. 95 *Use of a push-down stack in the evaluation of an expression.*

Once the RP form of an expression has been obtained, each symbol may be replaced by a low-level machine instruction, thus building a program segment for the evaluation of the expression. This is most conveniently done in a machine with a push-down stack which can be controlled by means of low-level instructions such as FETCH. The effect of the FETCH instruction is to copy the contents of the location named into the buffer register attached to the top of the stack, and to follow this operation with a PLACE command. Further, the arithmetic instructions in this type of machine refer to the top two cells of the stack, rather than to the accumulator and a main store address. This arrangement, together with definitions of typical arithmetic instructions are shown in

C3	C2	C1	Assembly language instruction
		A	FETCH A
	A	B	FETCH B
A	B	C	FETCH C
	A	B•C	MLT
A	B•C	D	FETCH D
	A	B•C-D	SUB
A	B•C-D	E	FETCH E
	A	(B•C-D)•E	MLT
		A+(B•C-D)•E	ADD

FIG. 96 *Stack contents in the evaluation of* $A+(B*C-D)*E$

Fig. 95, while Fig. 96 shows the successive stack contents in the evaluation of the expression A+(B*C−D)*E. Notice that the corresponding assembly language instructions are in exactly the same order as the reverse Polish string A B C*D−E*+ (the symbol * has been used for multiplication as is common to a number of high-level languages).

PROGRESS TEST 10

1. With reference to a machine code, explain the terms quasi instruction and pseudo instruction. (**2**)

2. Explain the difference between an assembly language and a problem-oriented language. (**5, 8**)

3. High-level languages are often said to be machine-independent. Can you explain why? (**8**)

4. What do you understand by the term compiler? Describe briefly the importance of syntax and semantics in the process of compilation. (**9, 10**)

5. Write down the reverse Polish equivalent of the BASIC instruction

LET P=Q*(S−T**U)

6. Explain the importance of a stack in the compilation of programs. How can a stack be implemented in hardware? (**14**)

7. What are rules of precedence as applied to the interpretation of arithmetic expressions? (**15**)

CHAPTER XI

Computer Programming Principles

ALGORITHMS AND FLOWCHARTS

1. Algorithms. In the preceding chapters we have examined the essential structure of computers and have seen how it is possible to provide them with viable instruction sets of considerable sophistication. There remains, however, the general question of getting the machine, with all its facilities, to assist us in the solution of a specific problem. To this end, we shall present some examples of the more important techniques of problem solving by computer, making use of both low-level and high-level programming languages.

The computer, prior to being programmed, is a witless collection of combinational and sequential circuits. Only by defining our problem in a logical and precise manner is it possible to persuade the machine to present us with anything like meaningful answers. The directions given must be completely unambiguous and number of steps required to reach a solution must be finite. A set of directions of this kind is referred to as an *algorithm*, a somewhat fuller definition of which is:

> *a finite unambiguous list of instructions specifying a sequence of basic operations such that if the instructions are obeyed and the operations carried out in the exact order stated, then a solution will always be obtained to any particular problem belonging to a given class of problems.*

2. Flowcharts. It would be quite possible to examine a given problem and, after some careful thought, write down an ordered set of sentences laying out the steps necessary to arrive at a solution. Such a procedure is, however, rather cumbersome. It is much more useful if we can communicate an algorithm in a form which clearly reveals its underlying structure. A suitable form with considerable visual impact is the *flowchart*. We have already used flowcharts in this book to illustrate certain processes relevant to computer operation (for example, to show how multiplication is carried out). The self-evident nature of the flowchart made it unnecessary to explain any rules which may apply to the flowcharting process. However, rules there are, and there is good flowcharting and bad.

3. The conventions of flowcharting. Before expressing any process in flowchart form it is necessary to be aware of certain simple conventions. First, a flowchart consists of a set of boxes connected by *flowlines*. The general direction of flow should be from top to bottom and from left to right, following the normal manner of reading adopted by many cultures (it is hoped that any Arabic students will not find this too much of a bind). Boxes come in different types, but the most important are the following.

(*a*) *Termination points.* These include start, stop, halt or delay.

(*b*) *Process boxes.* These contain any processing function, such as one causing change in the value, form or location of information.

(*c*) *Input/output boxes.* These show the general input/output function.

(*d*) *Decision boxes.* These show a decision or switching operation that determines which of a number of alternative paths followed.

These boxes and some other useful ones are shown in Fig. 97.

4. Creation of a flowchart. Flowcharting is an essential step in the overall process of problem-solving by computer. It is not only invaluable in the communication of algorithms to other people (who may later want to modify the method used) but also serves to clarify the problem for the programmer himself. Flowcharts make it possible to break down large and complex tasks into a number of interconnected sub-problems and greatly facilitate the conversion of an algorithm into coded form. The creation of a suitable flowchart should be seen as part of the process of moving from given problem to computed solution. This process is (naturally) shown in flowchart-form in Fig. 98.

PROGRAMMING AT A LOW LEVEL

Computer programs may be very lengthy and some are very subtle. Programs exist which play the game of chess (although not perfectly), and there are programs which can even clarify pictures radioed back from the surface of another planet. All these wonders cannot, however, be fully appreciated without the realisation that fundamentally the computer is slavishly following very many

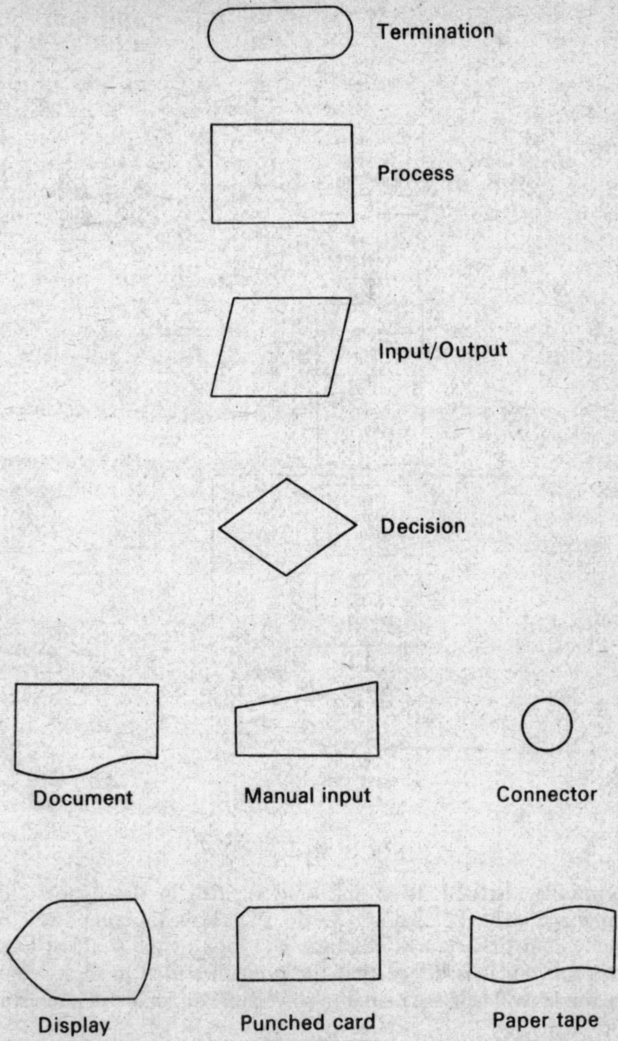

FIG. 97 *Flowchart symbols.*

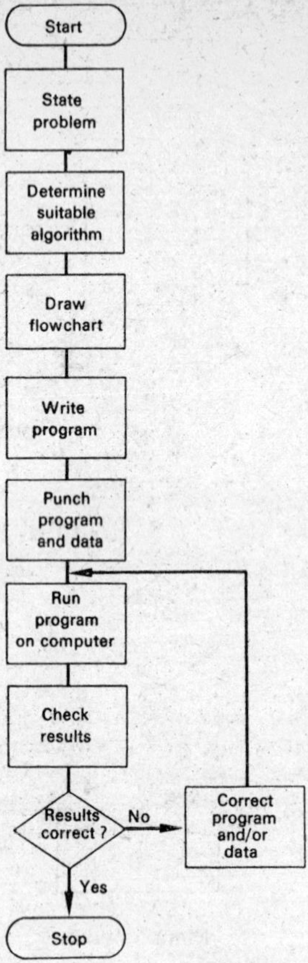

FIG. 98 *A typical flowchart.*

primitive instructions of the kind typified in the hypothetical language we have called LOCO. So, let us leave the computer chess game, and the pictures of Mars, and look at the simplest kinds of problem. It is hoped that the principles used in these simple examples will help the reader to solve more difficult and interesting problems.

5. Non-iterative processes. A non-iterative process is one in which one starts at the beginning and works through to the end without

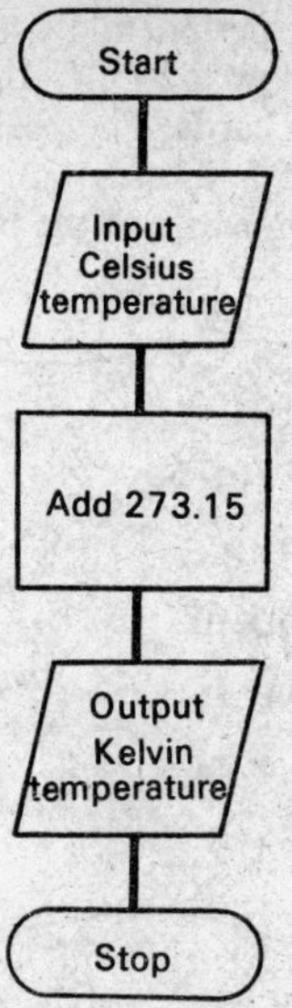

FIG. 99 *Algorithm for conversion of Celsius to Kelvin.*

any kind of cycling or repetition of sub-processes at any stage. A primitive example of this kind of process is the conversion of a temperature on the Celsius scale (°C) to its equivalent on the Kelvin scale (kelvins). The latter is obtained from the former simply by the addition of 273.15; the algorithm is shown in Fig. 99 and the LOCO program required to carry this out is in Fig. 100. Location 10 contains the necessary constant, entry to the program is made at location 11 and the process is terminated by a dynamic stop at location 14. Remember that the INP instruction places the input number into the accumulator, so the instruction ADD 10 has the effect of adding 273.15 to the Celsius temperature. The

	10	+273.15	Constant
Enter →	11	INP	
	12	ADD 10	
	13	ONP	
	14	JUN 14	

FIG. 100 *LOCO program for conversion of Celsius to Kelvin.*

result is sent to a suitable peripheral by means of the ONP instruction. Figure 101 shows how the LOCO program would probably be typed or punched on cards. The pseudo instructions S10 and E11 make the typing of addresses unnecessary and ensure that execution of the program starts at the correct instruction.

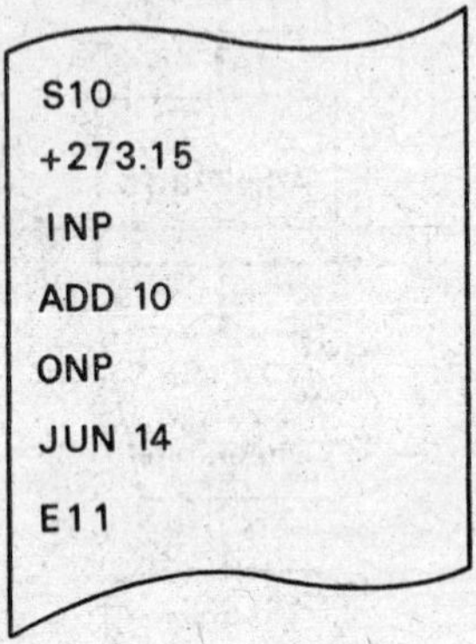

FIG. 101 *LOCO program for conversion of Celsius to Kelvin typed on cards.*

6. Iterative processes. Unlike most human beings, the computer does not become bored by performing monotonous and repetitive tasks. Because it is a high-speed automatic system it does not require the human faculty of concentration to avoid the making of mistakes. If we give the machine the same set of instructions to perform for the next hundred years, it will not complain, and if the hardware is well maintained it will not make a single mistake. Many useful tasks are of a repetitive nature: the totting up of bank balances, the preparation of wage slips, and many mathematical processes of great importance to scientists and technologists. The processes we are interested in are called *iterative*. An iterative process is

> *one which achieves a result by repeatedly performing a series of operations until some specified condition is obtained.*

7. Loops. The computer can carry out iterative processes by the use of *loops*. A loop is

> *a series of instructions which are performed repeatedly until some specified condition is satisfied.*

8. Jumps. Loops are made possible by the provision of *jumps* or *branch instructions.* A jump is

a departure from the normal sequence of program steps.

There are two kinds of jump instructions.

(*a*) *The unconditional jump* which causes a mandatory transfer of control out of the normal sequence, without reference to any condition. An example of this in LOCO is the instruction JUN which we have already met in VIII, **4**.

(*b*) *The conditional jump* which results in a transfer of control out of the normal sequence only if some condition is met. For example, in LOCO we have the instruction JAN. Whenever this instruction is encountered the machine examines the contents of the accumulator.

(*i*) If the contents are negative, transfer is made to the address specified in the jump instruction.

(*ii*) If the contents are *not* negative (i.e. zero or greater than zero) then the normal sequence of obeying instructions is followed.

Similar instructions are JAZ (jump if the accumulator is zero) and JIP (jump if the contents of the *index register* are greater than zero).

We shall now examine three very common methods for setting up a loop by making use of jumps and a few other ideas.

9. Loops controlled by markers. A simple algorithm for the totalling of a set of numbers is shown in Fig. 102. The data (set of numbers) are terminated by an *end-of-data marker* (or *stop number*), in this case −1. All the data are assumed positive. A certain location, which will ultimately contain the total, is initially set to zero (cleared). Each time a number is read in it is examined as to its sign; if it is positive it is added into the location to hold the total; if it is negative the marker will have been found. This signals the end of the data and the totalling process comes to an end with the subsequent outputting of the accumulated total. Examination of the corresponding LOCO program in Fig. 103 shows how the special location for the total is cleared using the first two instructions and how the program depends on the two jump instructions JAN and JUN at addresses 3 and 6 respectively.

10. Loops controlled by counters. Another way of controlling the number of times a loop is traversed is by using a specific location to count the number of traversals. Such a location is called a *counter*

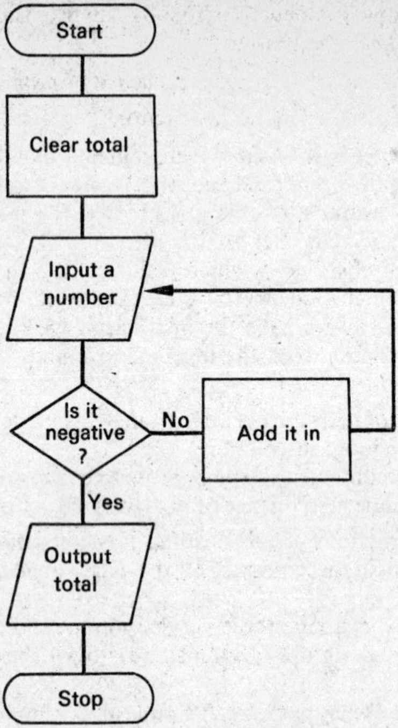

FIG. 102 *Algorithm for totalling set of numbers.*

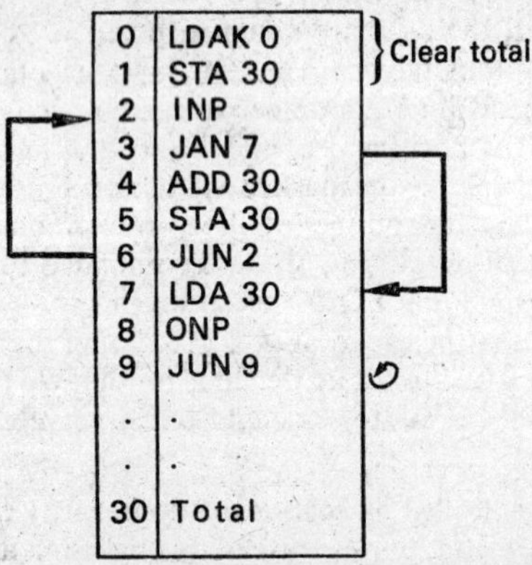

FIG. 103 *LOCO program for totalling set of numbers.*

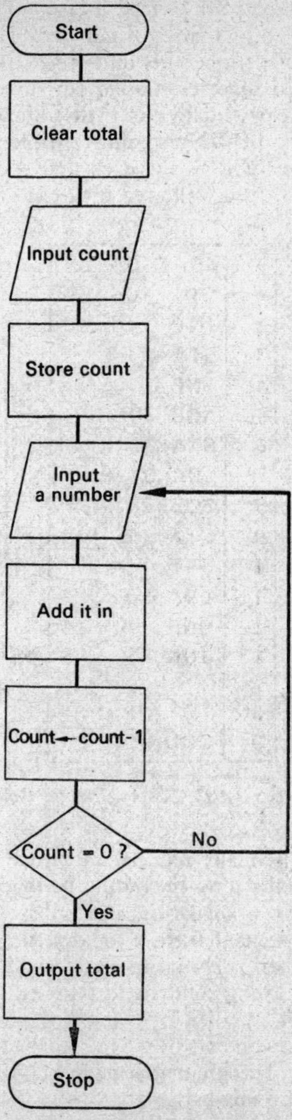

FIG. 104 *Algorithm for looping using a counter.*

and its contents are termed a *count*. The algorithm in Fig. 104 is designed to total a set of numbers. The *first* number presented to the input peripheral is interpreted as the number of numbers to be added together; this is our initial count. All subsequent numbers are potentially part of the ultimate total. Figure 105 shows one kind of LOCO program to achieve this end. The count is stored in location 31 and each time round the loop the count is decremented by 1, followed by a test on the accumulator. When

0	LDAK 0
1	STA 30
2	INP
3	STA 31
4	INP
5	ADD 30
6	STA 30
7	LDA 31
8	SUBK 1
9	STA 31
10	JAP 4
11	LDA 30
12	ONP
13	JUN 13
⋮	
30	TOTAL
31	COUNT

Count ←Count−1

FIG. 105 *A LOCO program for looping using a counter.*

the count is finally reduced to zero the iteration is terminated and the total sent to the output peripheral. The reader is advised to carry out a *manual trace* in order to fully appreciate what is going on. A manual trace (or dry run) is a method of checking a program on *paper* using limited and simple data. This is best done by drawing columns to represent each relevant location in the program and then following through the program step-by-step, entering the contents of the locations at each instruction. A trace for the above program appears in Fig. 106 where the test is carried out on just 3 numbers.

There are usually various ways of coding the same algorithm

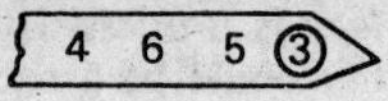

Accumulator	Loc. 30	Counter Loc. 31
0	0	3
3	5	2
5	11	1
5	15	0
3		
2		
6		
11		
2		
1		
4		
15		
1		
0		
(15) Total		

FIG. 106 *A trace of the LOCO program for looping using a counter.*

and the good programmer will make maximum use of the instruction set available to him. The LOCO language provides conditional transfers which refer to the index register and this fact can be put to good use in a more efficient coding of the last algorithm. This is shown in Fig. 107. Here, the count is held in the index register and use made of the INC instruction which is used to decrement the count each time round the loop. Notice that although the *total* number of instructions is only *one* less than in the previous case,

```
 0 LDAK 0
 1 STA 30
 2 INP
 3 STA 31
 4 LDI 31
 5 INP
 6 ADD 30
 7 STA 30
 8 INC-1
 9 JIP 5
10 LDA 30
11 ONP
12 JUN 12
 .
30 TOTAL
31 USED TO TRANSFER COUNT
```

FIG. 107 *LOCO program for looping using a counter in the index register.*

the number of instructions *in the loop* is *two* less. If the loop is traversed maybe a million times, this could be a real saving of time.

11. Loops using address modification. The facility of *indexing* was introduced in VIII, **5**. This facility gives rise to the very important technique of *address modification*. An instruction such as

ADDI 50

means

ADD CONTENTS OF LOCATION (50+(I))
TO THE ACCUMULATOR

If the contents of the index register are systematically changed by means of the INC instruction, then starting with (I)=0 and incrementing by 1 each time, the above instruction would mean

ADD 50
then ADD 51
then ADD 52

and so on.

In Fig. 108 we have a program which shows how this facility may be exploited. Locations 1 through 80 contain 80 numbers which are to be added together and the total is to be placed in location 0. The accumulator is first cleared and the index register

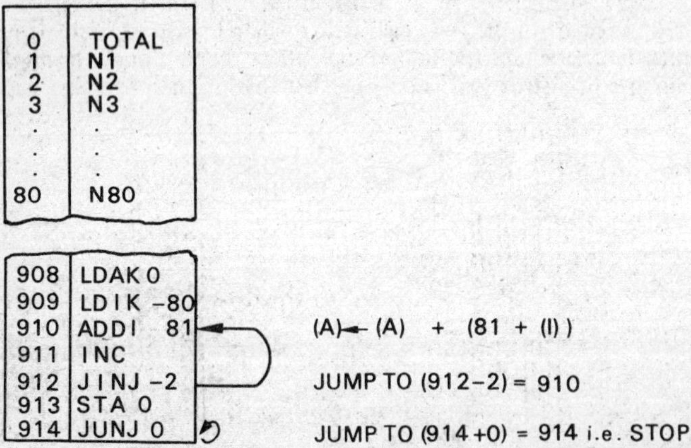

FIG. 108 *LOCO program illustrating address modification and relative addressing.*

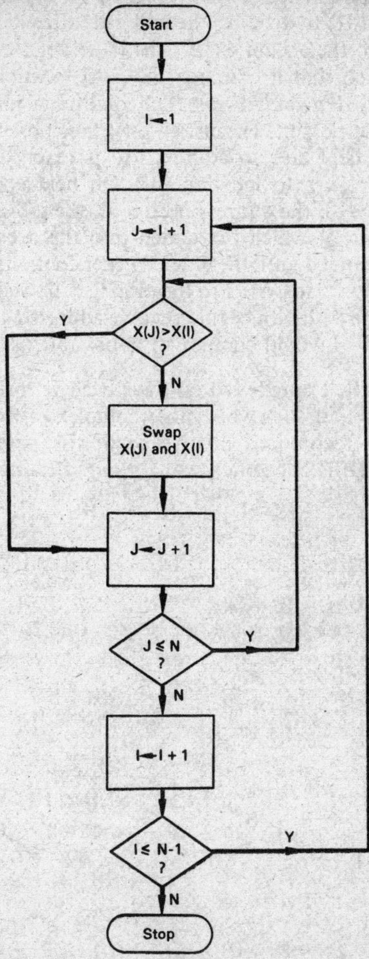

FIG. 109 *Bubble-sort algorithm.*

contains −80. The effect of the instruction at location 910 is as follows: the contents of the index register (−80) are added to the displacement (81) to produce the address 1, the contents of which are added into the accumulator. The index register is then incremented by 1 so that it contains −79. At location 912 we have an example of *relative addressing*. The conditional jump instruction, JIN 910, is not possible because of the range possible in a LOCO displacement field and so address 910 is reached by specifying its position *relative* to location 912. On next encountering the instruction at 910, the address produced (the *effective* address) is 2, the contents of which are added into the accumulator. This process is continued until the index register contains zero, at which point the sum is transferred to location 0, followed by a dynamic stop at location 914. Notice that relative addressing is again necessary as JUN 914 would contain an impossible displacement.

12. Sorting. The examples so far have been very simple, so let us take a second and somewhat more complex problem which can be solved by techniques involving address modification. The problem chosen is concerned with *sorting*. Sorting is the process of putting numeric (or alphabetic) data in ascending or descending

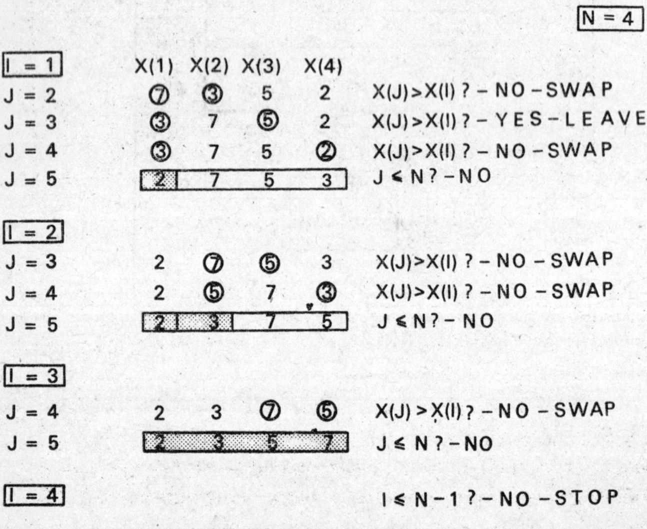

FIG. 110 *Manual trace of bubble sorting.*

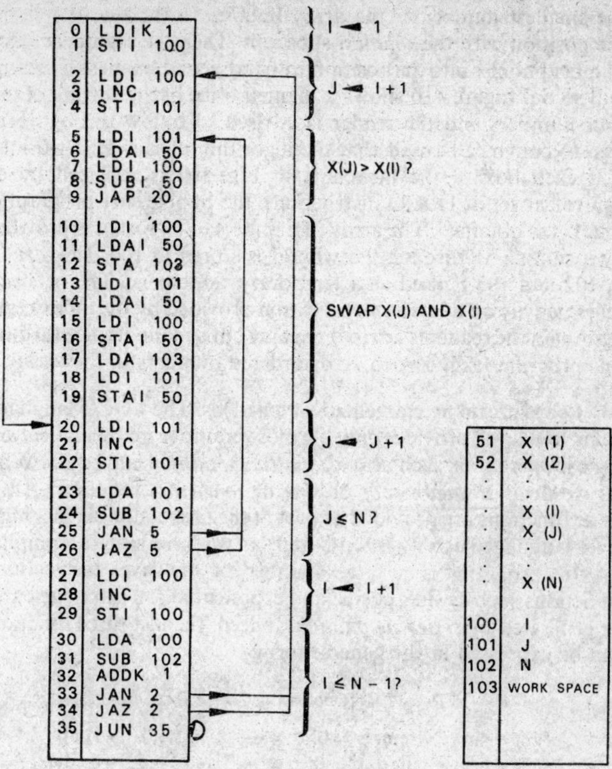

FIG. 111 *LOCO bubble-sort program.*

order. There are several well-known algorithms for carrying out this kind of process, some being more efficient than others. One such method is called the *bubble sort.* We start with N disordered numbers stored in the locations:

$$X(1), X(2), X(3), \ldots X(I), X(J), \ldots X(N)$$

A set of locations used in this way is called an *array*. The array *symbol* (or name) is X, and each member of the array is distinguished by a *subscript* (as in algebra we would write X_1, X_2, … X_i, X_j, … X_n).

The idea of the bubble sort algorithm (Fig. 109) is that first the smallest number in the array bubbles to the *top*, that is, to the position with the *smallest* subscript. Then the second smallest number bubbles into the position with the second smallest subscript, and so on. Figure 110 shows a manual trace of the sorting of just four numbers and the reader is advised to follow through each step to convince himself that the algorithm does indeed work.

If each box of the flowchart in Fig. 109 is replaced by an equivalent set of LOCO instructions, the bubble sort program of Fig. 111 is obtained. The array of numbers to be sorted is provided by locations 51 through 99, while I is stored in 100, J in 101, N in 102 and 103 is used as a temporary workspace. The program relies heavily on address modification provided by the index register. Again the reader is advised to carry out a manual trace through this program using say three disordered numbers in the array.

13. Loops providing mathematical functions. The LOCO language, being low-level, provides only the most primitive mathematical and logical operations such as *add*, *subtract*, *multiply* and so on. What do we do if a *square root* or *sine* or *tangent* is required? All of these functions are provided as part of the instruction set in a high-level language such as BASIC and, as we have seen, a compiled BASIC program, is a large number of low-level instructions. Functions such as sine, cosine and exponential (e^x) can quite easily be generated by *series summation*. Indeed, the last three functions can be expressed in the general form:

$$f(x) = p.\frac{x^0}{0!} + q.\frac{x^1}{1!} + p.\frac{x^2}{2!} + q.\frac{x^3}{3!} + p.\frac{x^4}{4!} + \dots$$

$f(x) = \sin x$ when: $p = 0$; $q = +1, -1, +1, -1$, etc.
$f(x) = \cos x$ when: $q = 0$; $p = +1, -1, +1, -1$, etc.
$f(x) = \exp x$ when: $p = q = 1$

By taking a sufficient number of terms it is possible to calculate these functions to any degree of required accuracy. It is left as an exercise for the reader to write LOCO program segments which will evaluate each of the above functions, but the provision of a very commonly occurring function other than the last three will be described.

Figure 112 shows a famous algorithm for the square root of a real positive number. Readers with a mathematical background will recognise this as a special case of the *Newton-Raphson iteration formula*. It is desired to obtain the square root of the number N. If x_n is taken as an approximation to the square root then it can be shown that x_{n+1} is a better approximation, where

$$x_{n+1} = \tfrac{1}{2}(x_n + N/x_n)$$

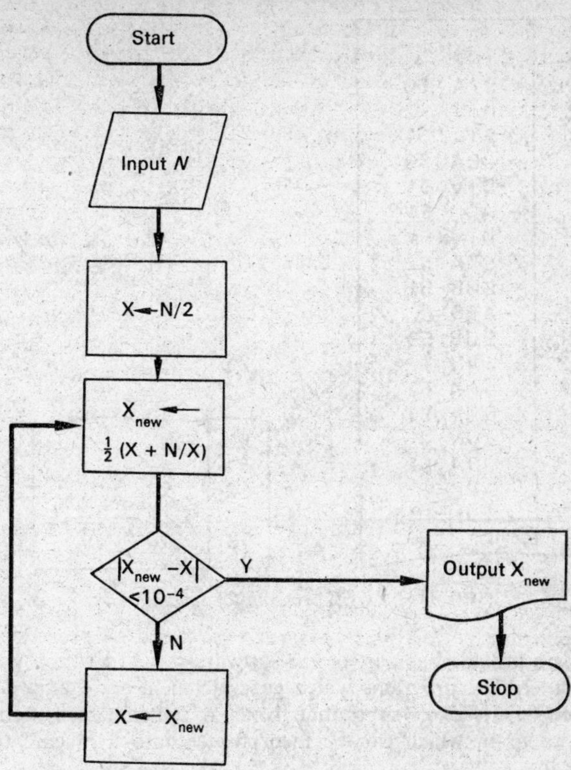

FIG. 112 *Hero's algorithm for the square root of a real positive number.*

In the algorithm, the first approximation is arbitrarily taken as $N/2$ and the *tolerance* (difference between successive approximations) is built in with a value of 0.0001. The method gives results which converge rapidly; for example, suppose $N = 10$.

First approximation		$= 10/2 = 5$	
Second	,,	$= \frac{1}{2}(5 + 10/5)$	$= 3.5$
Third	,,	$= \frac{1}{2}(3.5 + 10/3.5)$	$= 3.1785714$
Fourth	,,	$= \frac{1}{2}(3.1785714 + 10/3.1785714)$	$= 3.1623196$
Fifth	,,	$= \frac{1}{2}(3.1623196 + 10/3.1623196)$	$= 3.1622775$

A LOCO program coded from this algorithm is shown in Fig. 113 and the BASIC program in Fig. 114. Functions of the above

```
0    INP
1    STA  50
2    DIVK  2
3    STA  51
4    LDA  50
5    DIV  51
6    ADD  51
7    DIVK  2
8    STA  52
9    SUB  51
10   ABS
11   SUB  53
12   JAN  16
13   LDA  52
14   STA  51
15   JUN  4
16   LDA  52
17   ONP
18   JUN  18
```

50	N
51	X
52	X_{new}
53	10^{-4}

FIG. 113 *LOCO program for square root.*

type are provided as part of the software supplied with a given computer. The programs which generate them are examples of SUBROUTINES, a subroutine being a self-contained section of a program which can be incorporated into a much larger program.

```
 10 REM SQUARE ROOT BY HERO'S METHOD
 11 PRINT "VALUE OF N"
 30 INPUT N
 40 LET X = N/2
 50 LET XO = (X+N/X)/2
 60 IF ABS(XO-X) < 1E-4 THEN 90
 70 LET X = XO
 80 GO TO 50
 90 PRINT "SQUARE ROOT OF N =";  XO
100 END
```

FIG. 114 *Basic program for square root.*

MODIFIED TRANSFERS

We have already met one example of a jump instruction used with a set tag-bit when we saw the use of relative addressing. It is also possible to index a jump instruction and this provides us with more powerful programming techniques.

14. The multibranch switch. By using an indexed jump instruction like the one at location 20 in Fig. 115 it is possible to transfer control within the program to a number of different addresses. The destination address is determined in this example by the contents of the index register. If the index register contains 1, control is transferred initially to location 21. The instruction in location 21 is the first of a list of jumps constituting what is often called a *jump table.* If the index register contained 2, control would ultimately pass to location 67; if the index register contained zero, a dynamic stop would terminate the program. It should be noted that our example contains only unconditional jumps, but there is no reason why one should not use *conditional* indexed jumps such as JANI or JIPI.

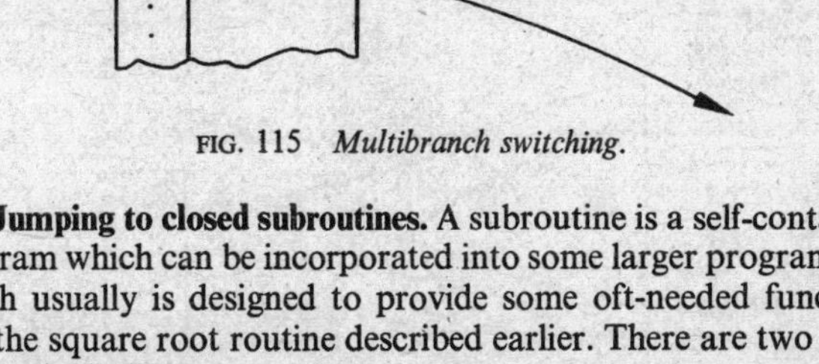

FIG. 115 *Multibranch switching.*

15. Jumping to closed subroutines. A subroutine is a self-contained program which can be incorporated into some larger program and which usually is designed to provide some oft-needed function, like the square root routine described earlier. There are two types of subroutine:

(*a*) *open subroutines* which are copied into the main program at those points where they are required, and

(*b*) *closed subroutines,* a single copy of which is inserted into the main program.

Using open subroutines can sometimes result in a *faster* main program but such usage is very wasteful of storage space. The closed subroutine is far commoner as it is copied only once into the main

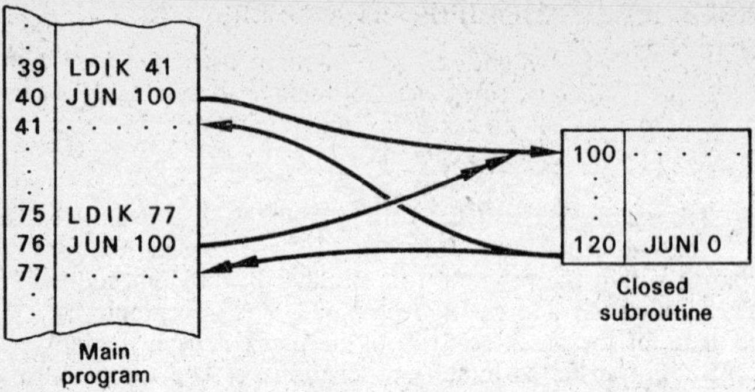

FIG. 116 *Jumping to a closed subroutine.*

program. It does, however, provide a small problem. We may wish to jump to the *same* subroutine from *different* parts of the main program and then *return* to the instruction which immediately follows the original jump. In other words, it is necessary to create some kind of *link* with the main program so that we can "find our way home" from the subroutine. This is most easily done by means of indexed jumps. Figure 116 illustrates the technique. A closed subroutine is stored in locations 100 through 120. Before jumping to the subroutine we have to *set the link* by means of

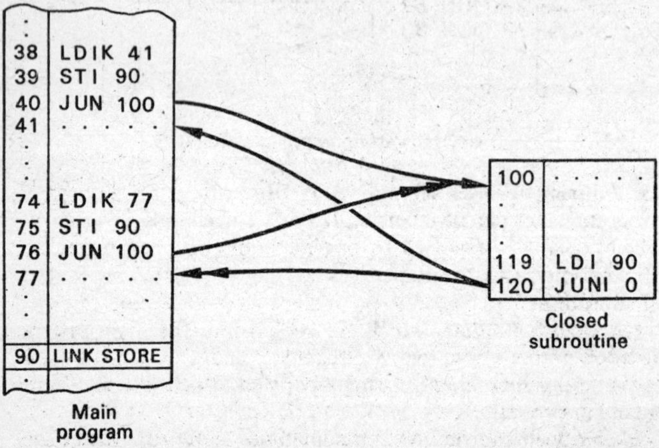

FIG. 117 *Jumping to a closed subroutine in which the index register is needed for some other purpose within the subroutine.*

the instruction LDIK 41. The effect of this is to place the first return address (41) in the index register. Provided the subroutine itself makes no use of the index register it is then an easy matter to return to the main program. The instruction, JUNI 0, will, in the first case be interpreted as JUN 41, and in the second excursion to the subroutine be interpreted as JUN 77, following the setting of a different link using LDIK 77. It is quite common to find that the index register is needed for some other purpose within the subroutine. In this case it is necessary to store the link in some other location as is illustrated in Fig. 117.

16. Nested subroutines. An interesting variation in the use of closed subroutines is when a subroutine *calls* another subroutine (which may call yet another subroutine, and so on). Such a system of subroutines are said to be *nested*. The idea is illustrated in Fig. 118 where the main program first calls subroutine 1 at location 10. During the execution of subroutine 1 a call is made to subroutine 2 at location 60. Notice that more than one link is necessary: the return from subroutine 1 to the main program is provided by

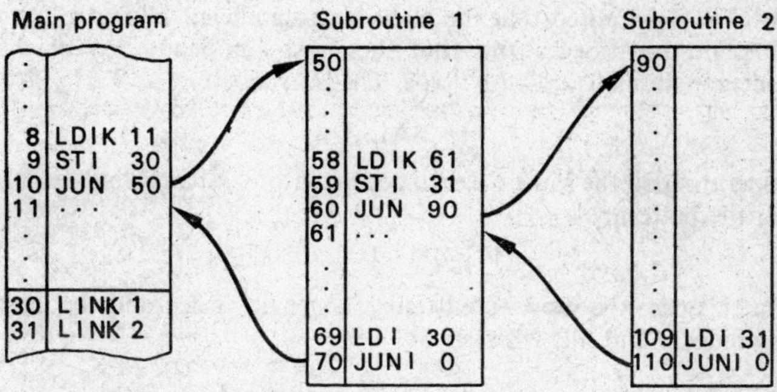

FIG. 118 *Nested subroutines.*

LINK 1 stored in location 30, while return from subroutine 2 to subroutine 1 is facilitated by LINK 2 stored in location 31. Locations 30 and 31 could be followed by locations 32 onwards containing further links for even more nested subroutines. These locations, containing the links, may be collectively referred to as a *link stack*. Computers with push-down stacks lend themselves readily to the storage of link addresses as return from each subroutine will consist simply in the removal of the link at the top of the stack, while calling further subroutines in the nest will be accomplished by the placing of the appropriate link on top of the stack (*see* Fig. 118).

SHIFTS AND LOGIC OPERATIONS

17. Shifts. The LOCO language provides two kinds of *logical shifts*. These are SAR, which shifts the contents of the accumulator to the *right*, and SAL, which shifts the accumulator contents *left*. The number of places shifted is determined by the value of the displacement field, suppose the accumulator contains the bit-pattern below:

0101 1111 0111 0001

then the instruction

SAR 8

will result in the accumulator holding the bit-pattern:

0000 0000 0101 1111

It should be noted that the eight least-significant bits have been lost in the process and that the most-significant end of the accumulator fills up with zeros. The instruction

SAL 4

operating on the same original accumulator contents would result in the pattern:

1111 0111 0001 0000

In this case the most significant bits are discarded and the least significant end fills with zeros.

18. Arithmetic shifts. The latter example illustrates the fact that logical shifts may result in alteration of the sign bit, as such shifts operate on *all* the bits in the accumulator. In certain applications it is desirable to *preserve the sign bit during shifting*. This is carried out by means of an *arithmetic shift*. In LOCO an arithmetic shift is obtained by setting the K-bit. The instruction

SARK D

means *halve the contents of the accumulator D times*

i.e. $(A) \leftarrow (A) \times 2^{-D}$

Suppose we are using the fractional format:

$$0.\ 10100000\ 00000000 \quad = +5/8$$

The effect of

SARK 1

would give the result

$$0.\ 01010000\ 00000000 \quad = +5/16$$

This correct result would also have been obtained using the logical shift SAR 1. But, suppose the fraction is negative; for example:

$$1.\ 0110000\ 00000000 \quad = -5/8$$

Then, SARK 1 would result in

$$1.\ 1011000\ 00000000 \quad = -5/16$$

It can be seen that the effect of the arithmetic right-shift is to discard bits at the LSE and to *introduce copies of the sign bit* on the left. It is left as an exercise for the reader to show the converse process—doubling—may be carried out by the simple use of a *logical* shift.

19. Logic operations. LOCO provides two logic operations (sometimes called Boolean operations). These are:

(*a*) not-equivalent, NEQ,

$$(A) \leftarrow (A) \not\equiv (D)$$

and

(*b*) collate, AND,

$$(A) \leftarrow (A).(D)$$

Both of these functions have been described in IV, **6** and **7**. The function NEQ is also recognised as the exclusive-or operation. Its effect is to produce a 1 bit wherever bits in corresponding positions are *different*. For example, suppose the accumulator contains the pattern:

1111 0001 1111 0101

and that location 50 contains:

0101 0001 1111 1111

then the instruction

NEQ 50

will produce the following pattern in the accumulator:

1010 0000 0000 1010

It should be clear from this example that NEQ has the effect of producing cleared regions (zeros) in those parts of the accumulator where the patterns are identical. In the latter case the middle 8 bits of location 50 and the accumulator were originally the same; the NEQ operation results in 8 zeros in the centre of the accumulator. The 4 bits at the end of the words have undergone *inversion*. This is another important property of the NEQ function. Suppose location 80 contains

1111 1010 1111 0101

then the instructions

```
LDA 80
NEQK-1
```

produce the accumulator pattern

0000 0101 0000 1010

Here we have used a literal with the NEQ function to obtain the pattern

1111 1111 1111 1111

which is −1 in twos complement form.

20. Masking. The function AND provides the *collate* operation in which a 1 is output where corresponding bits are themselves 1s; otherwise zeros result. The principal use of this function is in *masking*. A *mask* is just a word with a block of 1s confined to one part of it. Suppose we wanted to pick out the 8 least significant bits of the accumulator and that the latter contained the word:

1011 1101 1010 0010 (accumulator)

The necessary mask, held in location 50 (say), would be:

0000 0000 1111 1111 (location 50)

Execution of the instruction

```
AND 50
```

would produce the accumulator word

0000 0000 1010 0010

INPUT/OUTPUT OPERATIONS

21. Character transfers. LOCO provides two primitive functions for input and output of data: ICP and OCP. These functions were defined in VIII, **4**, and their effect is shown in Fig. 119. Suppose we want to input a string of 8-bit bytes from a specified peripheral and store them in a prescribed area of memory. This can be done by means of a short *character input routine*, i.e. a program segment which reads bytes and stores them in successive locations. Figure 120 shows such a routine where characters C1 through C20 are read and stored. The first instruction sets a count of 10 and the next reads a character to the LSE of the accumulator. A left shift

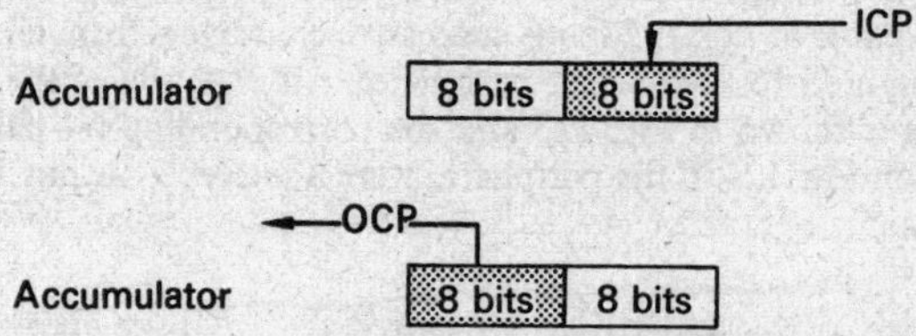

FIG. 119 *Action of input/output functions.*

makes room for the next character which is read in. The accumulator now contains two bytes and the contents are transferred to location (70+I), i.e. location 80 initially. The index register is decremented and a conditional jump permits the next pair of characters to be read in. This process continues until the jump test fails at instruction 26. The resulting contents of store are shown in Fig. 121.

```
20 LDIK 10
21 ICP
22 SAL 8
23 ICP
24 STAI 70
25 INC -1
26 JIP 21
```

FIG. 120 *Character input routine.*

71	C19	C20
72	C17	C18
	· · · ·	
79	C3	C4
80	C1	C2

FIG. 121 *Contents of store after character input.*

20	LDIK 6
21	LDAI 74
22	OCP
23	SAL 8
24	OCP
25	INC −1
26	JIP 21

FIG. 122 *Character output routine.*

75	S	!
76	L	K
77	F	O
78	O	SPACE
79	L	L
80	H	E

FIG. 123 *Examples of store contents.*

Output of characters may be achieved by a similar process. The *output routine* in Fig. 122 sends successive characters from location 80 through 75 to the chosen peripheral. An example of the store contents is shown in Fig. 123 and the corresponding bit patterns (ASCII) in Fig. 124. If the peripheral were a teletype, output would appear as in Fig. 125.

75	01010011 00100001
76	11001100 01001011
77	11000110 11001111
78	11001111 10100000
79	11001100 11001100
80	01001000 11000101

FIG. 124 *Corresponding bit patterns from example of store contents.*

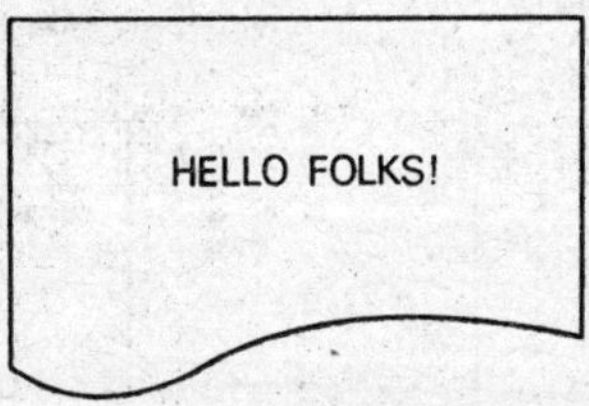

FIG. 125 *Printout from example of store contents.*

22. Numeral transfers. A point which is often not appreciated is that *all* alphanumeric input to the computer is in the form of characters, either letters, decimal digits or special characters. For

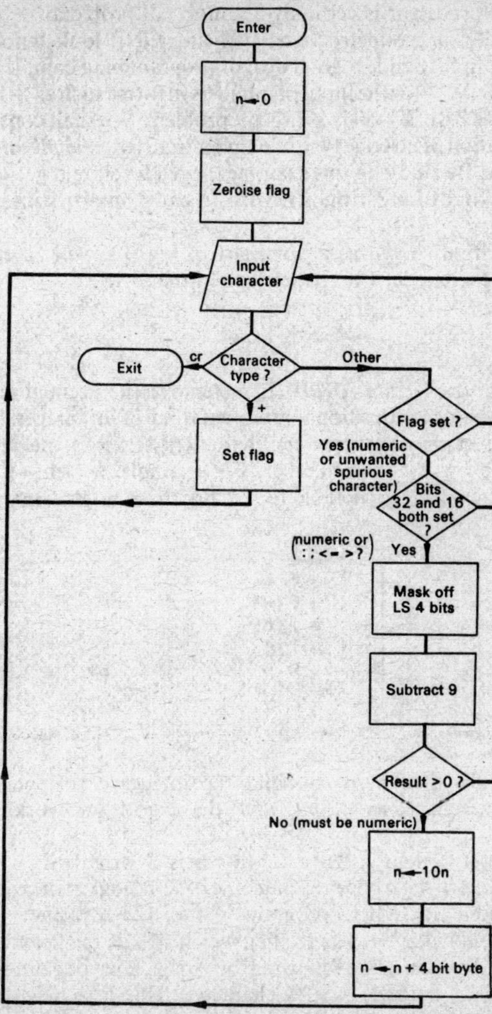

FIG. 126 *Simple integer input routine.*

this reason, the transfer of numeric information between peripherals and processor is certainly a non-trivial problem.

The LOCO macro-instructions INP and ONP look innocent enough but, in fact, hide a good deal of programming complexity. Providing facilities for the input of numbers in forms such as +16.1, −256.219, or 8.81 E−50 is a difficult problem. We shall consider here the solution of just one type of number transfer: a *simple integer input routine*. By studying this example the reader should get some idea of the kind of algorithms needed to enter numbers into the computer.

The algorithm shown as a flowchart in Fig. 126 will accept a *positive* integer punched on paper tape in the form:

$$+d_1d_2d_3 \ldots \text{cr}$$

where d_1, d_2, d_3, ... are ASCII characters for the decimal digits making up the usual positional representation of an integer. The + sign and carriage-return (cr) characters serve to mark the beginning and end of the number. For example, a print-out of the type of numerals acceptable to the algorithm might look like Fig. 127.

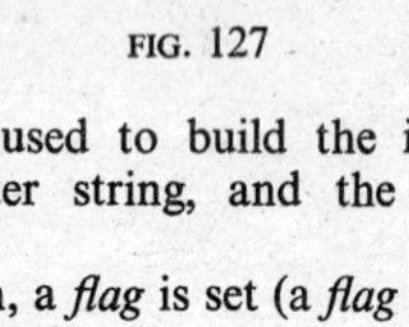

FIG. 127

The location n is used to build the integer corresponding to the input character string, and the algorithm works as follows:

On finding a + sign, a *flag* is set (a *flag* is a variable the value of which is used to determine the outcome of some logical decision). The corresponding LOCO program in Fig. 128 uses the index register contents (0 or −1) as the flag which signals the beginning of a number. Any character following the + sign must be examined to see if it is a numeric ASCII character. This is achieved by determining if the character is in the upper right block of sixteen characters in Fig. 4, all of which have bits 32 and 16 equal to 1. Six of these are, however, non-numerics like : or =. The non-numerics are eliminated by masking off the LS set of four bits

```
10 REM A SIMPLE PROGRAM
20 PRINT "CONVERSION OF CELSIUS TO KELVIN
   TEMPERATURES"
30 PRINT
40 PRINT "TYPE IN A CELSIUS TEMPERATURE"
50 INPUT T
60 PRINT "THE KELVIN EQUIVALENT IS"; T+273.15
70 END
```

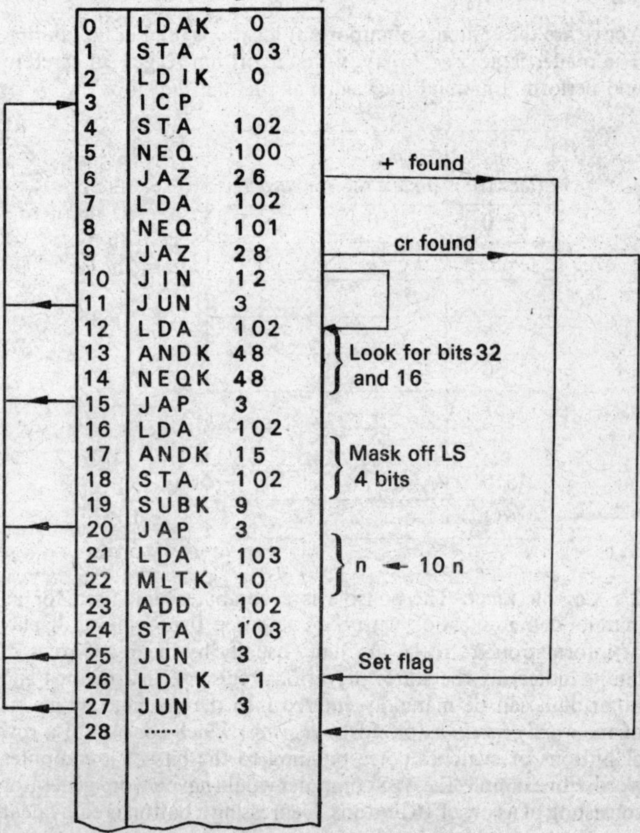

FIG. 128 *Simple integer input routine in LOCO.*

of the character to see if it is greater than 9. Once a numeric is found, the contents of n are multiplied by ten and the new numeric added in.

100	00000000 00101011	+
101	00000000 10001101	cr
102	TEMP. STORE	
103	n	

Above are the contents of important locations used in the routine. The reader is advised to study the algorithm (Fig. 126) carefully and perform a manual trace such as the one shown below.

n (*loc.* 103)	*flag* (*index reg.*)	*character*	
0	0	+	
	−1	5	
0			
5			
50		1	
51			
		2	
510			
512		cr	exit.

23. Console input. The console is a computer unit used for all manual communication with the computer. It provides a display of information from the machine, usually by means of rows of lamps indicating the states of various registers. Instructions and other data can be manually entered into the machine by means of the *word generator* (or *switch register*) which consists of a row of buttons or switches corresponding to the bits of a computer word. For example, the ASS computer would have a word generator consisting of a row of 16 buttons. Depressing a button is equivalent to setting up a logic 1, while an unpressed button represents a 0 state. The LOCO instruction WGA copies the state of the buttons on the word generator into the accumulator. By providing this facility it is possible to alter the path followed by a program containing WGA simply by pressing buttons on the console. For example, pressing the left-most button of the word generator is equivalent to setting the sign-bit of a computer word. Thus, a program containing the instruction-sequence

```
........
WGA
JAN 58
JAZ 75
........
```

would transfer control to location 58 if the left-most word-generator button was depressed, would transfer control to location 75 if all the buttons were clear, and would carry straight on otherwise.

HIGH-LEVEL PROGRAMMING

24. A simple example. The first algorithm we encountered was the conversion of Celsius to Kelvin (Fig. 99) and below is the BASIC-language equivalent of this.

Notice that English messages can be conveniently embedded in the program thus rendering the output of the program much more

```
CONVERSION OF CELSIUS TO KELVIN TEMPERATURES

TYPE IN A CELSIUS TEMPERATURE

?20

THE KELVIN TEMPERATURE IS 293·15
```

FIG. 129

meaningful. Line 20 causes the title in quotes to be printed out while line 30 causes a line to be skipped on the output paper. Line 40 prints another message and line 50 causes the machine to print a question mark and then wait for data input. The user then supplies a temperature, following which the machine prints its response in the form of English words and a numeric value. A sample run might look like Fig. 129.

25. Totalling. The BASIC equivalent of the first totalling algorithm (Fig. 102) is shown below.

```
 10 REM DEMONSTRATION OF SIMPLE LOOPING
 20 PRINT "TOTALLING NUMBERS"
 30 PRINT
 40 LET T=0
 50 READ N
 60 IF N=-1 THEN 90
 70 LET T=T+N
 80 GOTO 50
 90 PRINT "TOTAL=";T
100 STOP
110 DATA 5,7,4,8,12,1,5,23,5,6,9,35,-1
120 END
```

Line 50 contains a READ statement which assigns to the variable N successive values from the DATA statement at line 110. These are added into the initially zero location designated T at line 70. Each time round the loop a test is made at line 60 for the end of data marker. Line 70 illustrates the typical form of a high-level *assignment* statement, which should never be confused with an *equation*. Writing the instruction:

70 LET T=T+N

means "take the number currently in the location called T; add the number currently in location N and place the result in location T.

```
 10 REM COUNTER LOOPING
 20 PRINT "TOTALLING NUMBERS USING A COUNTER"
 30 PRINT
 40 LET T=0
 50 PRINT "TYPE IN NUMBER TO BE TOTALLED"
 60 INPUT CO
 70 FOR C=1 TO CO
 80 READ N
 90 LET T=T+N
100 NEXT C
110 PRINT "TOTAL OF"; CO; "NUMBERS="; T
120 STOP
---------------------------------------
130 DATA 5,7,4,8,12,64
140 DATA 7,3,56,34,36,78        } Data
 .  .                           } stack
 .  .
 .  .
400 DATA 77,4,32,89,69,5
---------------------------------------
999 END
```

FIG. 130 *Looping using a counter.*

26. Totalling using a counter. Figure 130 shows totalling in BASIC using a counter. The number of numbers to be added together is supplied at line 60 while the main loop consists of lines 70 through 100. BASIC provides the very useful facility termed a FOR-NEXT loop in which the initial and final values of the counter C are specified in one line (line 70). The amount by which the counter is increased each time round the loop is assumed by the compiler to be ONE unless otherwise specified. In the program shown the data to be totalled is held in DATA statements 130 through 400.

27. Bubble sorting. The bubble-sort algorithm of Fig. 120 is conveniently coded in BASIC as shown in Fig. 131. There are several points of interest. First, notice the ease with which an *array* of numbers can be handled. Lines 70 through 110 read an array from data provided at line 500, a test being made each time for the last item. In BASIC, X(N) specifies an element of the array X,

```
10 PRINT "BUBBLE SORT"
20 PRINT
30 DIM X(100)
40 PRINT "FUR NEW ARRAY INSERT DATA AT LINE 500"
50 PRINT
60 LET N=0
70 READ B
80 IF B=-1 THEN 120
90 LET N=N+1
100 LET X(N)=B
110 GOTO 70
120 PRINT "SORT BEGINS WITH ARRAY LENGTH= ";N
130 FUR I=1 TO N-1
140 FOR J=I+1 TO N
150 IF X(J)>X(I) THEN 190
160 LET T=X(I)
170 LET X(I)=X(J)
180 LET X(J)=T
190 NEXT J
200 NEXT I
210 PRINT "SORTED ARRAY IS:-"
220 PRINT
230 FOR I=1 TO N
240 PRINT X(I);
250 NEXT I
500 DATA 5,3,25,1,18,6,12,9,4,-1
999 END
```

FIG. 131 *Bubble-sort algorithm coded in BASIC.*

where N is termed a *subscript*. Thus the input loop in the bubble sort program sets X(1) = 5, X(2) = 3, X(3) = 25, ... X(9) = 4. Lines 130 through 200 contain two *nested loops* in which the input array is scanned and sorted. Swapping is carried out at lines 160 through 180. Finally, the sorted array is printed out using the loop at lines 230 through 250. A sample output appears in Fig. 132.

```
BUBBLE SORT

FOR NEW ARRAY INSERT DATA AT LINE 5ØØ


SORT BEGINS WITH ARRAY LENGTH= 9
SORTED ARRAY IS:-

 1    3    4    5    6    9    12    18    25

EXEC = Ø.Ø6 SEC
*END
```

FIG. 132 *Sample output from BASIC bubble-sort routine.*

28. Square root. The square-root algorithm of Fig. 112 is very easy to implement in BASIC and a version of this is shown in Fig. 114. Notice the quite complex decisions which can be made in a high-level language. Such a decision is made by means of the IF-statement at line 60. Several LOCO instructions would be needed to carry out the equivalent operation. The reader is advised to run this program on a computer to which he has access and should modify it so that appropriate action is taken if N is supplied with a value less than or equal to zero.

SOME HIGH-LEVEL FUNCTIONS

Finally, let us examine some of the functions commonly available in a high-level language. Although these do depend on the particular language concerned, a fair appreciation can be gained by once again referring to the widely used BASIC language and some of its *intrinsic functions*.

29. Fundamental mathematical functions. Square roots, trigonometrical, logarithmic, and exponential functions are all directly available:

e.g.

LET Y = SQR(X)	square root
LET Y = SIN(X)	sine (angle in radians)
LET Y = LOG(X)	natural logarithm
LET Y = EXP(X)	natural exponential

Here X is called the *argument*. An argument is an expression representing a value that the function is to act upon. The argument can be simple or complicated. For example:

LET Y = SQR(1 + SIN(B/F))

is a permissible BASIC instruction.

30. The Greatest-Integer function. In BASIC the function INT is very useful. For a given argument it produces the greatest integer that is less than or equal to the argument.

e.g.

INT(6.23) = 6
INT(12) = 12
INT(−2.4) = −3

To obtain the *nearest integer* to a given number, X, one may write:

LET N = INT(X + 0.5)

e.g. if X = 8.7,

N = INT(9.2) = 9

The following short program illustrates one of the many uses of this function; in this case the program determines whether a number is odd or even.

```
10 PRINT "WHAT IS YOUR NUMBER"
20 INPUT N
30 IF INT(N/2)=N/2 THEN 60
40 PRINT "YOUR NUMBER IS ODD"
50 GOTO 70
60 PRINT "YOUR NUMBER IS EVEN"
70 PRINT "GOODBYE"
80 END
```

31. Random-number generator. BASIC provides the intrinsic function RND which is used to provide a random number. The general form is:

LET X = RND(N)

The value of X is in the range below:

$$0 < X < 1$$

that is, X is a decimal fraction lying between 0 and 1 but not including these values. Thus, a typical value generated might be

0.415 762 7

If the argument of RND is zero, a new stream of random numbers is obtained starting with an unpredetermined number. If the argument is non-zero, the random number stream begins with the value of the argument. If no argument is specified, then X is set equal to the next number from a random stream.

Random integers may be produced by making use of the INT function. Thus, INT(10*RND) produces a random integer in the range 1 through 9; INT(11*RND) produces a random integer in the range 1 through 10.

There are many uses for random numbers in computing but just one example is shown below. This is a short conversational program for teaching addition to children. The reader is advised to try this program on the computer to which he has access and incorporate modifications and extensions such as the provision of other arithmetical processes and a means of printing out a record of the child's progress after a session at the computer.

```
 10 LET A = INT(11*RND)
 20 LET B = INT(11*RND)
 30 PRINT "WHAT IS";A;"PLUS";B
 40 LET I = 1
 50 INPUT R
 60 IF R = A+B THEN 130
 70 LET I = I+1
 80 IF I>3 THEN 110
 90 PRINT "SORRY—THAT'S WRONG. TRY AGAIN"
100 GOTO 50
110 PRINT "YOU ARE STILL WRONG. THE ANSWER
    IS"; A+B
120 GOTO 140
130 PRINT "CORRECT. VERY GOOD"
```

```
140 PRINT
150 PRINT "FOR ANOTHER QUESTION TYPE 1;
    OTHERWISE TYPE 0"
160 INPUT K
170 IF K=1 THEN 10
180 END
```

PROGRESS TEST 11

1. Explain the terms iteration, loop and counter. **(5, 7, 10)**
2. Define a jump (or branch). With reference to both low- and high-level languages, describe how unconditional and conditional jumps may be used in programming. **(8)**
3. Explain the use of a manual trace. **(10)**
4. What is meant by address modification? Illustrate your answer with a simple program segment in LOCO. Is address modification possible in BASIC? **(11)**
5. Describe two different uses for modified transfers. Illustrate your answer using program segments in LOCO and a high-level language with which you are familiar. **(14–16)**
6. What is a subroutine? Explain why subroutines are useful in programming a computer. Distinguish between a closed and an open subroutine. How may the speed of execution of a program be affected by choice of subroutine type? **(15)**
7. What is meant by a subroutine link? Explain how a stack is used in the implementation of nested subroutines. **(15, 16)**
8. Any mistake in a computer program is called a bug. Explain how the temporary inclusion of extra output instructions in a faulty program might assist in the process of debugging.
9. Prepare a flowchart for an algorithm that will read the coefficients a, b, and c of a quadratic equation $ax^2+bx+c=0$ and determine the roots of the equation using the well-known formula

$$x=\frac{-b\pm\sqrt{(b^2-4ac)}}{2a}$$

If the discriminent (b^2-4ac) is positive, output the two roots. If the discriminent is zero, output the double root $x=-b/2a$. If the discriminent is negative, output the message "The roots are complex".

10. Prepare the flowchart for an algorithm which calculates the

Fibonacci sequence 0, 1, 1, 2, 3, 5, 8, 13, ... The values of the terms are computed by means of the formula

$$F_{i+2}=F_{i+1}+F_i$$

11. Draw a flowchart illustrating the activities involved in making a telephone call from a public telephone box.

12. Write a LOCO program that computes the sum of the numbers $1+\frac{1}{2}+\frac{1}{3}+\frac{1}{4}+\ldots+1/100$.

13. Write a LOCO program to reverse any number from 0 to 100 i.e. 19 becomes 91; 36 becomes 63 etc.

14. Write a BASIC program to print out a table of the circumference and area of circles of radii from 10 mm to 100 mm in steps of 10 mm. Provide suitable headings with the output.

15. Write a LOCO subroutine to evaluate the square root of a number using the iteration formula

$$x_{n+1}=\tfrac{1}{2}(x_n+N/x_n).$$

Incorporate this subroutine into a program which calculates the length of the hypotenuse of a right-angled triangle from the values of the other two sides.

CHAPTER XII

Computer Applications

In this chapter are presented some of the many uses to which computers have been, and are being put in the modern world. It is in these applications that the computer is seen as a universal machine with almost limitless possibilities.

BUSINESS DATA PROCESSING

1. Nature of files. Although future innovations and changing human activity will doubtless alter the figures, it is now true that over 85% of computer applications are concerned with the handling of *files*. A file is simply an organised collection of *records*, a record being a set of data referring to a particular person or object. The keeping of files has a very long history and, though often regarded as a singularly dull business, it is a distinctly human and useful activity. The romantics were certainly disappointed when the famous tablets from the palace of Knossos were found to contain nothing more mysterious than storekeeping lists.

2. File maintenance. To be of maximum use a file should be *dynamic*, i.e. it should be capable of alteration as circumstances change. The process of modifying the contents of a file by adding, deleting or correcting records is termed *file maintenance*; it is this process which is right at the very heart of electronic data processing (EDP) applied principally to problems and organisation in the world of business. EDP may be defined as follows:

> *The operations performed on data to derive information, or to achieve order among* files *incorporated in a computer system.*

The maintenance of files consists in modifying the contents of a *master file* on the basis of new data called *transaction data*. The latter may consist of

(*a*) alteration to a record, or
(*b*) addition or deletion of a record.

There are two principal types of file maintenance in use today; one is that associated with sequential access mass memory devices while the other is relevant to mass memory with random (direct) access.

3. Sequential-access files. This type of file is maintained as follows (*see* Fig. 133).

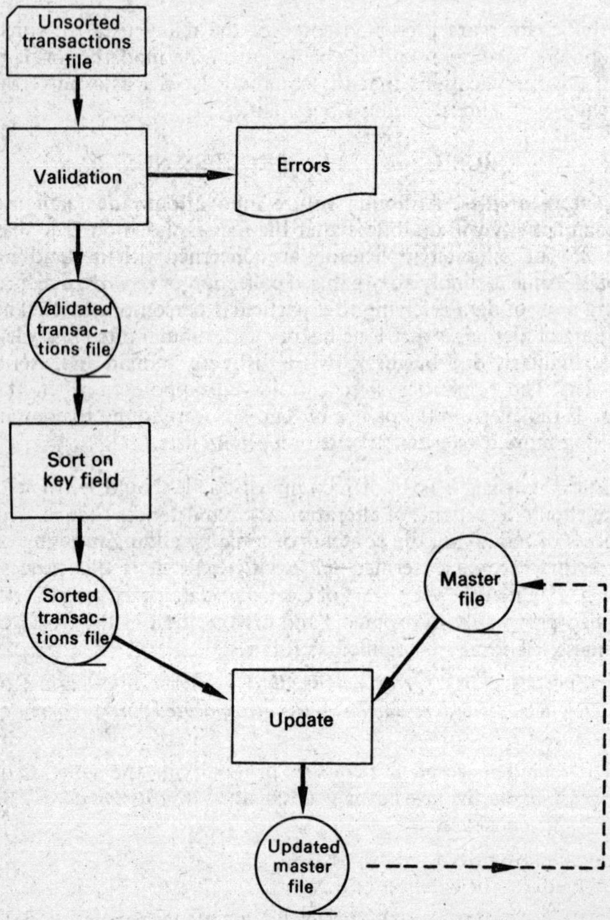

FIG. 133 *File maintenance (sequential access).*

(*a*) Transactions are collected into batches over a period to form an unsorted transactions file.

(*b*) Errors are looked for *before* the data is keyed into the system (a process termed *validation*—not to be confused with *verification*, which is a checking process carried out on data already punched on cards or tape).

(*c*) The unsorted transactions are then sorted into ascending or descending order by using a *key field* contained in each record. A key field is an item of data which can be *numeric* (e.g. a customer account number) or *non-numeric* (e.g. the customer's name). The transactions are thus sorted into the same order and on the same key as the master file.

(*d*) The computer next uses the key field in attempts to match records in the master file with records in the transaction file. This *update* creates the *new* master file.

It should be noticed that, in this type of maintenance, the *entire* master file is read. Even when there are few transactions, the complete master file is read and copied on to another tape, making a new master file which incorporates all the changes dictated by the transactions. The archetypal sequential-access file is, of course, the ubiquitous magnetic tape store.

4. Random-access files. If magnetic disk stores are used, information can be updated and written back to the same position on the file. Hence, it is not necessary to reproduce a completely new file. Random access also permits transactions to be processed in the order in which they are received, thus eliminating the need for sorting the transactions before updating the master file. The general process is illustrated in Fig. 134.

5. Data processing in banking. As an example of modern data processing in action we may take the business of *banking*. More than 1 000 000 cheques are handled daily by many banks and so without the computer, the handling of our financial affairs would be a formidable, if not impossible, task. MICR is used to read the cheques so that data from the latter can be read directly on to a file storage medium. MICR devices are also used OFF-LINE as cheque-sorters. This process is important because cheques received at head office have to be *cleared*, i.e. returned to the branch of origin.

Transactions may be transmitted from bank branches to the bank's computer centre either *off-line* or *on-line*.

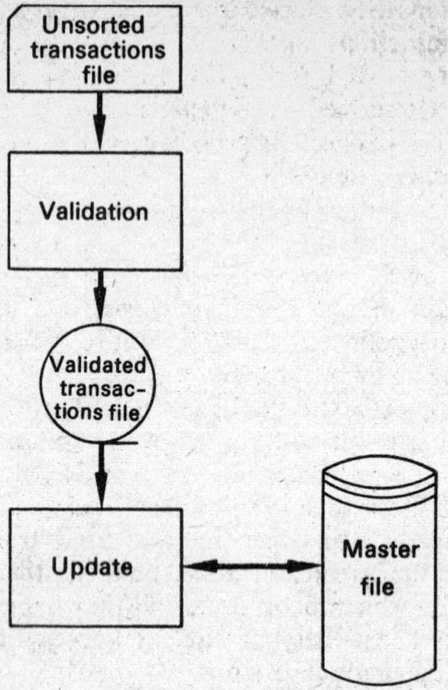

FIG. 134 *File maintenance (random access).*

(*a*) *Off-line transmission.* This kind of processing is shown in Fig. 135. Information is punched on paper tape at each branch and transmitted to the bank's computer centre where it is checked and filed on magnetic tape for later batch processing. During processing, transactions from the MICR and paper-tape transmissions are sorted on the same key field and are then *merged* on to a single magnetic tape. A second merge with the customers' accounts file creates an updated file which can be used in the preparation of statements to be sent by post to the customer.

(*b*) *On-line transmission.* A somewhat superior system is that which permits transactions to be sent continuously from remote terminals at bank branches. The transactions are filed on disk for subsequent processing.

6. Payroll processing. A second application of EDP is that of *payroll processing* in which monthly or weekly paypackets are prepared for workers of all kinds. This is a typical example of sequential-access file maintenance in which a master file is kept containing data such as employee number, employee's name, income-tax information, national insurance information, and other

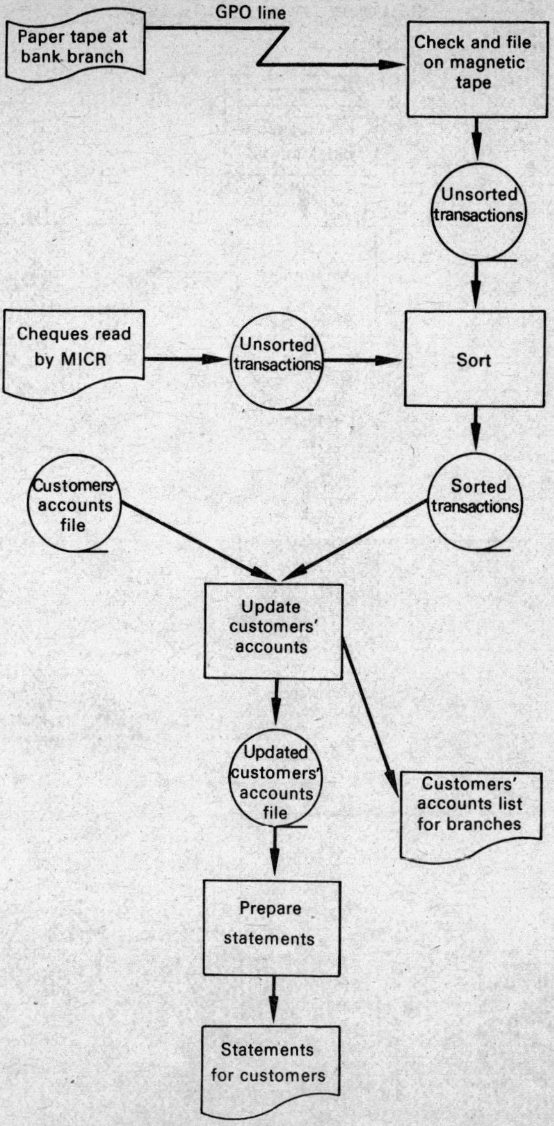

FIG. 135 *Data processing in banking.*

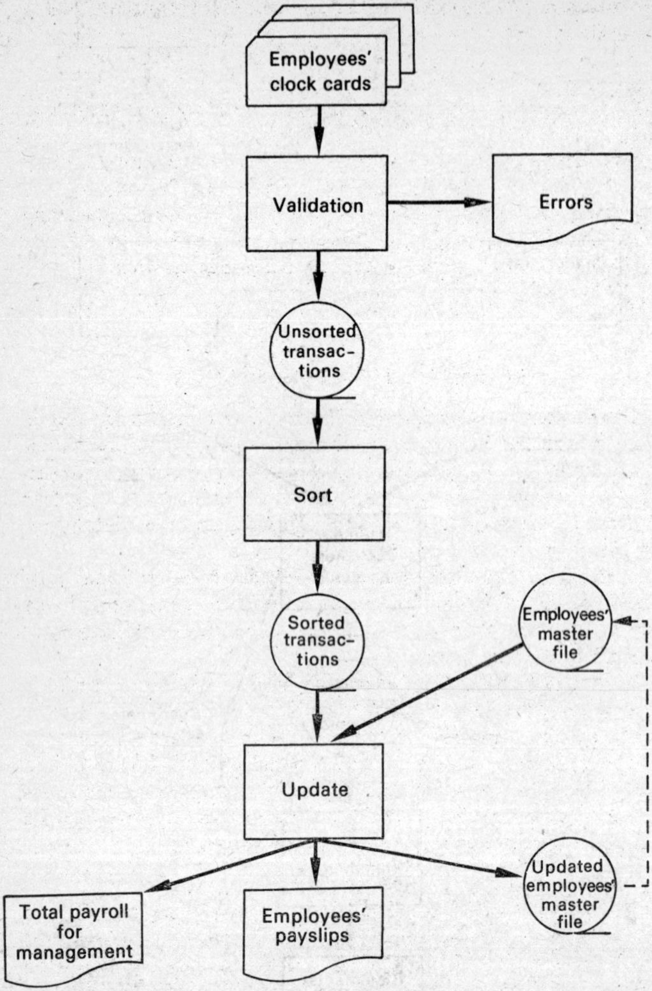

FIG. 136 *Payroll processing.*

personal details. Prior to payroll calculations being carried out, it is necessary to update the master file. Transactions affecting the updating are

(*a*) employee changes, and
(*b*) a record of the number of hours worked by each employee.

Industrial workers often supply the latter information on *clock cards*. When an employee arrives at work, he "clocks on" by inserting a card into a machine which records the time. On leaving work the card is again punched, thus providing data on total hours worked. The overall process in this application is shown in Fig. 136.

SCIENCE AND TECHNOLOGY

7. Conventional mathematical problems. The digital computer is firmly established in the general armoury of the physical scientist and technologist. Applications range from using the computer to evaluate problems about the sub-atomic world of the nuclear physicist to assisting the cosmologist in his grand speculations on the nature of the universe.

In many of these applications the basic computational processes are the same: the solving of differential equations of one sort or another. These equations are solved by using *numerical methods* of various kinds.

To illustrate the kind of approach used in numerical methods let us take a very simple differential equation which has a well-known solution: the problem of the simple harmonic oscillator (e.g. a body performing oscillations on the end of a string). Although this problem can be solved directly using straightforward mathematics, it is instructive to study an algorithmic approach to its solution. The differential equation to be solved is:

$$dv/dt = -k.x$$

where v is the velocity of the body at any time, t, and x is the displacement from equilibrium. The quantity, k, is a constant which depends on the mass of the body and the stiffness of the spring. The problem is to find the position x as a function of time, t.

If a small interval of time, Δt, is considered, the above equation can be written:

$$\Delta v \approx -k.x\Delta t$$

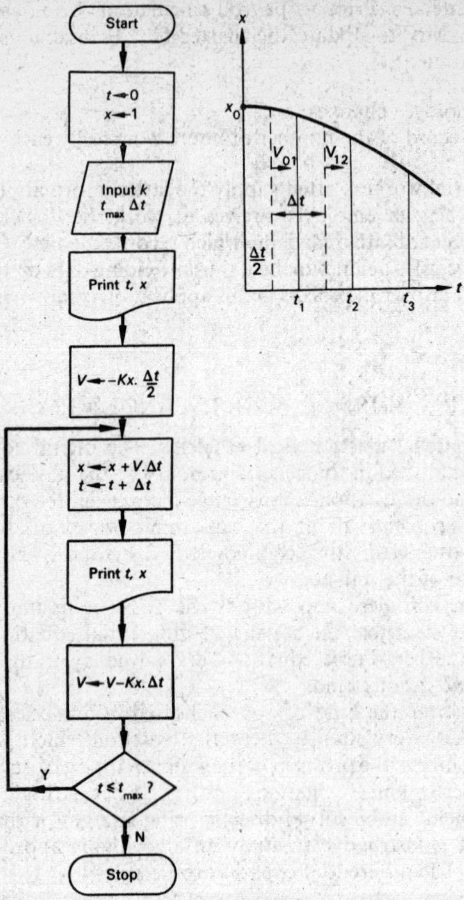

FIG. 137 *Algorithm for the SHM problem.*

Time is divided into small steps of duration Δt as shown in Fig. 137. Initial use of the last equation with $\Delta t/2$ rather than Δt gives a good estimate of the body's velocity half way through the first interval (V_{01}). This value is used to start the algorithm. A new position, Δt later is found from:

$$x_{new} \approx x_{old} + v.\Delta t$$

and subsequent velocity values approximated by:

$$v_{new} \approx v_{old} - k.x\Delta t$$

Proceeding in this way, the motion of the oscillating body can be calculated to a precision which is only determined by the small size of the time step. The reader is advised to study the flowchart of Fig. 137 and try out the algorithm with some simple data. The precision obtainable with a comparatively large time step is quite surprising. Figure 138 shows a BASIC program based on this algorithm and Fig. 139 shows a sample print-out of results obtained using $k = 1$ and $\Delta t = 0.1$.

```
10 PRINT "SHM EQUATION"
20 PRINT
30 LET T=0
40 LET X=1
50 PRINT "K,TMAX AND DELTA T"
60 INPUT K,T1,D
70 PRINT "T","X"
80 PRINT
90 PRINT T,X
100 LET V=-K*X*D/2
110 LET X=X+V*D
120 LET T=T+D
130 PRINT T,X
140 LET V=V-K*X*D
150 IF T<=T1 THEN 110
160 END
```

FIG. 138 *BASIC program for SHM problem.*

8. Non-conventional mathematical problems. Many problems in science are represented by equations which *cannot* be solved by conventional mathematical analysis and it is in these areas that computer-based numerical methods are used with great profit. An example of this kind is the famous Many-body Problem which concerns, in one form, the mutual interactions of a set of gravitating bodies in space. Now, using high-speed computers and sophisticated numerical methods, it is possible to study the evolution of a model galaxy consisting of some hundreds of simulated stars.

9. Application to X-ray crystallography. The microscopic world, as well as the macroscopic cosmos, is yielding more of its secrets under the combined attack of X-ray crystallography and computer processing. The central technique is based on X-ray diffraction in which the material under study is irradiated with X-radiation and the diffracted beams are intercepted by a photographic plate. The latter registers a diffraction pattern which can be interpreted by mathematical processes to give information about the atomic structure of the material. Unfortunately, the amount of arithmetic involved in these interpretations is prodigious and, before computer methods were available, it was not uncommon for a complete analysis of a single X-ray photograph of quite a simple molecule to take 2 or 3 years. Nowadays, the same job can be completed on the computer in just a few hours. The power of the computing technique in this field is well illustrated by the elucidation between 1954 and 1956, of the molecular structure of vitamin B_{12} (chemical formula: $C_{63}H_{88}O_{14}N_{14}PCO$) in which the positions of all the atoms were established to a precision of 25 picometres (a picometre is 10^{-12} m).

10. Engineering design. In engineering design very long calculations are often necessary, e.g. in designing a bridge it is important to calculate the stresses and strains in every member. Before the computer era, engineers were forced to make very risky simplifications in their analyses with a subsequent reduction in safety. Today it is possible to make detailed computer calculations and even explore such effects as high winds blowing on the structure from a variety of directions. The field of CAD (computer-aided design) is a growing one and the ability of the computer to present an engineering structure *visually* on a (possibly remote) VDU is a powerful facility. Using a light-pen, the engineer can modify a calculated structure in a flexible and natural way. Diagrams can be rotated, re-scaled, and even presented in perspective, thus enabling the designer to arrive more easily at the ideal compromise of economy and aesthetic appeal.

11. Process control. Many processes in research, engineering, and manufacturing industry require that a great deal of attention be paid to ensuring that all the working parameters are optimum. Such parameters include such things as temperature, pressure, flow-rates, linear and angular positions of moving parts and other factors. A *process-control computer* takes over the job of the technician who would otherwise have to spend a high proportion of his time checking instruments which indicate the state of a particular process. Input to the computer is provided by *transducers* of various kinds which translate process parameters into analog signals (for example, a thermocouple translates temperature into a small voltage). These signals are interfaced to the CPU via A/D converters so that digital information is available on all process parameters. The *process-control program* consists of instructions to examine values of the process parameters at prescribed intervals which may be fractions of a second. If a parameter goes out of its permitted range, the computer will type out an error message for the benefit of the human operators and will also send digital signals to D/A converters so that corrective analog information can restore the parameter (e.g. a temperature rising too quickly would, on detection, result in reduced current to a corresponding heater).

```
SHM EQUATION

K,TMAX AND DELTA T
?
1,5,.1
T                    X

 Ø                   1
 .1                  .995
 .2                  .98ØØ5
 .3ØØØØØ1            .9552994
 .4ØØØØØ1            .92Ø9959
 .5ØØØØØ1            .8774824
 .6ØØØØØ1            .8251941
 .7ØØØØØ2            .7646539
 .8ØØØØØ2            .6964671
 .9ØØØØØ2            .6213157
1                    .5399511
1.Ø99999             .453187
1.199999             .361891
1.299998             .2669762
1.399998             .1693916
1.499997             7.Ø113Ø6E-Ø2
1.599997            -2.986658E-Ø2
1.699996            -.1295475
1.799995            -.227933
1.899995            -.324Ø392
1.999994            -.4169Ø5
2.Ø99994            -.5Ø56Ø17
2.199993            -.5892424
2.299993            -.66699Ø7
2.399992            -.738Ø691
2.499991            -.8Ø17668
2.599991            -.8574468
```

FIG. 139 *Sample output from SHM program.*

MEDICINE

The computer has found extensive application in the medical field. It is possible to divide this application into five main areas: these are considered below.

12. Medical information systems. Many millions of pieces of paper are added to medical records yearly—their compilation and servicing amounting to considerable human effort. The sort of problem traditionally faced by hospital records clerks was that of sorting through shelves of folders containing shabby hand-written documents to find a case history vital to the treatment of some unfortunate patient. When found, the particular file would probably be retained by the doctor for several hours, thus making the patient's details completely unavailable to anyone else in the hospital or outside.

Nowadays computers are being increasingly used to maintain medical records on tape or disk files. These may hold information such as the patient's name, address, sex, blood group, date of hospital admission, present symptoms and a detailed medical history which can readily be updated.

An extension of this type of application is the establishment of *total hospital information systems*. One such system is installed in Peoria, USA, where it serves 11 hospitals in three states. These systems tie in accounting, service, and medical activities to a central computer to help control admissions, allocate beds, order drugs, schedule X-rays and operations, report results of laboratory tests, plan special diets and furnish doctors with updated records of patients' treatment and progress.

13. Patient monitoring. Computers can also be used to co-ordinate *patient monitoring systems*. At the San Francisco Presbyterian Medical Center a computer can monitor more than 20 physiological variables, including blood pressure, respiration rate, heart rate and body temperature and can compute from its measurements such things as the volume of blood pumped with each heart beat and the amount of lung movement with each breath.

14. Computerised instrumentation. The computer now plays a significant role in the automation of many routine but vital procedures carried out in a modern hospital.

One of these is the *automated clinical laboratory* where on-line data acquisition and analysis is proving extremely useful. In such a laboratory tests are carried out on blood and other material taken from patients. Large medical centres may carry out more than 700 000 tests in the course of one year. In the automated laboratory the computer collects signals from biochemical instrumentation and produces hardcopy analyses of medical samples. The analyses are also stored on a computer file for subsequent retrieval by hospital staff.

Another very powerful piece of equipment is the *computerised tomographic (CT) X-ray scanner* pioneered by EMI. The various forms of this device use precisely directed beams of X-radiation to scan sections of the brain (or other parts of the body). A set of detectors receives the radiation which has passed through the section of interest and produces signals which are processed by the computer. The output of the latter is used to drive a VDU on which a picture of the scanned section is displayed. CT scanners provide a means for the rapid detection and location of structures such as tumours. A highly developed scanner is being used at Leeds General Infirmary to obtain computer-generated maps of bone density and mineralisation.

15. Medical research. A very important use of the computer in medicine is in modelling parts of the human body in order to increase our understanding of the way in which various organs operate and interact with other systems of the body. An example is a model of the human inner ear which has been designed at IBM's Scientific Centre in Los Angeles using a 360/75 computer. Dr Alfred Inselberg, who has spent 11 years on the project, claims that the model is a "reasonable approximation" to the real thing, and has been able to draw some preliminary conclusions about the function of the inner ear, and hopes that the model and improved versions of it may be of use in improving the hearing capacity of people whose inner ear is damaged.

16. Computer-assisted diagnosis. Medical diagnosis has never been a fool-proof procedure. At any given time all a doctor can do is *identify a patient as belonging to one or other of the known treatable categories, and apply one or other of the known treatments for the category (or categories) identified.*

Medical knowledge has increased so rapidly that it is no longer a simple matter to categorise a patient, as there are upwards of 30 000 treatable categories continually being added to and modified, and no single doctor can hope to have detailed knowledge of more than a few per cent. It is for this reason that considerable effort is being put into research into diagnostic computer programs. The results of this research are encouraging. Here is an example.

A computer-aided diagnosis system developed by the IBM Scientific Centre in Haifa and the Sheba Medical Centre at Tel-Hashomer, allows doctors to interrogate a data base containing a comprehensive list of gynaecological complaints. The doctor inputs all the normal historical and clinical data from the patient together with certain specific endocrinological symptoms displayed by the patient. The program begins by informing the doctor that the patient could be suffering from one of some 60 possible disorders. As further data is entered the computer reduces the possible disorders to about five and advises the doctor to carry out final specific laboratory tests. The ultimate diagnostic decision is, of course, left to the doctor.

COMPUTERS IN EDUCATION

17. Science Education. The physical sciences provide a rich area for the application of computer techniques, but it was not until 1970 that any organised attempt was made to review the various ways in which computers can be used in the *teaching* of science. In the above-mentioned year the Conference on Computers in Undergraduate Science Education took place in Chicago, Illinois. Here were recognised four primary modes of computer usage in science teaching: calculator, simulator, tutor and administrator. However, the literature of CAI (Computer-Assisted Instruction) abounds in variations in this broad categorisation. For this reason, the author has, in a recent study, introduced the terms: T-mode (tutorial), S-mode (simulation), D-mode (demonstration), P-mode (preparation), M-mode (modelling) and C-mode (calculation).

In C-mode the science student writes his own programs to solve problems at a laboratory computer terminal. With the computer, the student can solve many more problems and they can be of a complexity which greatly increases his experience and feeling for physical problems. Simple examples of this mode are the plotting of projectile paths or the analysis of experimental data collected by students in the laboratory.

18. Simulation. In S-mode the student interacts with a computer program which has been specially written to behave like some physical apparatus or phenomenon. The justification for this mode is that the alternative real equipment may not be available because

```
00300 HEM MK5 HERMES MODEL : SCHROEDINGER HYDROGEN ATOM
00310 GOTO 400,430,450 ON 06
00320 DATA 1.602E-19,8.854E-12,9.109E-31,1.0544E-34
00330 READ E,E0,M,H
00340 PRINT "SCHROEDINGER EQUATION: HYDROGEN ATOM"
00350 PRINT
00360 PRINT "TOTAL (NEGATIVE) ENERGY IN ATTOJOULES"
00370 INPUT V0
00380 V0=V0*1E-18
00390 D=1E-15
00395 U1=1
00400 V=-E*E/(4*&PI*E0*D)
00410 D1=-2*M*(V0-V)*U3/(H*H)
415 $=U3*U3
00420 RETURN
00430 D3=U1
00440 RETURN
00450 PRINT "END OF RUN"
00460 RETURN
00470 END
```

FIG. 140 *Student-written model for solution of Schrödinger's equation.*

of expense, or there may be serious danger to the student in using the actual apparatus. Another justification is that the variables of a problem may present difficulties of access, as in the case of motion governed by gravitation on an astronomical scale, or the runaway of a nuclear reactor.

19. Modelling. In M-mode the student uses a special programming system enabling him to *create his own* mathematical model of a physical phenomenon (compare S-mode in which the student merely interacts with, but cannot alter, the model in the machine). The student uses his created model and may later modify it in the light of experience gained and compare its behaviour with that of the real world. The author has written software specifically designed for this mode and carried out successful experiments with a number of students. The program HERMES permits the user to write a simple subroutine in BASIC. This subroutine constitutes the student's model of his problem, an example of such a model being shown in Fig. 140. Here the student has written the well-known Schrödinger equation for the electron density distribution in a hydrogen atom. The physical equations are:

$$U_p = -e^2/4\pi\varepsilon_0 r$$
$$d\varphi/dr = -2m(U - U_p).A/\hbar^2$$
$$dA/dr = \varphi$$

```
SCHROEDINGER EQUATION: HYDROGEN ATOM

TOTAL (NEGATIVE) ENERGY IN ATTOJOULES
?
-.545
INT STEP
?
1E-13
OUT STEP
?
25E-12
RUN SPAN
?
600E-12
TO PLOT U1,U2,U3,U4,$ TYPE 1,2,3,4 OR 5: FOR TABLE TYPE 0
?
5

MAXIMUM ORDINATE
?
.5E-21
TYPE 1 FOR LEFT AXIS; TYPE 2 FOR CENTRAL AXIS
?
1

1.000E-15
2.500E-11
5.010E-11
7.519E-11
1.003E-10
1.254E-10
1.505E-10
1.756E-10
2.007E-10
2.258E-10
2.509E-10
2.759E-10
3.010E-10
3.261E-10
3.512E-10
3.763E-10
4.013E-10
4.264E-10
4.515E-10
4.766E-10
5.017E-10
5.267E-10
5.518E-10
5.769E-10
6.020E-10
END OF RUN
```

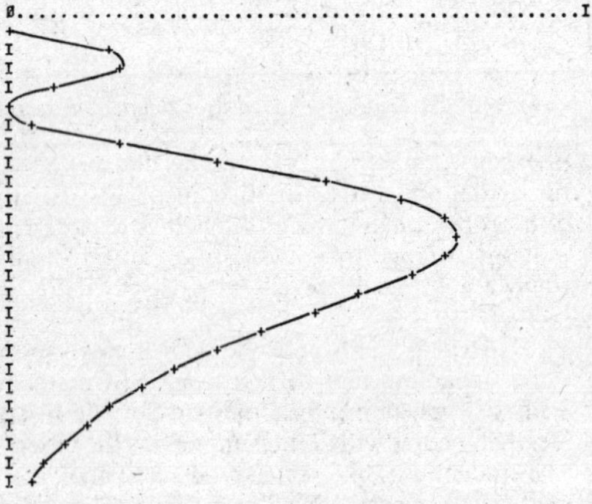

FIG. 141 *Sample computer run showing solution of Schrödinger's equation using the author's modelling program.*

Lines 400, 410 and 430 correspond exactly to the above equations. The main program carries out integration of these and permits the student to obtain either tabular or graphical output of the solution. A sample computer run giving graphical output at a teletype is shown in Fig. 141.

20. Demonstration. In D-mode the computer is used as a classroom aid. The computer enables the teacher to illustrate and explain phenomena which may be difficult to follow or visualise by other methods. D-mode has the same advantage over media such as films or television, as does the class demonstration: it permits interaction with the class and questions such as the "what if" type.

21. Preparation. P-mode concerns preparation: the computer is used by the teacher to generate material which can be used in the classroom or laboratory—tables of functions, deliberately randomised data, and so on. A sophisticated example of P-mode is the production of animated films which use numerical solutions of differential equations provided by the computer.

22. Tutorial. T-mode brings the student into active dialogue with the computer, which presents the student with situations, evaluates his response, possibly supplies remedial assistance and guides him to the next situation.

23. Non-numeric computing. Why should computers be considered the preserve of the numerate and not the literate? Response to this question has come from many educationalists in the form of a variety of computer packages for use in non-science subjects.

At Hatfield School the computer has been extensively used to enrich the study of history. One program is a general-purpose history test which outputs 100 questions to the student and analyses his responses. Advantages over normal testing methods include the following:

(*a*) The student gets his answers marked immediately; in this way the correct answer has far greater impact than in cases where he has to wait until the test has been completed.

(*b*) Students can work at their own speed.

(*c*) More freedom over the formation of questions exists.

Another program takes the student on an imaginary flight as a British pilot during World War II. During the flight a number or random hazards occur. The pilot must use his judgment to make the most of the events that happen. Thus he is able to experience some of the circumstances and strains under which these men worked and to recognise the part played by luck in affecting their chances of survival. A third program, BISVIX, simulates the situation in 1941 when the German battleship Bismarck tried to sail into the Atlantic. BISVIX invites the student to take the part of Admiral Lord Tovey of the Royal Navy. He has to find the Bismarck and send forces to intercept her. A user's pamphlet is provided for use with the program. Combined study of the background literature and an opportunity to take part in a famous historic event stimulate the student to learn more about the situation and bring it to life with the aid of the computer.

A different application has been in the teaching of Home Economics. A suite of programs developed at the University of Kent at Canterbury, called DIET, enables students to gain experience in the making up of diets in a variety of situations. The student working at a computer terminal is invited to suggest a diet under chosen circumstances and DIET then assesses it from several viewpoints: nutritional content; adequacy of diet under conditions of normal health; advice on remedies for inadequacy; vegetarianism; budgeting; price changes, and other factors.

THE ARTS

Computers are now capable of producing reasonable works of art, music and even poetry. An example of one of the early computer-created musical works was the Illiac Suite for String Quartet composed using a program developed by L. A. Hiller Jr. and L. M. Issacson. This was run on the ILLIAC computer at the University of Illinois.

Works of art produced by computer usually depend on a *random number generator*. The random numbers generated in the machine are used to represent notes, words, colours etc. As with human creations it is necessary to impose certain constraints during the composition and so rules must be built into such programs to restrict the way in which the random numbers are to be used.

PROGRESS TEST 12

1. What is a computer file? What requirements determine whether a file should be kept on magnetic tape or magnetic disks? Suggest an example of a file suitable for tape and another for disk. **(1, 3, 4)**

2. Distinguish between a master file and a transaction file. **(2)**

3. Explain the terms validation and verification as used in computer data processing. **(3)**

4. Why are numerical methods so important in scientific computing? **(7)**

5. Write a BASIC program to solve the equation of a damped oscillator

$$dv/dt = -k.x - c.v$$

where v is the velocity and x is the displacement of a particle at some time t. The constants k and c should be supplied as data. Use the simple step-wise numerical method of integration shown in the text. (7)

6. What do you understand by a process control program? (**11**)

7. What are the problems of applying computers to aid the diagnosis of disease?

8. Use your library to obtain information on:

(*a*) the use of computers in space exploration;
(*b*) computers in economics.

Write a short essay on each.

9. A popular saying in the computer world is: GARBAGE IN—GARBAGE OUT. Comment on this and point out its relevance in applying computers to practical problems.

APPENDIX I

Answers to Numerical Questions

Chapter 3

1.

Binary numeral	*Twos complement*
11 011	00 101
1	1
1 001	0 111
1 011	0 101

2. Decimal capacity of a 16-bit register
(*a*) in positive integer form $= 2^{16} - 1 = 65\ 535$
i.e. 0 through 65 535
(*b*) in twos complement negative form $= -2^{15}$ through $2^{15} - 1$
i.e. $-32\ 768$ through $+32\ 767$

3.

Binary	*Decimal*
101	5
1 011	11
111 101	61

4.

Decimal	*Binary*	*Octal*	*Hexadecimal*
396	110 001 100	614	18C
16	10 000	20	10
100	1 100 100	144	64
64	1 000 000	100	40
32	100 000	40	20
0	0	0	0

5.

Octal	*Decimal*
10	8
64	52
777	511

6.

Hexadecimal	*Decimal*
E3	227
EFF	1023

ABC	2748
9D31	40 241

8. Greatest positive number $= 2^7 - 1 =$ decimal $+127$
   Smallest positive number $= 2^{-9} =$ decimal $+1.953 \times 10^{-3}$
   Greatest negative number $= -2^7 =$ decimal -128
   Smallest negative number $= (-\frac{1}{2} - 1/128) \times 2^{-8}$
   $=$ decimal -1.938×10^{-3}

Chapter 6

1. (*a*) 110 011
   (*b*) 10 110 101
   (*c*) 1111.11
   (*d*) 1.100

2. (*a*) 11
   (*b*) 10
   (*c*) 100.0
   (*d*) −0.01

3. 320 microseconds

6. (*a*) 1110 = decimal −2
   (*b*) 1010 = decimal −6

7. (*a* 21 seconds
   (*b*) 5.1 milliseconds

Chapter 7

5. (*a*) 98 304
   (*b*) 24
   (*c*) 24
   (*d*) 24

Chapter 9

2. (*a*) 13 bits/cm^2
   (*b*) 4 bits/cm^2
   (*c*) 30 bits/cm^2
   (*d*) 2400 bits/cm^2

3. (*a*) 1600 ch/s
   (*b*) 2000 ch/s

APPENDIX II

Further Reading

M. Bohl, *Flowcharting Techniques*, SRA publication.

F. H. George and J. J. Humphries (Editors), *The Robots are Coming*, NCC Publications.

J. L. Gross and W. S. Brainerd, *Fundamental Programming Concepts*, Harper & Row.

F. G. Heath, *Digital Computer Design*, Oliver & Boyd.

H. Katzan, Jr, *Introduction to Computer Science*, Petrocelli/Charter.

M. Mandl, *Fundamentals of Electronic Computers: Digital and Analog*, Prentice-Hall.

N. M. Morris, *Logic Circuits*, McGraw-Hill.

C. A. Stewart and R. Atkinson, *Basic Analogue Computer Techniques*, McGraw-Hill.

R. Townsend, *Digital Computer Structure and Design*, Newnes-Butterworths.

APPENDIX III

Examination Technique

REVISION

1. Well before your examination draw up a revision timetable and keep to it.

2. Allocate a definite length of time, say about 30 minutes, for each revision session.

3. During the allocated time devote *all* your attention to a definite topic.

4. When you consider you have mastered a particular topic, test yourself by re-writing the main ideas as though explaining them to a group of people with no knowledge of that topic.

5. If you encounter an idea which you cannot understand, do not waste time in just worrying about it. Instead, make a careful note of the difficulty and seek help from a qualified teacher.

EXAMINATION TECHNIQUE

6. Read the rubric at the top of the paper *very* carefully to see exactly what you have to do.

7. Note how much time can be spent on each question and do not exceed it. Should you run out of time, write a shorter answer but make sure it contains the fundamentals asked for.

8. Read the question carefully. Do not repeat yourself. Do not waste time giving details that are not asked for, as no marks are awarded for irrelevancies.

9. Before writing each answer, jot down a brief plan of the order in which you are going to present your ideas.

10. Wherever possible *illustrate* your answer by means of clear, labelled diagrams. Credit is gained for *relevant* diagrams even if they have not been asked for in the wording of the questions. If diagrams have been *specifically* requested in the question, they must be drawn as marks will have been allocated for them.

11. Because of the lack of standardisation in the computer field, you should clearly define the symbols you use for hardware elements such as logic gates and two-state devices. The logic operators AND, OR and NOT also have a variety of alternative symbols in common use. You should therefore define briefly but clearly the operator symbols which *you* are using.

12. Written numerals can cause confusion for two main reasons:

(*a*) long uninterrupted strings of digits are difficult to read. Long numerals should be broken into groups of three digits separated by spaces. For example

53 296 145 . 013 773 9

is clearer than

53296145.0137739

This device is particularly useful when reading and writing binary numerals:

e.g. 10 111 010 111 . 010 111 01

rather than 10111010111.01011101

(*b*) numerals may be ambiguous if the particular radix is not specified. For example

15 = *thirteen* in octal
15 = *twenty-one* in hexadecimal
15 = *fifteen* in decimal.

It is recommended that you write *octal 15* or *decimal 15* for maximum clarity. Instead of this method many people write 15_8 and 15_{10}. If you opt to use this system, take care: 15_8 can easily turn into 158.

13. Keep your use of abbreviated forms to an absolute minimum. For example, if you write VDU (rather than Visual Display Unit), make sure that the term is explained at the point where you first introduce it.

14. In questions which involve calculations you should:

(*a*) summarise the information given, making the units explicitly clear;

(*b*) state the principles on which your method depends;

(*c*) perform the calculation in such a way that the examiner can easily follow your reasoning;

(*d*) always ask yourself if your answer is plausible. If you think it is not, then say so.

15. Good English and clear handwriting are essential: without them you cannot communicate.

Index